THE DYNAMICS OF FORCED FEMALE MIGRATION FROM CZECHOSLOVAKIA TO BRITAIN, 1938–1950

EXILE STUDIES

VOL. 18

Edited by
ANDREA HAMMEL

A series founded by
ALEXANDER STEPHAN

PETER LANG
Oxford · Bern · Berlin · Bruxelles · New York · Wien

Jana Barbora Buresova

THE DYNAMICS OF FORCED FEMALE MIGRATION FROM CZECHOSLOVAKIA TO BRITAIN, 1938–1950

PETER LANG

Oxford · Bern · Berlin · Bruxelles · New York · Wien

Bibliographic information published by Die Deutsche Nationalbibliothek
Die Deutsche Nationalbibliothek lists this publication in the Deutsche
Nationalbibliografie; detailed bibliographic data is available
on the Internet at http://dnb.d-nb.de.

A catalogue record for this book is available from the British Library.

Library of Congress Cataloging-in-Publication data
Names: Buresova, Jana B., 1950, author.
Title: The dynamics of forced female migration from
Czechoslovakia to Britain, 1938-1950 / Jana B. Buresova.
Description: First edition. | New York : Peter Lang, 2019. | Series: Exile studies ; 18 |
Includes bibliographical references and index.
Identifiers: LCCN 2018029885 | ISBN 9781788744461 (alk. paper)
Subjects: LCSH: Women refugees--Great Britain--History--20th century. | Women
refugees--Czechoslovakia--History--20th century. | Forced
migration--Czechoslovakia--History--20th century. | World War,
1939-1945--Refugees--Czechoslovakia. | Czechoslovakia--Emigration and
immigration--History--20th century. | Great Britain--Emigration and
immigration--History--20th century.
Classification: LCC HV640.5.C97 B87 2019 | DDC 940.53/1450820941--dc23 LC record
available at https://lccn.loc.gov/2018029885

Cover image: Nina Dobosharevich, Lady Milena Grenfell-Baines
and Hana Benešová (courtesy of Nadia de Vivo)

Cover design by Peter Lang Ltd.

ISSN 1072-0626
ISBN 978-1-78874-446-1 (print) • ISBN 978-1-78874-447-8 (ePDF)
ISBN 978-1-78874-448-5 (ePub) • ISBN 978-1-78874-449-2 (mobi)

© Peter Lang AG 2019

Published by Peter Lang Ltd, International Academic Publishers,
52 St Giles, Oxford, OX1 3LU, United Kingdom
oxford@peterlang.com, www.peterlang.com

This publication has been peer reviewed.

Printed in Germany

This book is dedicated to my mother, Barbora

Map of Czechoslovakia, 1918–1938, indicating areas of ethnic German settlement. Adapted from Paul Robert Magosci, *Historical Atlas of Central Europe*, Revised and Expanded Edition (Seattle: University of Washington Press, 2002).

Contents

Figures

Acknowledgements

It is thanks to Devana Pavliková, former Curator of the Czech and Slovak Collections at the British Library, who perceived a gap in the historiography, that this contribution to exile studies was undertaken, initially as a PhD thesis. It has been a privilege to interview the women (and some men) who animate the archival research, and are listed separately. An enduring memory is sitting with fatally ill Berta Freistadt in her attic, surrounded by family documents for me.

Special thanks are also gratefully expressed to the Martin Miller and Hannah Norbert-Miller Trust for its generous financial support for the publication of this book; to Emeritus Professors Charmian Brinson and Richard Dove for their guidance throughout the study on which it is based; to Professor Naomi Segal, Birkbeck, University of London; to Emeritus Regius Professor of Modern History Robert Evans, University of Oxford; and to local historian Neil Rees. Thanks are also extended to Peter Lang Senior Commissioning Editor Dr Laurel Plapp, for the opportunity to present the work to a wider audience, and to Editorial Assistant Simon Phillimore.

This author is indebted to many more people than can be named here, but whose assistance, interest and encouragement were nonetheless immensely appreciated, including British Czech and Slovak Association members.

The following libraries, archives and individuals have greatly assisted my research: Baťa Reminiscence and Resource Centre, East Tilbury Library; Bodleian Library, University of Oxford; British Library (Devana Pavliková); Finchley Reform Synagogue (David Rose); Fulneck School (Tony Sykes); Martin Hakel, former Director, Slovak Centre. Imperial War Museum; Institute of Advanced Legal Studies, University of London; Liberec Library (Kateřina Trojanová); London School of Economics and Political Science, also its Women's Library; Manx National Heritage Library (particularly Alan Franklin, Yvonne Cresswell and Wendy Thirkettle); Modern Records Centre, University of Warwick; Moravian

Church Archives (Lorraine Parsons); National Archives, Prague; Ladislav Potůček, Chairman, Czechoslovak Colony Club; School of Slavonic and East European Studies; Colonel Eduard Stehlík, military historian, Deputy Director, Institute for the Study of Totalitarian Regimes, Prague; The National Archives, London; University of Limerick, Centre for Irish-German Studies (Dr Gisela Holfter); Senate House Library, University of London; Wiener Library for the Study of the Holocaust and Genocide; YWCA archives (Eileen Hawkins).

Acronyms and Abbreviations

AI	Author's interview
ATS	Auxiliary Territorial Service
BBWs	British-born wives
BC	British Council
BCRC	British Committee for Refugees from Czechoslovakia
BL	British Library
BPC	British Pen Club
CBFC	Czechoslovak-British Friendship Club
CCC	Czechoslovak Cultural Commission
CCP	Czechoslovak Communist Party
CCWGB	Council of Czechoslovak Women in Great Britain
CCzW	Club of Czechoslovak Women
CI	Czechoslovak Institute
CNS	Czechoslovak National Socialist Party (not Fascist)
CPC	Czechoslovak Pen Club
CRC	Czechoslovak Red Cross
CRTF	Czech Refugee Trust Fund
CZ	*Československá žena [Czechoslovak Woman]* journal
DF	*Die Frau* journal (and its variations *Die Frau/P*)
DP/DPs	Displaced Person(s)
EVW	European Voluntary Workers Scheme
IGRS/IMLR	Institute of Germanic and Romance Studies (Institute of Modern Languages Research)
IoM	Isle of Man
IRO	International Refugee Organization
IWM	Imperial War Museum
JP	Justice of the Peace
LSE	London School of Economics and Political Science
MC	Moravian Church
MI5	British Internal Security agency

MIN	Minutes of meetings
MP	Member of Parliament
NAP	National Archives, Prague
PEN	Originally Poets, Essayists and Novelists club
PP	Private papers
RAF	Royal Air Force
RCLNU	Refugees Committee of the League of Nations Union
SGSD	Sudeten German Social Democrats
SHL	Senate House Library (University of London)
SSEES	School of Slavonic and East European Studies (University College London)
TNA	The National Archives (formerly PRO, Public Records Office), London
UN	United Nations
UNHCR	United Nations High Commissioner for Refugees
UNRRA	United Nations Relief and Rehabilitation Administration
WAAF	Women's Auxiliary Air Force
WIZO	Women's International Zionist Organization
WRNS	Women's Royal Naval Service
WVS	Women's Voluntary Service (later Royal – RWVS)
YC	Young Czechoslovakia club (also the title of its journal)
YWCA	Young Women's Christian Association

Introductory Notes

Territory and society

The Czechoslovak Republic (henceforth cited as Czechoslovakia), was created following the end of World War I and the Habsburg Empire's demise. Comprising the Czech Crown Lands of Bohemia and Moravia, plus Ruthenia and Slovakia, its 1918 borders were formally delineated in 1920. At a time of unstable regimes and political upheaval, Czechoslovakia was deemed a model of democracy in a Europe of so-called 'revolving door' democracies.

The historiography variously places Czechoslovakia in east or central Europe. The former is a political 'Cold War' reference, denoting Communist 'Eastern bloc' states allied to the Soviet Union, but on regaining its independence in 1989, Czechoslovakia (now separate Czech and Slovak Republics)[1] reverted to its *Mitteleuropa* geographical status. Its lengthy border with Germany contains the disputed N-S swathe known as the Sudetenland or frontier region(s), ceded to Nazi Germany under the 1938 Munich Agreement.

Czechoslovakia is currently spelt as one word, not Czecho-Slovakia, and *Czech(s), Czechoslovak(s)/ian(s)* embraces Czechs, Slovaks and ethnic minorities who were citizens during the period covered in this study (see Statistics, Appendix A). *Czechoslovak(s)/ian(s)* are the main terms used here. Distinctions are made, though, between, for example, specifically regional art or music and broader *Czechoslovak* cultural events.

---

[1] Slovakia seceded from Czechoslovakia, becoming the Slovak Republic on 1 January 1993. The renamed Czech Republic comprises Bohemia and Moravia.

1920 Constitution

Section I, Arts. 9, 14, granted full voting rights to all Czechoslovak citizens, including women. Section VI [although Czech was the official state language], granted equal civic and political rights to religious and racial minorities, with additional language rights, for example, use of German.

Germans

An important distinction is drawn between the Sudetenland and other predominantly ethnic German areas in Czechoslovakia,[2] also between ethnic Germans in or from Czechoslovakia known as *Volksdeutsche* (not a pejorative term), and Reich Germans. These terms are *not* synonymous historically, nor regarded as such here. Before 1945, ethnic Germans, a number of whom were Jewish, were predominantly German-speaking; some knew little or no Czech. Nonetheless, they were acknowledged Czechoslovak citizens.

2   The Sudetenland was not populated exclusively by Germans. 'Even excluding the numerous islands scattered over the whole territory of the Republic, there were [...] eight separate zones inhabited by the Germans, in which the proportion of Germans in the population varied between 80–95 per cent' pre-WWII, Czechoslovak Ministry of Foreign Affairs, Department of Information, *Two Years of German Oppression in Czechoslovakia* (Woking: Unwin, 1941), 23.

Ruthenians and Slovaks

Ruthenians and Slovaks are the least represented groups in this study due to political developments. Ruthenia declared its independence from Czechoslovakia mid-March 1939; in June 1945 Czechoslovakia ceded Sub-Carpathian Ruthenia (also known as Trans-Carpathian Ukraine) to the Soviet Union.

Martin Hakel, when Director of the Slovak Centre, London, explained that having no reason to leave initially, not many Slovaks came to Britain.[3] Following negotiations with Germany, Slovak People's Party leader Jozef Tiso, became Slovakia's President, and declared its independence on 14 March 1939 (until reunification in 1945). Anti-Fascists then had great difficulty fleeing the German 'puppet-state' in Nazi-occupied Europe.

Names

Although a 'puppet-government' existed in Slovakia, the national government in exile in wartime Britain comprised Czechs and Slovaks, and is cited as *Czechoslovak*. Czech place names are generally given, with some former German ones. Spellings of personal names vary according to individual preference, official usage or error, for example, Edvard/Eduard, Tschapek (German), Čapek (Czech). The 'ová' suffix denotes the feminine in Czechoslovak surnames; though differing slightly from the masculine, they are nevertheless correct.

N. B. An interviewee's married name is used in the main text, her maiden name added in brackets in the footnotes. (See also Appendix C listing key interviewees).

---

3   Oral and email communications.

Diacritics are used except when quoting from sources that have omitted them, for example, English-language documents and publications, or where the customary usage is unknown. Unlike the British format, Czech titles, for example, of books and clubs are mostly lower case except for the first word.

Terminology

In exile discourse there is some dispute as to whether the terms *émigré(e)*, *exile, refugee*, are interchangeable or not. They are used to broadly describe someone 'taking refuge, especially in [a] foreign country from religious or political persecution, or from war',[4] not in the legalistic sense defined by the League of Nations or the later UNHCR 1951 Convention Relating to Refugee Status.[5] Despite perceived nuances, in this work the terms are treated as interchangeable, though the preferred, more explicit term 'refugee' is mainly used.

Currency, weights and measures

Czechoslovak currency was and remains the Czech koruna (Kč), whereas pre-decimalization in 1971, British currency comprised pounds, shillings and pence (£sd), for example, £5; 1/-; 6d; hence, for example, £5.2.6; for example, 2/6 also given as 2/6d. (12 pence = 1 shilling, 20 shillings = £1).

1 pound (lb) in weight = 0.45359237 kilograms (kg). 12 inches = 1 foot (approx. 30cm).

---

4   J. B. Sykes, ed., *Concise Oxford Dictionary of Current English*, 6th edn (Oxford: Oxford University Press, 1976), 941.

5   UNHCR, *Handbook on Procedures and Criteria for Determining Refugee Status Under the 1951 Convention and the 1967 Protocol Relating to the Status of Refugees* (Geneva: United Nations High Commissioner for Refugees, 1988), 58.

Introduction

'Exile is one of the saddest fates', posited writer and academic Edward Said in his third 1993 Reith Lecture. 'The exile [...] therefore exists in a median state, neither completely at one with the new setting, nor fully disencumbered of the old [...] nostalgic and sentimental'.[1] It is at once a profound and challenging statement open to debate, for although Said drew upon his own experiences, his observations have a universal resonance: they might equally apply to the 2015–16 surge of refugees predominantly from the Middle East and Africa, entering Europe in numbers unprecedented since World War II (WWII), and to WWII refugees from the former Czechoslovakia; but if so, to what extent in the latter case? This book examines that question and endeavours to fill a gap in Anglo-Czechoslovak historiography. It highlights refugee women's diverse experiences, dilemmas and contribution to Britain 1938–50 within a socio-political context, commencing with the 1938 Munich Agreement that precipitated exile. Oral interviews complement archival research, providing an insight into individual lives rather than the broad sweep of history. There has been a dearth of literature concerning Czechoslovak refugees in Britain during the given period, and the works that have been published deal almost exclusively with men, focusing on military service and the government in exile; women appear, if at all, merely as subsidiary figures. The specific topic of Czechoslovak women refugees in Britain has apparently not been investigated previously in English, and thus represents a striking gap in current research.

This study therefore links two totalitarian regimes, Fascism and Communism; the ramifications of the causal effect of major political upheavals, and the resultant successive cohorts of migration, are fundamental to both periods. Its aim was to research and document the reasons

---

1   Said, Edward, 'Intellectual exile: expatriates and marginals', *The Independent* (8 July 1993).

for Czechoslovak women's forced migration, and their experiences in exile in Britain including, where they are inextricably intertwined, those of Czechoslovak men and children. The essential difference between this and some other studies of exiles is the focus on nationality (Czechoslovak) and gender (women), rather than language, for example, German, as the common factor. Discrete publications pertaining to Czechoslovak women exist, but they are not comprehensive or always relevant to the period in question. Some wider Austrian and German exile studies have touched tangentially on refugees from Czechoslovakia (notably from the Sudetenland and ethnic German enclaves), but do not differentiate between *Czechoslovak* German-speaking refugees and those arriving in Britain from Reich Germany or Austria, nor is their focus on women.

I am not, however, suggesting here that the Czechoslovak refugee experience was unique; it could also exemplify pressures on women and girl migrants from other countries, at other times. Certainly literature on German and Austrian exile issues reflects shared experiences such as domestic service, internment, and cultural activities – aspects pursued in this study from the Czechoslovak perspective. Nevertheless, as will be demonstrated, the Czechoslovak refugee trajectory differs markedly for specific reasons. It is driven by historical and socio-political factors peculiar to that country, such as the Sudetenland question and its aftermath and Slovak wartime independence (see Introductory Note), and it is distinguished by the charitable support of the British Committee for Refugees from Czechoslovakia (BCRC), followed by Britain's funding of the Czech Refugee Trust Fund (CRTF), its work and refugee hostels or flats. The Czechoslovak refugee trajectory is further distinguished by the role of the Czechoslovak Red Cross in Britain, and the opening of Czechoslovak state schools in Britain by the Czechoslovak government in exile in London; all these entities are discussed in subsequent chapters in relation to the women's lives. In contrast, the only Reich Germans and Austrians to benefit from BCRC or CRTF assistance were (a) women who gained Czechoslovak citizenship on marriage to Czechoslovak men or (b) racial and/or political refugees who had initially fled to Czechoslovakia, and were later helped together with Czechoslovaks at risk to reach Britain, where they remained until WWII ended or emigrated to another country pre-/post-war. As the statistics show

(Chapter 1), Reich Germans and Austrians constituted minority groups in the two agencies' care: there was no parallel or directly comparable care for Reich German or Austrian refugees in general in Britain.

Most Czechoslovak women, regardless of their ethnic origin, were totally unprepared for the vicissitudes of life as an exile, and did not initially contemplate settling in Britain, focusing instead on their eventual repatriation to the homeland. Yet many of the women came to play an active part in the Czechoslovak and host communities; moreover, like their Reich German and Austrian counterparts (and British women in wartime conditions), some Czechoslovak women perforce became the breadwinner or main family supporter. 'Gender role swap', the reversal of traditional male/female roles, was a major social phenomenon during WWII when men were away in the armed forces or elsewhere. It extended to peacetime where Czechoslovak ex-servicemen lacked suitable skills for civilian employment or remained absent for whatever reason (as noted in the Conclusion). As yet, however, the individual and collective roles or contributions of Czechoslovak women, particularly regarding the British war effort and their post-war achievements, remain largely unrecognized, and thus risk falling into historical obscurity. This study addresses and helps redress that imbalance by

(a) examining what informed and shaped the women's lives 1938–50;
(b) recording findings for future reference, especially when the period is no longer within living memory.

To achieve this, the work examines the dynamics of forced female migration specifically from Czechoslovakia to Britain between 1938 and 1950 by adopting a dual archival and oral history approach. This places the experiences of Czechoslovak refugee women in relation to the underlying historical, geo-political and social factors that shaped and influenced their lives throughout the given period, both in the homeland and in the host country. It must be stressed that within this context 'forced migration' (whether of a literal physical or psychological nature), was usually a life-and-death matter – not one of economic betterment as some critics claimed then and now. Escape was potentially dangerous, followed by exile and an indeterminate future. Hence, exile was not only about leaving one's home, it was about leaving, and perhaps losing, everything that one held dear.

The principal migration elements considered here therefore include diverse 'pull-push' factors dictating the refugees' flight according to individual circumstances and the period in time (see Chronology), the women's arrival and reception in Britain (Chapter 1), repatriation and, in some instances, post-war (re)migration to Britain (Chapter 6). The dynamic effects of these factors on women's personal development are also considered, since Czechoslovak women in exile did not live in a vacuum; they were part of the wider society. Moreover, their relationships and responsibilities (familial and otherwise) underpinned their experiences and impacted on their endeavours. They remained closely bound to their respective families, and were affected by the latter's needs and actions. For this reason, attention has also been paid to the lives of the Czechoslovak refugee children (especially in Chapter 4), and men with whom the women were associated. Instances where men's lives have direct consequences on those of women are presented throughout the study. Attention is similarly paid to the situation for British-born wives (BBWs) of Czechoslovak men, who under Czechoslovak and British legislation became Czechoslovak nationals on marriage. The collective experiences of these women therefore form part of the discourse on British, as well as Czechoslovak history.

The intention here is not merely to examine who came to Britain, when and why, but more particularly to present an insight into issues regarding the women's lives pre-/post-arrival in Britain, hence the more detailed and nuanced micro approach, rather than a macro broad sweep of history that subsumes all but the most prominent individuals. Consequently, although the chapters connect structurally and contain a chronological thread, each chapter emphasizes particular facets of exile life. Sources of aid, problems and pressures are considered, for example how the women coped (alone or with a partner), raised their families and spent their leisure time. Additional aspects central to the topic include women's activities within the exile community, and whether they (with their family members where applicable), were accepted by the host communities across Britain, or formed a 'parallel society'. Other important questions are also addressed: was their fate as exiles really as sad as Said argues? Were they deracinated victims devoid of any sense of purpose, or liberated and empowered by the agents of change forced upon them? There are two schools of thought on this. One holds that women in exile were downtrodden and suffering, which some inter-viewees had certainly felt at times, the other posits that emigration was an opportunity to become more independent, despite initial exploitation or setbacks. Tony Kushner, writing (more broadly) on women refugees in *Second Chance*, inclined to the latter view,[2] as did several interviewees who maintained that things were already changing in the homeland, especially regarding the younger generation whose goals and opportunities extended beyond traditional early marriage, home-making and childbearing; women studied at university, pursued careers, voted and entered parliament. The issue raises further points for discussion. That Czechoslovak women as well as men migrated to Britain in 1938–50 is made clear, but were women merely passive beneficiaries, or active contributors to Britain?

Reference is also made in this study to interaction between the exiled groups, drawing out positive joint endeavours as well as tensions, rup-tures and factors undermining them. Though from the same country, Czechoslovak refugees were notably not a homogeneous unit, as evidenced by their ethnic origins (Appendix A), with numerous ethno-political per-mutations. The resultant political and cultural diversity variously tran-scended difference or engendered disputes between the refugees. Since adult refugees had already formed their perspectives and opinions before going into exile, exile itself was not necessarily the unifying or bonding factor some observers might assume it to have been. Instead, exile could aggravate differences, causing divisions in the homeland to be perpetu-ated rather than accommodated in the host country. Indeed, concepts of the homeland itself varied according to regional and cultural identi-ties, as did the mother-tongue. Whilst it does not follow that all refugees from the Sudetenland region were native German-speakers rather than Czech-speakers, the need to deconstruct the generic approach and not conflate perspectives rapidly became apparent. The shifting complexities of cultural identity, political allegiance and conflicting national loyalties constitute recurring elements throughout this work, interfacing at every

---

2   Tony Kushner, 'Domestic Service', in Werner E. Mosse, ed., *Second Chance. Two Centuries of German-Speaking Jews in the United Kingdom* (Tubingen: Mohr Siebeck, 1991), 553–78 (here 555).

level, even within families. Of particular significance since a number of children became young adults in the diaspora, was a form of matrilineal nationalism (see Chapter 4). It is an interesting concept whereby women took a particularly active part in developing a new state's sense of national identity, and is adopted here. Refugee women from Czechoslovakia, then still a young state, acted as role models and mothers or carers guided and influenced the young regarding identity, patriotism and remembrance. Remembrance remains important. Czech and Slovak organizations in Britain continue to commemorate key figures and observe anniversaries of major occasions especially during 2018, marking the 100th anniversary of the foundation of the Czechoslovak state and fifty years since its invasion by Warsaw Pact soldiers at the Kremlin's behest.

Literature regarding Czechoslovaks and the exile situation

It is worth considering that for much of the period in question, the primary literature was produced or initiated in exile by exiles (discussed in Chapter 5), augmented later by literature in the field of Jewish studies which has broadened exile studies since the war. Whereas, however, Britain, Germany and Austria can boast a host of publications in German and English on exile issues, the narrow spectrum of Czechoslovak exile discourse highlights the dearth of literature observed by Devana Pavliková, former Curator of the Czech and Slovak Collections at the British Library. One explanation is that the topic would not have been tolerated during the Communist era, a view held by Lewis M. White, editor of *On All Fronts* which comprises written testimonies of former Czechoslovak servicemen who had served with the Allies, and is supported by Antonin Petrak: 'In school children learned about "western warmongers" and the "bad imperialists".[3] The received ideology was

3   Antonin Petrak, 'From Dunkirk to Mirov Prison', in Lewis M. White, ed., *On All Fronts in World War II, Part III, East European Monographs*, DLVIII (New York: Columbia University Press/Boulder, 2000), 307–15.

all-pervasive. With travel and external contact restricted during the 'Cold War' Communist era, many Czechoslovaks were totally unaware of what life in exile had been like or believed a distorted view of it, and former émigré(e)s feared to speak about it. Interest has grown with increased awareness of this historical gap following Czechoslovakia's return to democracy in 1989, but the literature from both sides of the former 'Iron Curtain' remains incomplete.

Without in any way wishing to undermine the contribution of contemporary studies in English specifically about Czechoslovak women, they notably tend to place women either within Czechoslovakia itself, like Melissa Feinberg's *Democracy and Its Limits*,[4] and Wilma Iggers' *Women of Prague*[5] or, even if regarding Czechoslovak refugees, do not locate them in Britain. Iggers' 'Refugee Women from Czechoslovakia in Canada: An Eyewitness Report' for instance,[6] and the Czechoslovak Society of Arts and Sciences founded in the USA, which publishes writings of and about Czech and Slovak immigrants and their descendants' lives in America. Three modern novels characterized by the themes of Czechoslovak emigration and repatriation, are likewise situated outside Britain. *The Visible World* by Mark Slouka, the son of Czech immigrants, is set in New York, USA,[7] while Czech-born author Milan Kundera sets *Ignorance* in the Czech Republic,[8] and Simon Mawer's *The Glass Room* depicts fictional lives in the former Czechoslovakia, but bases his novel on the real and famous Tugendhat Villa in Brno.[9] Interviewee Dorrit Epstein (née Fuhrmann) disliked his approach intensely, having visited her mother's relations there as a child. In contrast,

---

4   Melissa Feinberg, 'Democracy and Its Limits: Gender and Rights in the Czech Lands, 1918–1938', in *Nationalities Papers: The Journal of Nationalism and Ethnicity*, 30/4 (30 December 2002), 553–70.

5   Wilma A. Iggers, *Women of Prague: Ethnic Diversity and Social Change From the Eighteenth Century to the Present* (Oxford: Berghahn Books, 1995).

6   Iggers, 'Refugee Women from Czechoslovakia in Canada', in Sibylle Quack, ed., *Between Sorrow and Strength. Women Refugees of the Nazi Period* (Washington, DC: German Historical Institute and Cambridge University Press, 1995).

7   Mark Slouka, *The Visible World* (London: Portobello Books, 2008).

8   Milan Kundera, *Ignorance* (London: Faber and Faber, 2002).

9   Simon Mawer, *The Glass Room* (London: Abacus, 2010).

whilst Martin Brown's detailed reference work *Dealing With Democrats*[10] indisputably concerns Czechoslovak exiles in Britain, it is at a highly political and official level not representative of quotidian refugee life, and in no way focuses on women. Much broader, *Exile in and From Czechoslovakia During the 1930s and 1940s*, comprises papers of the 2008 conference at the University of London;[11] again, Czechoslovak women were not a key topic, and though they featured in the 2014 *Exile and Gender* conference and subsequent publication,[12] there is scope for further documentation.

Literature in Czech on the topic of women émigrées in Britain between 1938 and 1950 is likewise apparently limited. Jana Burešová's[13] *Proměny společenského postavení českých žen v první polovině 20. století* [*The Changing Position of Czech Women in Society In the First Half of the 20th Century*] certainly focuses on women, but in Czechoslovakia.[14] *Česko-slovenská Británie* [*Czechoslovak Britain*] by London-based Milan Kocourek and Zuzana Slobodová, goes some way to bridging the gap with profiles of selected Czechoslovak immigrants who have gained recognition in Britain.[15] These immigrants, however, range from the seventeenth to the twentieth centuries. Furthermore, the work does not focus on women, and being in Czech the majority of second generation children would be unable to read it. Personal

---

10   Martin David Brown, *Dealing With Democrats. The British Foreign Office and the Czechoslovak Emigrés in Great Britain, 1939 to 1945* (Frankfurt am Main: Peter Lang, 2006).

11   Charmian Brinson and Marian Malet, eds, *Exile in and From Czechoslovakia During the 1930s and 1940s: Yearbook of the Research Centre for German and Austrian Exile Studies*, vol. 11 (2009).

12   Charmian Brinson, Jana Barbora Buresova, and Andrea Hammel, eds, *Exile and Gender II. Politics, Education and the Arts: Yearbook of the Research Centre for German and Austrian Exile Studies*, vol. 18 (2017).

13   The present author is *not* the author of the Czech book, despite her identical name.

14   Jana Burešová, *Proměny společenského postavení českých žen v první polovině 20. století* [*The Changing Position of Czech Women in Society In the First Half of the 20th Century*]; Czech with English Summary (Olomouc, Czechoslovakia: Katedra historie, Univerzita Palackého, 2001).

15   Milan Kocourek and Zuzana Slobodová, *Česko-slovenská Británie* [*Czecho-Slovak Britain*], UK Chapter of the Czechoslovak Society of Arts and Sciences (Trebon, Czech Republic: Carpio, 2006).

accounts in English specifically concerning Czechoslovak women's lives in wartime Britain are relatively uncommon in published form, and generally produced privately like Josephine Bruegel's *Joza: Memories of My Life and Times*.[16] However, Bohuslava Bradbrook's *The Liberating Beauty of Little Things*, is noteworthy for its narration of her escape after the 1948 Communist coup, conditions in British and American refugee camps in Austria, and bureaucratic procedures that problematically delayed her arrival in Britain.[17]

Wider exile studies

Although some works concentrate on the Jewish experience, their strength lies in contextual details. Hana Demetz's *The House on Prague Street*[18] helpfully substantiates anecdotal reflections on the high degree of acculturation of Czechoslovak Jewry, which had mostly adopted the Czechoslovak non-Jewish culture frequently mentioned by this author's interviewees. As a descendant of Rabbi Löw, Demetz's comments give credence and validity to such claims, and are supported by Hana Greenfield in *Fragments of Memory from Kolin to Jerusalem*.[19] Two major features of exile in 1938–45 were Britain's immigration and wartime internment policies. Louise London criticizes 'British Immigration Control Procedures and Jewish Refugees, 1933–1939' in *Second* Chance,[20] and in *Whitehall and the Jews, 1933–1948*,

---

16 Josephine Bruegel, with Sylva Simsova, *Joza: Memories of My Life and Times* (London: privately printed by Kuperon Press, 2002).

17 Bohuslava Bradbrook, *The Liberating Beauty of Little Things. Decision, Adversity and Reckoning in a Refugee's Journey from Prague to Cambridge* (Brighton: Alpha Press, 2000).

18 Hana Demetz, *The House on Prague Street* (London: Allen, 1980).

19 Hana Greenfield, *Fragments of Memory from Kolin to Jerusalem* (Jerusalem: Gefen, 1998).

20 Mosse, ed., *Second Chance, op. cit.*, 492.

she devotes a chapter to Czechoslovak Jewry, asserting that 'discrimination was based on the principle of opposing mass Jewish emigration from Czechoslovakia' in the aftermath of the 1938 Munich Agreement.[21] Records do not, though, always distinguish between men and women refugees, or between Czechs and Slovaks. More generally, Yvonne Kapp and Margaret Mynatt, as employees of the CRTF, were well placed to critique internment policy in practice (Chapter 2), and Kapp's *Time Will Tell* provides some details about Czechoslovak refugees and the work of the CRTF;[22] however, their Communist bias and overt sympathies for refugees in their care were viewed as one-sided by some commentators.

Kushner, writing on women in domestic service in Britain in *Second Chance*, concentrates on the situation for Jewish refugees which narrows the subject focus, but blurs distinctions based on nationality essential to this study, so it should be borne in mind that numerous Czechoslovaks who were not Jewish also became domestic servants in Britain. Jews constituted only 1.39 per cent of the total Czechoslovak population according to the 1930 census[23] (Appendix A), but it is known that many Jewish families, including those of some interviewees, registered as Germans instead, while others inter-married or converted to Christianity. Even descendants of the famous Rabbi Löw[24] described by Demetz ate ham, and her grandfather disliked those who 'thought of themselves as Jews rather than Czechs'.[25] It was therefore imperative that an appropriately broader approach to this study be adopted, which spanned the spectrum of ethnicity, religion and political affiliation.

21   Louise London, *Whitehall and the Jews, 1933–1948. British Immigration Policy, Jewish Refugees and the Holocaust* (Cambridge: Cambridge University Press, 2000), 142.

22   Yvonne Kapp, *Time Will Tell: Memoirs*, eds C. Brinson and B. Lewis (London: Verso, 2004).

23   Czechoslovak Ministry of Foreign Affairs, Department of Information, *Statistická příručka Československé republiky/Statistical Handbook of the Czechoslovak Republic* (joint Czech/English) (London: 1942), 10–11.

24   Demetz, *op. cit.*; Rabbi Jehuda Löw was a Chief Rabbi of Prague associated with the Golem myth.

25   *Ibid.*, 53, 87.

Certain shortcomings, however, hampered research for this study. Governmental and organizational records are not always open for scrutiny, or if they are, are neither always complete nor always impartial. Many records have been lost or destroyed through the ravages of time, or for security reasons. Some personal files in The National Archives could not be accessed; others remain inaccessible for some years yet. Refugees' personal records at the Religious Society of Friends (Quakers) archives in London have been destroyed due to the UK's Data Protection Act 1998, depriving researchers of a valuable resource. Privately held documents, too, concerning the Western Hats factory, in Castlebar near Dublin, which had employed refugees during WWII, were destroyed by the Czechoslovak General Manager's daughter twenty-five years before this author contacted her.[26]

The destruction of documents has been a notable factor on the Czechoslovak side too, though for different reasons. Archivists in London and Prague have suggested that bulk and weight limited the removal of files from London to Prague after WWII, causing some archives to be either 'thinned' or disposed of; yet the bulky personal possessions of repatriates were transported across Europe despite the war damage. Of the documents that reached Czechoslovakia, it is believed that many were lost due to poor storage conditions or 'purged' during the Communist era as ideologically unacceptable. The archivists' views were substantiated when this author was researching Czechoslovak Young Women's Christian Association (YWCA) files in Prague's National Archives. A document was stamped by the Ministry of National Security, Archive and Study Division in November 1952, with four signatories whose ranks suggest certain authorities rather than archivists.

Even where official archives do exist and are open to scrutiny, they mostly reflect policies and events from a governmental or official point of view, 'a view from above'; as such, recognition of the role and importance of the individual may be suppressed. Organizational sources may also, to some extent, present 'a view from above', particularly where people are presented as recipients of financial and/or material aid, as is the case of

---

26   Franci Dražil(ová) (Šmolková), re: her uncle, František Šmolka/Franz Schmolka, and his daughter, author's interview [AI].

refugees helped by the CRTF and YWCA in Britain. Furthermore, few of the secondary academic sources on anti-Nazi migration are specific to Czechoslovak refugees, let alone the difficulties of Czechoslovak women refugees in Britain; these women have consequently become marginalized in exile studies. The various shortcomings of official records therefore necessitate a more balanced approach, and in this regard the study follows social historian Raphael Samuel, who advocated 'history from below' and promoted women's history.[27] Astrid Erll's *Memory in Culture*[28] is also very appropriate, presenting elements of memory in terms of 'human activity' through remembrance and commemoration at individual, institutional and collective levels. Individual women refugees thus have a 'voice' here via interviews, to comment on policies concerning them – essentially the 'view from below' of the 'ordinary people' as they were (or became) on arrival in Britain.

Oral history

In the light of the preceding observations, oral interviews as a means of accessing the past became an important feature of this work. By supplementing official records with personal histories and private papers, interviewees not only provided details that might otherwise never have been recorded, but also provided nuanced perspectives absent in extant records that focus on the 'broad sweep' of events or on the prominent agents involved in them. Moreover, it was imperative that the interviews be conducted and recorded while it was still feasible to do so; the main actors were elderly or unwell, and several have since died. Invaluable though the interviews were, the process nevertheless required critical examination and consideration

27   '*Making History. Historian Profiles. Professor Raphael Elkan Samuel (1934–1996)*', The
      Institute of Historical Research, University of London (2008), <http://www.history.
      ac.uk/makinghistory/historians/samuel_raphael.html>, accessed 31 May 2018.
28   Astrid Erll, *Memory in Culture* (Basingstoke: Palgrave Macmillan, 2011), 1–8.

of the drawbacks and pitfalls. Like the archives, the views and experiences presented by interviewees may not be impartial, and there is 'no one truth', as is compellingly argued by authorities on the subject, Paul Thompson in *The Voice of the Past. Oral History*[29] and John Tosh in *The Pursuit of History*, who also asserts that as 'history is not a single fixed event or a smooth sequence, context must be respected at every point' – a view this author strongly supports.[30]

Questionnaire and interviews

For consistency, a set 'life history' format questionnaire comprising twenty questions was prepared for Czechoslovak interviewees or their adult children (see Appendix B, Questionnaire), designed to elicit a range of data that could be collated, evaluated, compared and/or contrasted. (Separate questions were prepared for English interviewees). This form of qualitative, in-depth interviewing added layers of meaning to the topic of refugee women in exile. It must be stressed, however, that interviewees were drawn from as wide a spectrum of people as possible (see Appendix C);[31] they were not pre-selected, nor were they deemed middle or upper class simply because their family had had a maid. This author knew only a minimal amount about them in advance, thereby pre-empting deliberately skewed or pre-determined conclusions. Interviews lasted approximately two to three hours, and were mostly conducted in the interviewee's home. Physical and temporal distance from painful events enabled most interviewees to

---

29   Paul Thompson, *The Voice of the Past. Oral History* (Oxford/New York: Oxford University Press, 1988), 2nd edn, 101–49, especially 137–9 re: 'false memory'.

30   John Tosh, *The Pursuit of History. Aims, Methods and New Directions in the Study of Modern History* (Harlow: Longman, 2000), 3rd edn, 1, 8, 194, 198, 202.

31   For clarification regarding relationships, the names of interviewees' mothers or relatives have also been listed in Appendix C if substantive references have been made to them.

speak frankly about their experiences, feelings and opinions. In a marked shift in attitude about 'not talking about things in the past', interviewees saw the importance of doing so for an academic study, and for posterity. As Bohuslava Bradbrook commented in her autobiography, 'As one grows older, perhaps it is natural to look back and ask what turn our lives would have taken if we had acted differently in vital situations in the past'.[32]

In sum, seemingly disparate sources have surprisingly linked discrete strands of the study, and provided useful cross-references. Records in Britain and the Czech Republic referring to interviewees and/or family members significantly verified their narratives. A wealth of interviewees' private documents comprising reports, official or personal documents, letters and testimonies, have also illustrated aspects of this work, supporting and substantiating the interviewees' statements. Thus, the interviewees' oral history accounts complement historiography and policies, and provide a 'live' dynamic in this academic study, connecting it directly to identifiable Czechoslovak refugee women. Overall, it is hoped that this study will provide an insight into the quotidian lives of Czechoslovak refugee women in Britain from 1938 to 1950, treating women as individuals in their own right, rather than as 'appendages' to their menfolk.

32   Bradbrook, *op. cit.*, vi.

Arrival and Adjustment in Britain

'Munich' reverberates

While upper class young women in 1938 Britain were planning their 'coming out' programme for the 1939 season, few would have heeded the growing crisis in central Europe or its consequences. Yet the Munich Agreement of 29 September 1938 was the foreseeable, if unintended, cause of the first period of forced migration from Czechoslovakia in 1938–50, and underpinned successive ones. For Czechoslovakia, it was a case of 'o nas, bez nas' [about us, without us] – a popular term adapted from Czechoslovak Foreign Minister Kamil Krofta's announcement of 30 September 1938, that 'we submit to the decisions adopted in Munich without us and against us'.[1] For Britain, 'The achievement at Munich was the postponement of war. Except for the unfortunate Czechs, the whole western world was delirious with joy and thankfulness': such was the opinion of historian, academic and War Office Intelligence member, R. G. D. Laffan.[2] Britain's Prime Minister, Neville Chamberlain, was the hero of the day, advocating appeasement and declaring 'Peace for

1   Ministry of Foreign Affairs of the U. S. S. R., *Documents and Materials Relating to the Eve of the Second World War*, vol. 1, November 1937–8, From the Archives of the German Ministry of Foreign Affairs (Moscow: Foreign Languages Publishing House, 1948), 269.

2   R. D. G. Laffan, *Survey of International Affairs 1938*, vol. II, *The Crisis Over Czechoslovakia January to September 1938*, Royal Institute of International Affairs (London: Oxford University Press, 1951), 450.

our time',[3] but the euphoria was not to last; complex and far-reaching ramifications of the Agreement were soon manifested.

The ceding of the Sudetenland region to Hitler under the Munich Agreement on the pretext of German self-determination, touched upon the lives of all who lived there (see map on p. vii; the shaded areas denote ethnic German settlements in the Sudetenland). Susan Grant Duff argues that despite pockets of nineteenth-century German settlement in the Sudetenland, most Czechoslovak territory had belonged to the Austro-Hungarian Empire before 1918, not to Germany.[4] Nevertheless, the Agreement 'increased the population of the Reich by some 3 million Germans, together with about three-quarters of a million of unnoticed Czechs';[5] but whilst Germany's occupation of the Sudetenland from 1 October 1938 expanded its territory, it did *not* provide 3 million additional Nazi supporters and potential German combatants loyal to the Reich. Instead, Germany acquired the diverse and sometimes divided ethnic and political groups based on Czechoslovak citizenship or residency rather than a shared language. Although demographically the majority of people in the Sudetenland were ethnic Germans (*Volksdeutsche*), they were politically polarized, mostly supporting either Konrad Henlein's pro-Hitler Sudeten German Party which dominated the Sudetenland, or anti-Fascist groups such as Wenzel Jaksch's Sudeten-German Social Democrats which constituted a minority in that region, and whose opposition to Fascism placed them in considerable danger.

3   '1 October 1938: Chamberlain returns from Munich and declares "Peace for our time"', *Manchester Guardian* (1 October 1938), <http://www.guardian.co.uk/theguardian/from-the-archive-blog/2011/may/25/guardian-190-chamberlain-returns-from-munich>, accessed 31 May 2018.
4   Susan Grant Duff, *Europe and the Czechs* (Harmondsworth: Penguin Books, 1938), 94.
5   Laffan, *op. cit.*, 450–1.

First migration period: The Sudetenland

Fear of Germany's treatment of its 'acquired subjects' was widespread among the Sudetenland's anti-Fascists, precipitating the first cohort of migrants in 1938 for political, religious and racial reasons. The cohort comprised a broad spectrum of ethnic Germans: Jews, Christians, Communists, Social Democrats, MPs and trade union leaders and activists. They fled, if possible with their families, predominantly to Prague and its environs where German was widely spoken. Czech Slav counterparts similarly at risk did likewise. Some people had followed developments in Germany and Austria closely, hence left before the Munich Agreement, but in émigrée Elizabeth Weiss's opinion, 'few people anticipated events' in Czechoslovakia.[6] Most Czechoslovak Jews consequently only belatedly understood that their high degree of acculturation would not protect them from Nazi anti-Semitism. Gerda Mayer, for example, recalls her girlish notions of 'romantic poverty and adventure' in *Prague Winter*, whereas her father's diary entry notes 'We *had* to flee from Karlsbad' [his italics].[7] Thus, the family joined the exodus to rump Czechoslovakia.

In *Pearls of Childhood* Vera Gissing highlights just how frantic the exodus from the Sudetenland was, describing a new girl's arrival at school minus shoes and overcoat, there having been no time to dress or collect personal belongings. Gissings's father hastily had Vera and her sister Eva baptized as a 'wise precaution', though like others he did not think that Germany would invade rump Czechoslovakia.[8] By 23 November 1938, 91,625 refugees were sheltering there, comprising some 72,912 uprooted Czechs, 10,817 Germans, 190 Poles, 6,765 Czechoslovak Jews and 340 Jews of other nationalities, plus an estimated 10,000–15,000 refugees evading registration. Furthermore, reports stated, although 750,000 Czechs had remained in some occupied regions, various displaced minorities and hundreds of Czech teachers, lawyers and civil servants, who had been serving in ceded

6   Elizabeth Weiss, author's interview [AI].
7   Gerda Mayer (Stein), *Prague Winter* (London: Hearing Eye, 2005), 10, 17.
8   Vera Gissing, *Pearls of Childhood* (London: Robson Books, 1994), 24–5.

parts of Ruthenia and Slovakia, all converged on Czechoslovakia's trun-
cated territory.[9] This territory was further reduced from 1 November 1938
when Hungary claimed part of Slovakia, while Poland (re)claimed Těšín,
commencing its 'evacuation' on 2 October 1938. It caused Milena Roth's
mother, Anna, to write in December 1938 from Prague to an English friend
about 'thousands of families, that from one day to the other [...] have
become German, Polish or Hungarian citizens'.[10] For a small country it was
a huge upheaval, illustrated by Appendix A, the 1930 population census
extract, highlighting the country's ethnic composition and size of each
grouping as a percentage of the total population. In the melee, thousands
of Czechoslovak nationals effectively became refugees in what had been
their own country.

A 'special cause'

Czechoslovakia's 'dismemberment' was reflected in the gradual break-up of
many nuclear families. In Mayer's case, she slept in a drawer on the floor of
an aunt's home in Prague, while her parents stayed with another aunt until
rooms could be found pending their (planned but never realized) family
migration to another country.[11] Refugees without extended family connections or helpful friends in rump Czechoslovakia endured much harsher
conditions. The problem was compounded by the loss of Czechoslovakia's
industrial heartland, and the fact that while the available territory for a supposed safe haven had decreased, the number of people seeking refuge within

9   Imperial War Museum [IWM], Private Papers of M D Layton [Layton], Documents
     16055, box no. 07/70/1–2, box 2, Reports on Prague file: International Centre for
     Aid in Czechoslovakia and attachment, The Refugee Question in Czechoslovakia,
     statistical data to 23 November 1938.
10   Milena Roth, *Lifesaving Letters. A Child's Flight From the Holocaust* (Seattle:
     University of Washington Press, 2004), 49–50.
11   Mayer, *op. cit.*, 10, 17–18.

it increased. *Staging Point Prague German Exiles 1933–1939*, put the number of political refugees at 12,500, 14,500 Jewish and over 150,000 Czech refugees. A small number of Reich Germans sheltering in the Sudetenland since Hitler's appointment as Chancellor on 30 January 1933, and Austrians since the 12 March 1938 *Anschluss* [Annexation by Germany] fled for the second time; their group, reportedly comprising some 600 political and 5,000 Jewish émigrés, joined compatriots in rump Czechoslovakia.[12] The ensuing chaos, over-stretched essential services and starvation in inadequate refugee camps,[13] rendered Czechoslovakia a 'special cause' according to several charities in Britain. This dire situation was aggravated by nationality and citizenship issues, which were to have serious repercussions on refugees in wartime Britain (expanded in Chapter 2). Czechoslovak policy was split in the inter-war years (and again post-war). The Ministry of Foreign Affairs favoured 'openness and tolerance towards refugees', supported by Edvard Beneš when Prime Minister, and then President 1935–8, whereas the Ministry of the Interior 'was more restrictive'.[14] Nevertheless, 'it must be noted that Czechoslovakia did not grant "asylum" in the twenties and thirties; it just had very flexible legislation, which enabled many people to stay for long or "indefinite" periods of time'.[15] Attitudes hardened after the Sudetenland debacle however, leading to forced migration due to 'push' factors in rump Czechoslovakia too.

A 1938 report observed that because German Social Democrats and Communists (whether Czech-born or post-1933 arrivals) had fled

---

12   Peter Becher and Peter and Sigrid Canz, eds, *Drehscheibe Prag: Deutsche Emigranten/ Staging Point Prague: German Exiles 1933–1939* (joint German/English) (Munich: Adalbert Stifter Verein, 1989), 150; see also Peter Becher and Peter Heumos, eds, *Drehscheibe Prag: Zur Deutschen Emigrantion in der Tschechoslowakei 1923–1939* [*Staging Post Prague: German Exiles in Czechoslovakia 1933–1939*] (München: Oldenbourg, 1992), 182–3.

13   IWM, Layton, *op. cit.*, box 2, Reports on Prague file; Warriner later reported on the situation to Layton, letter, 29 November 1938.

14   'Czechoslovakia: "Island of Democracy" and Refuge Between the Wars', Radio Prague, Czech Radio (20 October 2005), <http://www.radio.cz/en/article/71864>, accessed 31 May 2018.

15   *Ibid.*

for political reasons, and despite their 'valiant' resistance to Henlein, it
was thought that 'they cannot be kept in Czechoslovakia since their presence there a) gives rise to the possibility of continued bad feeling between
Germany and Czechoslovakia, b) due [...] to increased pressure on
Czechoslovakia from Germany, c) greatly adds to the economic problem'.[16]
Furthermore, for the same reasons regarding 'Czech-born Jews who owned
factories and employed Czechs' in the occupied areas, and post-1933 refugees, 'it is considered impossible to keep these Jews'; 'those not Czech-
born should have first consideration in state plans for emigration'. This
approach was not confined to factory owners. 'Where can they go?' Anna
Roth(ová) asked her English friend, appealing for contacts in the colonies.
I have relatives who must emigrate, because they have no other choice'.[17]
Britain, however, like other countries, did not have (then or subsequently)
an 'open-door' policy. Nonetheless, the magnitude of these socio-political
developments ultimately came to the attention of the British public and
parliament. The Munich Agreement had given rise to considerable rifts and
shifts in opinion, but a sense of guilt regarding its outcome spurred some
people into action. The plight of the 'unfortunate' as described by Laffan
was also championed by MPs such as Eleanor Rathbone, who opposed
Chamberlain's appeasement policy; she cited the thousands of refugees
in danger, and pressed Home Secretary Samuel Hoare to substantially
increase the 350 entry permits to Britain granted pending permanent settlement elsewhere.[18] In a lengthy Commons policy debate on 5 October 1938,
Harold Nicolson challenged the government's 'hypocritical dealings with
regard to Czechoslovakia', asserting that it had given Hitler the three things
he sought: the Sudeten Germans, the destruction of Czechoslovakia as 'a

16   IWM, Layton, box 2, Reports on Prague file, International Centre for Aid in
       Czechoslovakia', *op. cit.*
17   Roth, *op. cit.*, 50.
18   Hansard, Parliamentary Reports, House of Commons, 340 H. C. DEB. 5 s., Oral
       Answers, 'Czechoslovakia (Refugees)', cols 369–70, 3 November 1938; Rathbone
       became Honorary Secretary of the Parliamentary Committee on Refugees. See also
       Susan Cohen, *Rescue the Perishing. Eleanor Rathbone and the Refugees*, especially
       Chapter 5 re: Czechoslovakia.

barrier to his "Drang nach Osten" [Hitler's plan to seize 'living space' east of Germany], and the opportunity to 'assure the world that Germany was now the dominant Power in Europe'.[19] Winston Churchill duly intoned, 'All is over. Silent, mournful, abandoned, broken, Czechoslovakia recedes into the darkness'.[20] Czechoslovakia did not, though, recede into oblivion, for others outside Parliament took up the Czechoslovak cause too, albeit not without opposition.

Czechoslovak refugees arrive in London

In contrast to the official government stance, the Refugees Committee of the League of Nations Union (RCLNU) sent a communication in October 1938 to Britain's Foreign Secretary, Lord Halifax, placing the onus of responsibility fully on the British and French governments for the consequences of their part in the Munich Agreement. Immediate government action was urged, 'irrespective of the relief which can be afforded to the sufferers by private charity', stressing that 'circumstances place the problem of Czech refugees on a different plane from those other categories of refugees'.[21] It was not, however, government aid which initially assisted refugees in or from Czechoslovakia, but voluntary charitable action. Widespread public sympathy prompted not only fund-raising sales and concerts, but also subscriptions to major appeals like the *News Chronicle* Fund (launched by the newspaper's Liberal chairman, Sir Walter Layton), and the Lord Mayor's Fund for Czech Refugees, launched primarily to provide humanitarian relief in Czechoslovakia. £360,000 was raised by the Lord Mayor's Fund by the end of December 1938, and shared among a number of

---

19   Hansard, House of Commons Official Report 339 H. C. DEB. 5 s., 'Government Policy', cols 427–34, 5, October 1938.

20   *Ibid.*, col. 364.

21   IWM, Layton, box 2, Refugees Committee of the League of Nations Union, Refugees in Czechoslovakia. Draft Communication to the Foreign Secretary, 13 October 1938.

organizations, including £260,000 for 'relief administration in the new [rump] Czechoslovakia', and '£80,000 ... for relief in the United Kingdom through the British Committee for Refugees from Czechoslovakia'.[22] The Trades Union Congress also contributed £2,000 'for transport for the Social Democrats' to emigrate.[23] Press coverage sustained the momentum. The *Evening Standard* of 31 October 1938, for example, announced 'Czech Refugees Come to London', and photographed them disembarking at Hay's Wharf, London Bridge, after their journey via Gdynia, Poland. 'Their future is not yet settled, and in the meantime they are being "billeted" in private houses', the caption read.[24] Many more refugees were to follow, drastically augmenting Britain's inter-war Czechoslovak community of merely around 500.[25]

Second migration period: Initial groups

The second period of migration overlapped with the first, initially on a small scale. A nexus of political and socio-economic obstacles in Britain prevented a mass influx of refugees, but as problems in Czechoslovakia escalated, it was increasingly held that the way to alleviate matters was to provide temporary shelter in Britain or its dominions. BCRC Prague Representative, Doreen Warriner, emphasized this in 'Aiding Czechs to Emigrate. Immediate Need for Action', a letter to the Editor of *The Daily Telegraph and Morning Post*, dated 11 December 1938. 'Any other way is a palliative for one's own conscience only', she wrote, recommending the

---

22   The National Archives London [TNA], HO 294/87, Lord Mayor's Fund Administration March 1944-August 1975, Note to Trustees, 24 April 1950.

23   IWM, Layton, box 1, Report on the Czechoslovakian Refugee Problem, and the Best Use of the Lord Mayor's Fund, 3; undated, with documents dated 1938.

24   'Czech Refugees Come to London', *Evening Standard* (31 October 1938), 10.

25   TNA, HO 294/72, British Council circular: founding of the Czechoslovak Institute in London 21 January 1941, undated, around December 1940/January 1941.

granting of block visas and funds for overseas settlement.[26] Numerous individuals and organizations including the Moravian Church, and RCLNU members such as the Christian Council for Refugees, Jewish Refugees Committee, Save the Children Fund, the Society of Friends (Quakers) and the Society for the Protection of Science and Learning endeavoured to help refugees reach Britain and/or care for them on arrival. The main focus here, though, is on the work of two key organizations, the BCRC and its successor, the Czech Refugee Trust Fund (CRTF), with emphasis throughout this study on the latter due to its greater duration. As an example of a smaller-scale relief effort, this chapter also presents the little known involvement of the Young Women's Christian Association (YWCA) with Czechoslovakia during the period 1938 to 1939.

British Committee for Refugees from Czechoslovakia

The BCRC was founded in October 1938 in direct response to the consequences of the Munich Agreement, for 'refugees whose prominence in opposition to Nazism and Fascism had brought their liberty and even their lives into danger', and who therefore needed to be rescued.[27] The charity actively helped such people to escape to Britain, principally Communists, Social Democrats, trade unionists, PEN members,[28] Jews and their families. Kate Thornycroft, who became head of the hospitality section and oversaw the housing of some 3,000 refugees, was involved in the Committee's work from its inception to her resignation in 1940.

26 Warriner, Doreen, 'Aiding Czechs to Emigrate. Immediate Need for Action', *Daily Telegraph and Morning Post*, letter to Editor, 11 December 1938 (14 December 1938), 14.
27 TNA, HO 294/5, History of CRTF, CRTF Advisory Council. General Report of the Director, 15 November 1939.
28 PEN helped support Czechoslovak refugee members financially.

The first discussion was held at economist Maynard Keynes' Bloomsbury home, Thornycroft recalled, but large dedicated premises were soon needed to deal with 'the great snowball of humanity – all people uprooted by intolerance'.[29] A report headed 'Action of the Committee to Date', 21 February 1939, noted that in October 1938 alone, some 250 men had been rescued from the Sudetenland, plus 100 German and Austrian refugees from Prague. Over a thousand more were awaited in Britain, with emigration plans being made for them all.[30] Then as now, criticism of such assistance was expressed. In a letter to the Editor of the *Evening Standard* published on 28 December 1938, the correspondent pointed out that 'We have nearly two million unemployed', and noted the cost of feeding, housing and training 'alien refugees, mainly ex-enemy', alluding to Germany and WWI.[31]

Such statements were noticed by refugees able to read English newspapers and who relayed information to their compatriots, but BCRC Chief Executive Officer and Secretary, Margaret Layton,[32] responded by emphasizing the 'pull-push' predicament refugees were locked into, in 'The Victims of Munich. An Appeal to British Co-operative Youth', published by the Co-operative Youth Movement in January 1939. She explained that although the Committee had accepted responsibility for 350 refugees and their families who were therefore allowed to enter Britain, 'some 4,000 Sudeten Germans, most of them Social Democrats' remained in appalling emergency camps, the only alternative being a German concentration camp. There were also 'some 15,000 Jews from the Sudeten areas who will find no place in the new [rump] Czechoslovakia', plus 'some 5,000 Germans and Austrians [...] who must leave [...] or be turned back to the Reich', she stated.[33] The BCRC resolutely continued

---

29   Hermann and Kate Field (Thornycroft), *Trapped in the Cold War. The Ordeal of an American Family* (Stanford, CA: Stanford University Press, 1999), 122–4, 280.
30   IWM, Layton, box 1, Action of the Committee to Date, 21 February 1939.
31   Letter to Editor, *Evening Standard* (28 December 1938), 15.
32   Walter Layton's daughter, a Cambridge graduate like Thornycroft.
33   Margaret Layton, 'The Victims of Munich', *Co-operative Youth* (January 1939), 57, 64.

with its work, and by mid-February 1939 numbers 'under direct charge' of the Committee had risen to 870, with some 400 Sudeten heads of families, 120 German and Austrian heads of families, 200 women and 150 children under 18.[34]

Dispersal

It can be deduced from Layton's report that the disruption to family life caused by events in the homeland was perpetuated and even heightened in Britain, as existing family units began to break up too. This was not an intentional but a causal effect of early accommodation problems, necessitating a policy of refugee dispersal. Consequently, Sudeten Germans at this juncture were mostly placed in large groups in guest houses in Guildford, Dorking and Haywards Heath, or in youth hostels; 130, though, were placed in 'private hospitality' in London or dispersed in small groups in Essex, Leicester, Oxford, Kendal, Bristol, Manchester, Leeds and Cheshire.[35] Many English people across the country had responded to appeals for help and short-term hospitality for newly arrived refugees, published for instance in 'The Victims of Fascism', *New Statesman and Nation*, 19 November 1938.[36] Some women were sent for domestic training with the YWCA in Seaford, but in general it remained necessary for the BCRC to subsidize basic expenses, since refugees were prohibited from working as a condition of entry into Britain (subject to certain exceptions discussed here later), even if they spoke English adequately. Minors attended British schools or received technical training. Thus the refugees were safe, but obliged to adjust rapidly to their new environment, which presented many challenges.

34   IWM, Layton, box 1, Action of the Committee to Date, 21 February 1939.
35   *Ibid.*
36   'The Victims of Fascism', *New Statesman and Nation* (19 November 1938), 814.

Early challenges

The *Evening Standard* of 4 February 1939 recorded some of these challenges
in 'Refugee Lawyers, Doctors, Dentists Attend School to Learn English'[37] in
Albury, Surrey, observing that most 'were over 40' with 'only two or three of
the workman class'. Asked what their prospects were 'in beginning life again',
the Reverend Philip Gray replied, 'Pretty grim'. The Lord Mayor's Fund (via
the BCRC) provided board and lodging in guest houses and 2/6d per week per
person pocket money (see Introductory Note, pre-decimalization currency),
while 'private benevolence' supplied clothes and 'extra comforts', but 'finding
these very intelligent men [and women] something to do is one of our chief
problems', he commented. 'The aimlessness of life, the blankness of the future,
weighs on their minds more than anything else'. Some seventy refugees therefore studied English for two hours daily and attended lectures on England,
which would ultimately help them to integrate, but initially helped to pass the
time. The women also learnt practical skills such as cookery, dressmaking and
'various crafts', and ten were placed in domestic service. Each guest house, the
piece concluded, was run by a democratically elected committee, 'For these
people [...] were all workers in the democratic cause in the Sudetenland – that
is why they are here – and they are meticulous in carrying on the tradition of
popular government in their exile'. This observation was borne out by Fortis
Green CRTF hostel residents (as noted below), and similar self-organization
manifested by women interned on the Isle of Man (discussed in Chapter 2).

A further insight into refugee life at this early stage is via the vexed question of suitability or acceptability, that is, 'the right sort' of person, which arose
in connection with charitable refugee groups and regional refugee committees, and recurred in numerous instances. On 26 October 1938, for example,
Ellen Champness wrote on behalf of the National Committee of Brotherhood
Movement to Layton about practical issues concerning any refugees it might

---

37   'Refugee Lawyers, Doctors, Dentists Attend School to Learn English', *Evening
      Standard* (4 February 1939), 15. [120 refugees had originally arrived in Albury
      November–December 1938, and were lodged in Tree Tops holiday camp, and Surrey
      Hills and Brook Lodge guest houses].

accommodate, adding that its members were 'mostly men and women attached to the Anglican and Free Churches and would make the right type of hosts and hostesses'. Layton replied on 27 October 1938, explaining that hospitality could be for a limited period, though preferably for three months, noted the financial arrangements previously described here, and advised that the inability to speak German 'does not matter, but hostesses should be warned that few of the refugees know English'. Given the highly political. secular background of most BCRC refugees at that time, Layton astutely ended by stating that it would be useful to know 'what type of refugee would be most congenial to the hostess, as they come from all classes and occupations'. Ostensibly, Champness's approach was discriminatory, though it was also a practical one and efforts were made to 'match' hosts with refugees;[38] but for dislocated women refugees accustomed to running their own home and to Czech or German cuisine, living as a 'guest', albeit a helpful one, could still be trying in a foreign country with unfamiliar customs and traditions. The psychological and emotional importance of one's own home and personal objects is highlighted in *The Meaning of Things; Domestic Symbols and the Self*, since 'the things that surround us are inseparable from who we are'.[39]

Second migration period: Main surge

While debutantes in Britain were being presented at court, Germany seized rump Czechoslovakia during 14–15 March, consolidating its hold over *Mitteleuropa*. 'On 16 March 1939 news of the German invasion of Czechoslovakia ousted the Court Circular, with its report of the previous evening's presentations, from the pages of *The Times*'; further presentations were suspended during WWII, causing parents 'great practical problems

---

38   IWM, Layton, box 1, letter 26 October 1938, and BCRC reply 27 October 1938.
39   Mihaly Csikszentmihalyi and Eugene Rochberg-Halton, *The Meaning of Things; Domestic Symbols and the Self* (Cambridge: Cambridge University Press, 1981), 16.

in bringing out their daughters'.[40] For the BCRC, the problems were of a very different kind. By 14 March 1939 it was responsible for 2,900 individuals[41] for whom, regardless of age, the 'push' of enforced migration from the homeland marked years of adjustment and insecurity, while the 'pull' of freedom was countered by the wrench of separation from family members left behind (sometimes including the breadwinner or head of family), for varying periods of time or permanently in many cases. The dates 14–15 March 1939 were therefore highly significant, adding to the worries of those refugees in safety, and providing the impetus for a surge in the migration of diverse Czechoslovaks. Alice Masaryk, the first President's daughter, reportedly stated that 'March 15 was not the end of history',[42] which indeed it was not. Nevertheless, it denoted the end of an era in Czechoslovak social history. Moreover, it constituted a watershed for hundreds of women and children whose lives were entwined with the fate of their men-folk who believed everyone would be safe in rump Czechoslovakia. Instead, they all had to flee (some for the third time); this time, though, not to a neighbouring region, or a country with a shared culture and language inherited from the Habsburg Empire, but to a distant and unknown land.

As the Gestapo sought out intellectuals and 'politically undesirable' anti-Fascists, particularly those named on a blacklist,[43] members of the Fascist *Flag* organization were ordered to 'inform on the Jews, Communists, followers of Beneš, illegal leaflets and whispered propaganda'.[44] Wives and family members were consequently also at risk due to their own political engagement, imputed political opinion, or because they were suspected of aiding wanted men in hiding. With heightened fears for their safety, and concerns for Jews who soon lived *de facto* under the so-called Nuremberg laws in what became

---

40   Fiona MacCarthy, *Last Curtsey. The End of the Debutantes* (London: Faber and Faber, 2006), 12.
41   TNA, HO 294/5, History of the CRTF, *op. cit.,* 15 November 1939, item 3.
42   Gordon H. Skilling, *Mother and Daughter. Charlotte and Alice Masaryk* (Prague: Gender Studies o. p. s., 2001), 160.
43   IWM, Layton, box 1, Preliminary Report, undated, around early to mid-1939.
44   Michael Burian, *et al., Assassination. Operation Anthropoid 1941–1942* (Prague: Defence Ministry of the Czech Republic, 2002), 13.

the German Protectorate of Bohemia and Moravia from 16 March 1939,[45] the BCRC's work became increasingly urgent. The situation worsened in July 1939 when Adolf Eichmann, Director of the Gestapo's Department of Jews in Vienna, arrived in Prague and began 'regulating' the Central Office for Jewish Immigration,[46] but Zionists like LS from Teplice [Teplitz-Schönau] had fortunately emigrated to Palestine in February 1939.[47] Slovakia, having declared its independence from Czechoslovakia on 14 March 1939, was (theoretically) an autonomous state. Hence it was suggested that a separate Commission be established in Bratislava with a British Mission representative, to select small groups of families drawn from different professional backgrounds 'which could lead an independent existence' abroad.[48] Nevertheless, the situation for Jews in Slovakia generally came to mirror that of the Protectorate. Slovak anti-Jewish legislation based on the Nuremberg Laws was passed on 9 September 1941, and 57,628 people were deported to Poland between March and October 1942. Most of the remaining approximately 24,000 Jews either had a particular role, or were sent to work camps;[49] some hid in the mountains or joined the partisans there – few could escape across increasingly Nazi-occupied Europe.

BCRC rescue efforts had thus centred on Prague until it became too dangerous to continue, as described in Warriner's report, 'The Winter in Prague'.[50] Thanks largely to Warriner, some 500 women and children escaped by train from Prague via Poland on 14 March 1939, though around

45 IWM, R. J. S. Stopford [Stopford], ref: RJS 3/13–3/15, Baumgarten's confidential Report on the Position of Jews in the Bohemian-Moravian Protectorate, 23 July 1939. Reich Protector Decrees enforced parts of the 1935 Nuremberg Declaration on racial issues in June and July 1939.
46 *Ibid.*, outline of procedures.
47 LS, AI.
48 IWM, Layton, box 2, Wisconsin file, Emigration in Slovakia, Report of Ludwig Kemeny, Bratislava, undated, with correspondence dated 1939.
49 Shari Cohen, *Politics Without a Past. The Absence of History in Postcommunist Nationalism* (London: Duke University Press, 1999), xii, 68–9.
50 Doreen Warriner, report, 'The Winter in Prague', June 1939, Fromings (Huenigen), private papers [PP].

240 more waited to do so.[51] Others furtively approached her for help, like Anna Tschapek, a German-speaking Sudeten Communist and her 10-year-old son Walter, who narrowly escaped deportation to a concentration camp when a policeman 'turned a blind eye'. They sheltered in Prague's Miramar Hotel at the BCRC's expense, but following a Gestapo raid were hidden in a Czech home with ten other refugees until their departure. The Tschapeks hid in the train's luggage section when the Gestapo retained Anna's passport and searched the carriages, but reached Britain safely on 27 April 1939 at the second attempt (see Figure 1).[52]

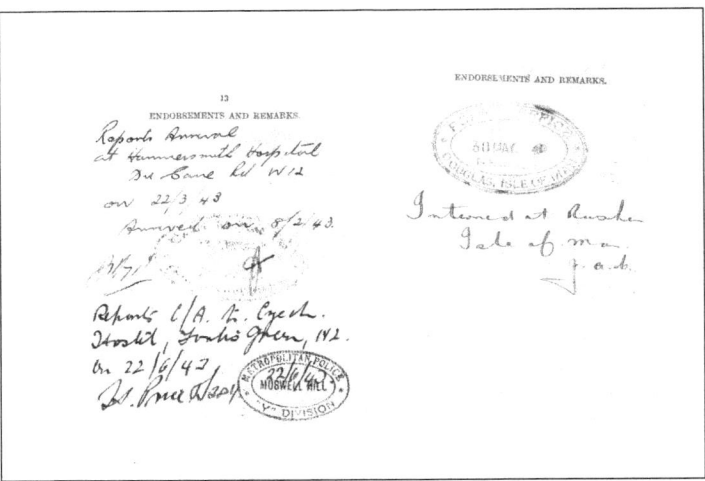

Figure 1. Anna Tschapek's British Registration Certificate showing endorsements re: Fortis Green CRTF hostel, internment, Hammersmith Hospital [Czechoslovak section], 1940s. Courtesy of son, Walter.

Escape was fraught with danger and the risk of last-minute arrests on trains. Exit permits (valid for just a few days) were compulsory from 16 March 1939, and granted only to non-Jews, who had to present their birth certificate.[53]

51   Warriner, report, *op. cit.*, 26–7.
52   Walter Tschapek, AI, PP.
53   IWM, Layton, box 1, Report of Evacuation of Refugees From Prague Since March 13th [1939].

Significantly, 'izr', that is, Izraelita/Izraelitka [Israelite] as on Zora Karas's birth certificate, plainly indicated Jewish origins.[54] As Gestapo scrutiny of applications for permits gradually increased, Warriner wrote, applications were submitted via Čedok travel agency 'without mentioning that they [the women] were communists or political refugees. The men, of course, had to go illegally'. Hundreds of people crossed the Tatra mountain region into Poland on foot en route to Gdynia, but risked being passed to the Gestapo, or returned to Czechoslovakia by nervous Polish authorities[55] as were Pavel Seifter's Communist parents Karel and Anna, who finally arrived in Britain with him in September 1939.[56]

Special lists of refugees

Anxious individuals and groups competed for help, and the difficulty of selecting those to be assisted is evidenced by lists of approximately 600 people deemed most at risk on a scale of one to six, as agreed by the BCRC in January 1939.[57] These pertain to prominent men, known political leaders and activists or those who had been imprisoned by the Nazi authorities, but women came too, as proven by lists and documents among Layton's papers containing the names of interviewees and/or close relatives the BCRC helped to reach Britain, including women and children due to join their menfolk who had gone ahead of them. Among them are the Tschapeks (given as Tschappek), journalist Ludvik Freund's first wife and 6-year-old son Tommy.[58] Liberec MP Edmund Huenigen was a Sudeten German listed as an important Communist at risk,

---

54   'Sarah' was also used in some countries re: Jewish females.
55   Warriner report, June 1939, *op. cit.*, 35.
56   Pavel Seifter, AI.
57   IWM, Layton, box 1, Central Committee lists file, undated but with documents dated 1939.
58   Freund was later changed to Frejk(a) to appear less Jewish.

but he refused to leave without his family.[59] He was subsequently arrested by the Gestapo in Prague on 17 March 1939. Perceived as German, his teenage son Edmund was obliged to remain in Czechoslovakia, while Huenigen's wife Hedwig and apprehensive 12-year-old daughter Hedy escaped in July 1939, after a 'tip off' not to board a particular train (see Figure 2). Their journey was rendered all the more dangerous by pretending that a Jewish girl joining family members in Britain was Hedy's sister.[60] The last group of women in Doreen Warriner's care also travelled by train from Prague's Wilson Station across Germany to Holland, arriving at Liverpool Street Station on 22 May 1939, and her colleague Beatrice Wellington helped the final group of women to escape from Prague in July 1939.[61]

Figure 2. Where the journey began: interviewee Hedy Fromings by the Kindertransport memorial, platform 1, Wilson Station, Prague, 2011. Author's image.

59   IWM, Layton, box 1, Central Committee lists file 1939, Spanish file; Vera Vohlídalová (Tomášková), AI.

60   Fromings (Huenigen), AI, PP.

61   Warriner report, June 1939, *op. cit.*, 51.

Another list of special interest, dated 11 November 1939, concerns Jaksch supporters from the Sudetenland, providing socio-historical data in terms of their age, skills, date of birth and their early location in Britain.[52] While the men's occupations ranged from lawyer, journalist, student, to mason, furrier, porcelain worker, chemical worker, merchant and metalworker, the word 'housewife' appeared frequently by the women's names, especially in the case of older women born in the late nineteenth or early twentieth centuries. Perhaps unmarried or widowed, Marie Altschul, a cook born in 1881, and Margaret Adler, a dressmaker born in 1899, were notable exceptions; both went to Margate. Many of the women appear to have come alone, or with their daughter(s), and although most of the names are German, Czech names (minus diacritics) such as Dub, Dubsky and Dvořák also appear. Friederike Cerny, a nurse born in 1915, had a German first name but Czech surname, suggesting mixed German-Czech parentage, which would not have been unusual. She too went to Margate, as did embroiderer Marie Dannler, born in 1911, whereas lace-worker Anna Denk went to Cark-in-Cartmel, a Cumbrian village, and sales-woman Gertrude Brueckner, also born in 1906, lived at 199 Goldhawk Road, in Shepherds Bush, London. Other women included a hairdresser and a 'domestic'. Like most civilian exiles from Czechoslovakia they were aided in some way by the BCRC's successor, the CRTF.

Czech Refugee Trust Fund

By March 1939 the BCRC's funds were almost exhausted. The charity evolved, however, into the Czech Refugee Trust Fund due to a shift in British government policy that, despite some opposition, adhered closely to the previously spurned League of Nations 1938 recommendations. Events had

---

62   IWM, Layton, box 1, Central Committee lists file 1939, Communists and List of Members of Jaksch Group, 11 September 1939.

necessitated the protection of a) refugees in the second (for some third) migration periods to Britain and other countries, and b) the balance of the British Grant of £4 million, a gift to the Czechoslovak government as set out in *Financial Assistance to Czecho-Slovakia* for the assistance of refugees from the Sudetenland. Only £500,000–600,000 had been used by 15 March 1939,[63] mostly by the Jewish Agency for the permanent settlement of Czechoslovak Jews in Palestine.[64] The British government consequently established the Czech Refugee Trust Fund by Deed on 21 July 1939, 'for the purpose of assisting emigration and settlement of refugees' from the territory which prior to 1 October 1938 'belonged to the Republic of Czechoslovakia', and for the refugees' maintenance and training in Britain pending their final settlement, that is, somewhere other than Britain.[65] When rump Czechoslovakia was seized, 'H. M. Government took prompt steps to safeguard from Germany the unexpended portion',[66] and the Grant was transferred from the Bank of England to the Treasury under the Czecho-Slovakia (Financial Claims and Refugees) Act, 1940.[67] As a public Trust, the CRTF came directly under the aegis of the Secretary of State for the Home Department and the Treasury. Thus, apart from the Czechoslovak state boarding schools opened in Britain and a hospital wing in London, the welfare of the majority of civilian refugees from

63   IWM, Stopford, RJS 3/13–3/17, file 3/14, Czech Refugee Trust Fund, Note from Home Office (dated only as 1971). For terms of the Agreement see Treaty Series No. 9 (1939), *Financial Assistance to Czecho-Slovakia*, Cmd. 5933 (London: HMSO, 27 January 1939).

64   IWM, Stopford, RJS 3/13–3/17, folder 04/14/2, file 3/15, [translated] letter from Presidium of [Czechoslovak] Ministry of Finance, 13 January 1939, agreeing to transfer of funds to the Jewish Agency.

65   TNA, HO 213/292, Trust Deed. See also Home Office, *Czech Refugee Trust Fund and Directions to the Trustees* (London: HMSO, July 1939).

66   Layton Papers, box 1, Note on the Financial Position Regarding Refugees from Czechoslovakia, undated but attached to House of Commons notepaper stamped 18 July 1939, for debate in Parliament by Eleanor Rathbone, MP; Stopford Papers, RJS 3/13–3/17, folder 04/14/2, Minute Sheet with earlier 'Secret' correspondence; National Bank of Czechoslovakia and Bank of England, May 1939, also deals with this matter.

67   IWM, Stopford, RJS 3/13–3/17, file 3/14, CRTF, Note from Home Office [given as 1971].

Czechoslovakia was, in the main, administered by the CRTF, not President Beneš's government in exile. This level of British support for Czechoslovak refugees distinguished the Czechoslovak exile experience in Britain from others, both immediately prior to, and during WWII. To a lesser extent, that support was extended post-war thereby linking two totalitarian regimes, Fascism and Communism.

Britain's declaration of war on Germany

In the Trust's first phase 1939–48 (the second, 1948–50, is dealt with in Chapter 6), it took over the BCRC's 170 staff and adopted its administrative structure. Refugees like Berta Freistadt's Slovak father therefore retained their BCRC registration number, but received a new CRTF card. Six weeks after the Trust's creation, Britain declared war on Germany on 3 September 1939, causing major policy shifts: 'There was no longer any question of the rescue of refugees whether legally or illegally', stated the Trust's Advisory Council, General Report of the Director, 15 November 1939.[68] Nonetheless, item 10 on the Position as to Immigration, acknowledged the immense pressure to leave Czechoslovakia on account of the 'known hostility of the German authorities towards the wives of political refugees who have succeeded in escaping', and on account of Nazi transfers of Jews to Ljublin in Poland, while an unknown number of refugees 'is believed to have made its way in to the territories now occupied by Russians'. Jews in particular were caught up in a 'catch 22' situation whereby 'The policy of H. M. Government hitherto has not been to close the door altogether, but to admit refugee immigrants only in very special circumstances and only after they have succeeded in making their way into a neutral country' – which did not allow legal entry without the assurance of early admission to another country.[69]

68   TNA, HO 294/5, History of the CRTF, *op. cit.*, 15 November 1939.
69   *Ibid.*

The Trust did, though, take responsibility for an additional 200 refugee families from the Protectorate and Slovakia (mostly those stranded in Poland) as at August 1939,[70] and honoured the Committee's prior commitment to meet the emigration costs of over 1,600 refugees to Canada, Palestine and Sweden. It also assisted 365 individual refugees who emigrated to the British Empire, the USA, South America and other countries at a cost of £34,000. Most of those refugees had sailed by December 1940, as the number of prospective host countries had dwindled and voyages were dangerous.[71] Thus, contrary to expectations, the Trust's intended focus on emigration to other countries perforce shifted from September 1939 to the 'inherited' 'static block of some 8,000 human beings who might not be able to leave this country [Britain] for a very long time'.[72] That figure rose to nearly 12,000 refugees from Czechoslovakia by December 1939, including those who had first sought refuge there and later became refugees for a second or even third time. They comprised 6,000 Czechoslovaks, 3,000 Sudeten Germans, 300 'other Czech minorities', 1,000 Reich Germans, 800 Austrians and 800 'unclassified'; more than half of these refugees were 'wholly dependent upon the Trust for financial support'.[73] The need to re-plan was clearly pressing.

CRTF hostels and the *Arbeitskreis* system

One of the many problems to confront the Trust was how to adapt a scheme for short-term assistance that had not envisaged accommodating and maintaining refugees in Britain for an indefinite period, and certainly not in

70   IWM, Layton, box 1, CRTF to Cooper, Home Office Aliens Department, 15 August 1939.
71   TNA, HO 294/7, CRTF, Outline of Events in the Period July 1939 (date of commencement) to 31 December 1941.
72   TNA, HO 294/5, History of the CRTF, *op. cit.*, items 4, 7.
73   TNA, HO 294/7, CRTF, Consideration of Future Activities, undated but with CRTF correspondence dated September 1947.

such large numbers. A solution lay in the hostel system, with two different kinds of hostel: those managed and financed entirely by the Trust, and those managed by local British refugee committees but wholly or partly financed by the Trust. This was more economical than individual private accommodation, and became a major feature of the Trust's first phase of existence. The present focus is therefore on the Trust's hostels and their impact on those who dwelled in them. There were seventeen 'directly controlled' hostels when the Trust commenced, and twenty-two new ones were opened in the period to March 1940. They were located as far afield as Wales and Inverness in order to disperse the refugees, but were opened or closed depending upon cost, the state of the building, and changing needs. For example, for security reasons the Aliens (Protected Areas) Order of April 1940 obliged the Trust to close hostels situated near the coast, and open new ones elsewhere.[74]

By then, each hostel was required to have a British warden, with an elected refugee 'house mother or father' responsible for organizing the general running of it. Coping with a large influx of refugees with disparate and sometimes conflicting backgrounds and needs was no easy task so, where possible, residents placed in hostels were of the same ethnicity and/ or political persuasion. Like the BCRC, the Trust depended heavily on the *Arbeitskreis*, essentially a group system devised in rump Czechoslovakia comprising political, ethnic and religious refugee groups, with a committee comprising representatives of all the groups[75] (though the majority of those arriving in Britain after the *Einmarsch* [invasion] were described by the Trust as *not* specifically political). Known by the leader's surname, groups were headed by prominent representatives who liaised with their group members and the Trust, if not always with each other due to political differences indicated here by the spectrum of parties:

Sudeten Communists, Gustav Beuer
Sudeten Liberals, Alfred Peres
German Social Democrats, Wilhelm Sander

74   TNA, HO 294/7, CRTF, Outline of Events, 1941, *op. cit.*
75   IWM, Layton, Box 2, CRTF, Minutes of Meeting 9 December [1939], 3.

German Salda Committee (i.e. Communists), Heinz Schmidt
German Democratic Committee, Otto Wollenberg
Hicem (Jewish group), Paul Rehfeldt
Thomas Mann (group of German and Austrian writers and intellectuals),
Bernhard Menne
Austrian Social Democrats, Johann Svitanics
Austrian Salda Committee (i.e. Communists), Hans Winterberg
There was also a general Czech group comprising Miloš Ambros, Josef
Bělina, the Communist Anežka Hodinová (later Hodinová-Spurná), and
Sudeten Trade Union representative, Josef Lenk[76] joined by (*inter alios*)
Pavel Kavan and Otto Šling.[77]

Although, inexplicably, no women became group leaders, they did play an
increasing role in both the exile and host community, and were represented
by active women members of the Czechoslovak government in exile like
Marie Jurnečková, Social Democrat member of the Czechoslovak State
Council in exile with special responsibility for women's movements and
interests. Hodinová was a leading member of the Czechoslovak Communist
Party, and later became a Communist member of the Czechoslovak State
Council too.

Fortis Green CRTF hostel

It fell to group leaders to explain the need for hostels to refugees, and
appeal for their co-operation[78] – not always successfully. Adjustment to
life in Britain was much harder than some refugees had anticipated or

---

76   TNA, HO 294/74, *Arbeitskreis General*, undated, with correspondence dated 1939.
77   School of Slavonic and East European Studies [SSEES], Lisicky Collection, LIS
     3/3/8, letter to CRTF on group membership, 13 June 1939.
78   IWM, Layton, box 2, Advisory Committee members file, *Arbeitskreis*, 8 December 1939.

would have wished, and communal hostel life contrasted immensely with a private home life, leading to considerable tension, even friction at times, especially at Canterbury Hall in Bloomsbury, London, Bournemouth and Margate.[79] Nonetheless, there was a degree of equality between men and women sharing duties and tasks in their respective hostels, particularly where political affiliation or leadership bonded them. Two 'model hostels' were renowned for their success: one for unaccompanied children (Chapter 4), and Fortis Green hostel in East Finchley, London, which opened in June 1940, primarily to house some fifty women and children (dependents of Czechoslovak servicemen) according to CRTF Minutes dated 8 April 1940 (see Figure 3).[80] Hetty Bower, a qualified book-keeper whose calculations on comparative accommodation costs had helped shape the Trust's hostel policy, became the warden, earning 5/- (see Introductory Notes) per week. She had suggested the adoption of Fortis Green School as a hostel after boarders and day pupils were evacuated due to the Blitz, since the grounds, large dining room, kitchens and range of rooms rendered it 'eminently suitable'.[81] British-born but of Silesian Jewish origin, Bower welcomed the first busloads of forty to fifty refugees, most of whom had been transferred from coastal zones. She recalled that 'it was an amazing experience [...] to observe how disciplined and efficient these people were. Really, the organization was superbly managed'. She also observed how quickly 'they elected their own committee from among their members, about twelve adults' who elected a chairman, but it was 'the efficient way the committee set about arranging which rooms were to be occupied by whom, and how people were immediately taken to their room, shared by a whole family', that greatly impressed her. 'They then appointed four cooks from the women, two to be on duty for two or three days, then the other two. Assistants to the main cooks were also selected'. While all this

79 See, for example, TNA, HO 294/19, CRTF, Hostels, Canterbury Hall; TNA, HO 294/20, CRTF, Political Intrigues – Margate.

80 CRTF Minutes, 8 April 1940, Private papers of Yvonne Kapp [originally lodged with the Women's Library, ref: 7YVK; transferred to the London School of Economics and Political Science archives 2013]; see also Senate House Library.

81 Esther (Hetty) Bower (Rimel), AI, PP.

was taking place, beds, wardrobes, vacuum cleaners and other essential equipment arrived from the CRTF. 'It was all done in a day. By evening we could assess how many more people we could accommodate if necessary'.

Figure 3. Early days: women refugees in Fortis Green CRTF hostel, London, c.1940/1.
Courtesy of Fritz Koehler, son of 'house-father' Frederic Kohler [sic].
Front row (l. to r.), 1-7: 2 Hilde Weber, 3 Marte Richter, 7 Marga Tomašková/Tomasek/
Tomaschek. Second row (l. to r.): Marte Masopust, Gisa Grünwald, Hanna Grossman
(Struz), Schellenberger, Marie Köhler, Ida Antusch, Anna Seifter.
Back row (l. to r.): Epstein [not interviewee Dorrit Epstein], Vogel, Elvira Kühn.

Approximately 85 per cent of the hostel's residents were German-speaking *Volksdeutsche* activists from the Sudetenland, who certainly reinforced the *Evening Standard*'s statement above about Sudeten refugees maintaining the 'tradition of popular government in their exile'. The residents included a small number of non-observant Jews, plus some Hungarians, Poles and Slovaks, and generally comprised Communists, Social Democrats and trade unionists. 'Many of course had known each other in Czechoslovakia', Bower commented. Despite some personal problems confided in her, to her knowledge 'there was never any personal animosity or open antagonism', and the respected 'house-father', Frederic Kohler, fostered an enduring communal spirit that was to help sustain the refugees through difficult times. To some extent, it might be said that the refugees constituted a 'parallel community' at that juncture, but their life was hardly one of secluded contemplation; on the contrary. Somewhat paradoxically given the supposedly transient nature of the refugees' stay in Britain, English language classes were organized by the British Council as a matter of government policy, initially to enhance integration. A female teacher therefore visited the hostel weekly, although women 'had to fit in English lessons with work in the hostel such as cleaning and dining room schedules', Bower noted. Men and women formed convenient reading and study groups, aided by the warden and two or three English-speaking former teachers among the residents, so the majority of refugees soon learnt enough English for basic communication, amidst confusion and hilarity on the women's part over different meanings of words such as 'dummy' and certain German and English verbs. Pregnant women or those with very small children stayed in the hostel and were advised on health and welfare matters by a district nurse, but most of the younger residents worked outside the hostel when legally permitted to.[82]

Britain's new Order in Council of 17 November 1939 (revoked July 1940) briefly allowed the employment of refugees in a wide range of work. Whilst Labour Exchanges did not purport to offer personally fulfilling employment, being usefully occupied was important for refugee morale and well-being. It left less time to brood over problems, as the Albury refugees had done, and curtailed accusations of 'sponging' on the state. Employment also helped to finance the hostel, since all CRTF hostels had to be self-sufficient, with properly kept accounts available for inspection. Thus, while residents involved in the hostel's maintenance, such as the cooks and gardener, received a small additional payment for their work from the CRTF, external wage-earners paid 10/- per week inclusive to the warden for their keep. For every maintained resident, the Trust sent Bower 10/- per adult, plus somewhat less per child. Minimal resources, however, were maximized by individual enterprise. Free second-hand clothes had initially been supplied to each hostel according to its needs by the Trust's Clothing Department at 130 Westbourne Terrace, London W2, but under a new 1940 policy, they would only be distributed to maintained refugees in hostels,[83] and the £2 clothing allowance ceased

82 Bower, AI.
83 TNA, HO 294/1, CRTF letter, Dudding to Kapp, 25 February 1940.

in 1941.[84] Two tailoresses therefore helped by sewing children's clothes and women's skirts and blouses for fellow residents. A former farmer grew vegetables and raised rabbits (their white fur was later transformed into a little girl's jacket, replicating traditions in the homeland). Buying a piglet did more than satisfy the Czechoslovak appetite for pork and pork products; it met wartime requirements not to waste food leftovers,[85] and provided quantities of fat for cooking. This did not offend Jewish residents: as Pavel Seifter remarked, as a hostel child he 'did not know what religion was'; his parents were, after all, committed Communists.[86]

Yet for all the positive attitudes and activities, certain refugee experiences were thought to be beyond the comprehension of most British citizens however kindly, like homesickness for a country few British people knew anything about. Headaches and depression were acknowledged ailments in hostels, compounded by deaths, the absence of comforting familiar objects, or even family photographs (too incriminating for escapees to carry) to show to children, friends or hosts. The support and companionship of fellow countrymen and women, and social acceptance on the part of British 'hosts', was therefore crucial to the general well-being of refugees and their efforts to integrate and contribute to Britain, as is recounted in subsequent chapters.

YWCA domestic service project

In the longer term, refugee women aided by the BCRC or CRTF benefited from greater security than those who arrived in Britain via the YWCA's domestic service project, which operated on a much smaller scale and for a relatively short period. A sense of guilt, however, regarding the repercussions

---

84   TNA, HO 294/2, CRTF, Dudding correspondence, March-April 1941.

85   The piglet was replaced by another and similarly despatched with the local authority's requisite approval. See also poster encouraging pig-rearing, Imperial War Museum: Britain, WWII display.

86   Seifter, AI.

of the Munich Agreement, and a Christian obligation to alleviate them, had prompted the YWCA to establish its domestic service project for refugees from Czechoslovakia. Its aims were idealistic but ill-fated, notably concerning funding, the credibility of so-called refugees, and Jewish trainees in particular, as will be explained. None of this was anticipated, however, when six women met with May Curwen, National General Secretary, at the YWCA Central Building in Great Russell Street, London WC1, on 12 December 1938. The 'Czechoslovak predicament' was reflected in the newly created YWCA Refugee Committee's three terms of reference:

1. To help in any way possible with the problem of refugees, particularly Czechoslovakian refugees.
2. To consider the plan for opening Bainbridge House, Seaford,[87] for a period of domestic training for approximately forty-two people, and that this period should be up to three months if possible.
3. To consider what can be done in recruiting from Prague and from Czechoslovakia generally for applicants for the International Employment Department.[88]

It was, the Committee Minutes noted, to be 'made clear to the trainees that they were being trained to take posts of a general domestic nature in English households'.[89] Prague YWCA Secretary General, Mrs Lewisova [*sic*], had reported that members were 'stretched to the utmost to deal not only with their normal work but other emergency problems', such as 'help in the care of refugees from the frontier places' (namely the Sudetenland).[90] Thus when Curwen visited Prague and Brno YWCAs on 20–27 November 1938, her suggestion to place Czechoslovak 'girls' (then an acceptable term for young women) with English families as

---

87 The YWCA Holiday Centre in Heathfield Road, Seaford, with Protestant and Catholic churches nearby, and a synagogue in Brighton.
88 Modern Records Centre [MRC], University of Warwick, Papers of the Young Women's Association [YWCA], MSS.243/92/1, 1938–9, Refugee Committee, Minutes, 12 December 1938.
89 MRC, YWCA, MSS.243/92/1, *ibid.*
90 MRC, YWCA, MSS.243/92/2, draft circular from Curwen, Czechoslovakia Fund No. 2, October 1938.

servants, was warmly welcomed as a legal means of both escape from the situation and entering Britain.[91]

Women with some experience of cookery or domestic work could be placed immediately, others would need training. An intensive training plan including English lessons was therefore agreed at the British YWCA's second Refugee Committee Meeting on 13 January 1939.[92] The course proposed ought to be quite simple work, it was asserted. The maximum number of trainees was reduced to thirty-six, but the staff increased from two to four, a warden plus deputy, preferably German-speaking. Trainees would be divided into three groups of twelve, rotating so that they each had three weeks' training in (a) kitchen, (b) housework, (c) odd jobs – mending, cleaning silver, etc. According to the Budget of Expenditure January–March 1939, 'it could all be done for 15/- per head per week quite easily' including board and administrative costs.[93] The estimated total cost of the course was £350.[94] Funds to implement it were expected from three sources: the BCRC which would make a grant of about 10/- per head for women it nominated, an appeal in *The Times* newspaper, plus contributions to the YWCA Czech Refugee Fund, subject to Prague YWCA's approval.[95] The plan seemed promising and uncomplicated; it was not to prove so, nor did it suit everyone – at least one trainee 'opted out'.

91 MRC, YWCA, MSS.243/92/1, Correspondence with Prague YWCA [includes that with Brno YWCA]; Brno YWCA, letter 6 December 1938 to Curwen.
92 *Ibid.*, Refugee Committee, Minutes, 13 January 1939.
93 *Ibid.*, Minutes, 12 December 1938.
94 MRC, YWCA, Correspondence with Prague YWCA, letter to Molnarová, 8 December 1938.
95 MRC, YWCA, Refugee Committee, Minutes, 12 December 1938, *op. cit.* [BCRC incorrectly given as Czech British Refugee Committee].

Setbacks

A British YWCA Executive Committee appeal of October 1938 to Committee and Council members was launched with Curwen's emotive circular in the belief that: 'We have all secured immediate peace but Czechoslovakia has paid the highest price for it. Here we have a chance [...] to redeem some sense of our debt to them'.[96] Goodwill abounded. Putney Branch sent 15/-,[97] but the appeal was overshadowed by more prominent ones. M. K. Ashby, Principal of Hillcroft Residential College for Working Women, in Surbiton, was keen to support the Czech Association as 'we have had several students through them', but replied, 'I am only able to enclose 5/- as I have just subscribed what I can to the Lord Mayor's Fund'.[98] Others wrote similarly. Hence an appeal for funds in *The Times* was postponed indefinitely in January 1939, with serious consequences.[99] The target sum of £1,000–£1,200 set in the hope of continuing the training scheme 'for some time', was never realized, nor, it appears, was any major funding obtained. Points to have been included in the draft appeal[100] are indicative of future difficulties. It was thought, for example, best to present the plan not only as an aid to refugees, 'but as a contribution towards the problem created by the shortage of domestic servants' and moreover, as a way of remedying 'the fact that so many foreign servants coming to this country were proving unsatisfactory through their unfamiliarity with English work and its customs'. Further points explained that the trainees would be 'Sudeten Germans and Czech Social Democrats from the Sudeten areas, and Jews' who would be 'chosen by the YWCA in Czechoslovakia', and the scheme

96   MRC, YWCA, MSS.243/92/2, Curwen, draft circular, Czechoslovak Fund, 6 October 1938 for despatch 14 October 1938.
97   Near President Beneš's London residence, it was at 12 Ravenna Road, SW15, until around 2008.
98   MRC, YWCA, MSS.243/92/2, Czech Fund No. 2; renamed, Hillcroft College still exists.
99   MRC, YWCA, MSS.243/92/1, Refugee Committee, Minutes, 13 January 1939. British YWCA had hoped to be a beneficiary of the larger appeals.
100 *Ibid.*

operated 'in co-operation between the two organisations' (Czechoslovak and British).

Selection of trainees

The importance of interviewing applicants in Prague and Brno[101] 'so that only suitable people were accepted' was raised at the very first YWCA Refugee Committee Meeting in December 1938, but 'suitable' was unfortunately never defined. 'Is it possible to send some Jewish girls, who are very nice?' Běla Rezníková, Brno YWCA General Secretary, inquired on 8 December 1938. In a confidential letter dated 3 January 1939 to May Curwen, C. Beresford of the YWCA Social and Industrial Section, described some candidates she had met in Brno: Mrs R, for instance, 'a very superior German-Czech' whose husband had headed a Sudeten hospital. 'They are now refugees and she is very anxious to undertake household employment in England [...] a fine woman, attractive in appearance and of a dependable type'. In the same letter she wrote, 'Anna M [...] also appeared to be a superior woman, rather frail in appearance but has a good health record [...]. She was quite worried for fear that you would think her too old because she is forty-five, but as she speaks excellent English and has had household experience in Canada, I feel persuaded she will be a comfort and help to people who prefer to have older [...] employees'.[102]

Despite their subjectivity and class-consciousness of the time, these letters reflect an open attitude to religion and age. The Czechoslovak authorities, however, adopted very different criteria as to who was suitable, which Prague YWCA conveyed to May Curwen on 6 January 1939, as follows:

---

101 Brno YWCA had a degree of autonomy but was answerable to Prague's central YWCA; Slovakia (then still part of Czechoslovakia) did not appear to be greatly involved in these plans as most refugees were in or around Prague and Brno.

102 MRC, YWCA, Correspondence with Prague YWCA, Brno YWCA to Curwen, 8 December 1938.

1. Purely Czech or Slovak girls or women … we are to recommend to you, for your training course, only this category.
2. German or Jewish girls or women – Czechoslovak citizens … we are to send directly to the Refugee Section of the Czechoslovak Ministry of Social Welfare that will give them further advice and help.
3. Girls and women refugees from other countries who have foreign passports, or who have been given only interim passports and hospitality in our country, and have to leave Czechoslovakia now [e.g. those from Reich Germany and Austria].[103]

Regarding the last group, Prague YWCA added, 'These are the most difficult cases, and in order to help them, we are sending them to Miss Lee's office (International Employment Department in London). She tries to help them as best she can'. Whether this approach was due to Czechoslovak protectionism, pressure from German authorities or dictated by Britain's restrictive immigration policy as described by Louise London, Bernard Wasserstein and others[104] remains debatable – possibly a combination of all three factors.[105] The matter was finally resolved, albeit not entirely satisfactorily, following representations by Curwen to J. Pitlick, Consul at the Czechoslovak Republic's Consulate in London.[106] The Czechoslovak authorities directed that 'of the twenty-six trainees [formerly thirty-six], not more than six should be Jews'.[107] The course was due to run from January to March 1939, yet at the time of the second Refugee Committee meeting on 13 January 1939, only sixteen names were submitted. Of fifteen names submitted by Brno YWCA, one was rejected by a Prague Central Labour Exchange (CLE). The applicant was Jewish; no explanation was given.[108] The names listed changed frequently.

103 *Ibid.*, Molnarová, Prague YWCA to Curwen, 6 January 1939.
104 See Bibliography.
105 IWM, Layton, box 1, unofficial English translation of [Czechoslovak] *Government's Decree 27 January 1939 which completes the prescriptions about the stay of foreigners as far as they are emigrants*, highlights the problem.
106 MRC, YWCA, Correspondence with Prague YWCA, letters, Curwen to Pitlíck, 30 December 1938 and 10 January 1939. The consulate was at 8 Grosvenor Place, SW1.
107 MRC, YWCA, MSS.243/92/1, Refugee Committee, Minutes, 13 January 1939.
108 MRC, YWCA, Correspondence with Prague YWCA, Prague YWCA to Curwen, 11 January 1939.

Prospects brightened temporarily by 22 January 1939. London Central YWCA received twenty-six applications for the first training course, complete with CLE questionnaires, police and medical testimonies. Even better, the Czechoslovak Legation in London had approved the plan, and all twenty-six women would have 'an emigrant passport' valid for two years. Travel arrangements were in progress via Čedok travel agency for 31 January, ready for trainees to commence the course on 1 February 1939.[109] 'You cannot imagine the expectations of these girls', Brno's YWCA representative exclaimed on 19 January 1939.[110] Some applicants even borrowed money from the organization to pay for the course, it was noted.[111] Curwen's response was swift and terse, unlike the customary warm exchanges. 'Applicants must be *bona fide* Refugees'. This had always been the plan; public funds could not be raised otherwise, she reminded Prague thence Brno YWCAs on 26 January 1939. 'From [...] your last two letters we wonder if some of the girls are not merely coming here for a change of work and scene and for the expansion of their horizon [...] we do not want to spend money on training them'.[112]

Brno YWCA had advertised in a newspaper. Pavla Molnarová, National General Secretary, Czech YWCA in Prague had (like Ellen Champness regarding the BCRC's refugees), considered whether the applicants were 'the right type', in this instance 'the right kind' of women for the training course 'and their home conditions', claiming that 'all of them are in equal need of help', but admitted that only fourteen were refugees. In the 'numerous refugee camps' around Prague, the girls were either too young or unsuitable. It would take some time to find more girls, she stated.[113] British Home Office entry permits for the given trainees were finally granted in late January 1939 – with three exceptions:[114] Miss D 'because she is German', Miss R 'because she is stateless'; they would require visas. Mrs R, despite

109   *Ibid.*, letter to Curwen, 22 January 1939.
110   *Ibid.*, Brno YWCA to Curwen, 19 January 1939.
111   Prague YWCA to Curwen, 25 January 1939.
112   Curwen to Prague YWCA following her telegram, 26 January 1939.
113   Prague YWCA to Curwen, 26 January 1939.
114   Curwen to Prague YWCA, 28 January 1939.

being a genuine refugee, could not be accepted for the project 'because she is married', not widowed or divorced. The obstacles seemed endless. By 30 January 1939, the Home Office had refused all but genuine refugees for the course.[115] Only thirteen trainees commenced it on 14 February 1939. Places were offered to other organizations for refugees through the Central Office for Refugees, known as Bloomsbury House,[116] and short courses for non-refugees discussed. A second group of eight trainees arrived in Britain on 6 March 1939, but overall it was an inauspicious time.[117]

The project's demise

Germany's invasion of rump Czechoslovakia mid-March 1939 caused trainees in Britain immense anxiety about family members left behind. Work placements were found for the first trainees, but few new ones arrived. Grete Reichl was among six applicants granted Home Office permits, but she never arrived for the course. She only reached Britain on 13 May 1939 via a British Committee for Children Kindertransport from Prague.[118] Britain's subsequent declaration of war on Germany on 3 September 1939 effectively ended the scheme for refugees from Czechoslovakia. 'Unforeseen circumstances have made this necessary', E. A. Rattray, the course warden wrote emotionally to the 'flüchtlinge' [*sic*, 'refugees'] on 4 October 1939, expressing the hope that the course had helped them 'to start a new life', and entreating them to 'uphold the honour of Czecho-Slovakia'. They were not alone she told them, the YWCA was always there for them.[119] Her offer of help was soon taken up as fresh challenges arose. Remembering Rattray's words, some lonely Jewish trainees attempted to socialize with local YWCAs or church groups, to their

---

115   Curwen to Prague YWCA, 30 January 1939.
116   Located in Bloomsbury Street, London WC1 (now an hotel).
117   MRC, YWCA, MSS.243/92/1, Refugee Committee, Minutes, 6 March 1939.
118   Greta Reichl (Bader), PP held by niece, Kate Ottevanger (Sterne).
119   Circular, E. A. Rattray to trainees from Czechoslovakia, 4 October 1939.

mutual discomfiture, having little in common. Some trainees had left their jobs due to lack of aptitude or ill-health; others had to leave coastal areas for security reasons.[120] Unable, however, to assist for lack of funds except in a minimal way, the YWCA directed women to the CRTF.

The Trust declined to help, assuming that the British YWCA had a contractual responsibility for the unemployed former trainees, even intimating that it was 'not properly looking after the girls' it had brought to Britain.[121] It was yet another blow to the project, the deadlock ameliorated by Alexander Maxwell at the Home Office. He confirmed in September 1940 that the YWCA had no legal responsibility to maintain the trainees after their course, but neither did the Trust according to its Terms of Reference. However, changes in government policy arising from the war, he explained, allowed these women to seek Public Assistance if, for example, displaced by security regulations. Furthermore, under the Order in Council of 17 November 1939, women who had entered the country as domestic servants or trainees were no longer limited to such work or to nursing, and 'free to accept other work', subject to Ministry of Labour approval. 'Any foreign woman who is unemployed should therefore register at the nearest Employment Exchange', Maxwell advised.[122] This development gave alien women in Britain infinitely wider scope, but the YWCA's inability to aid its former trainees when requested, seems an undeservedly ignominious end to an altruistic and meritorious scheme.

The project's demise, plus certain restrictions governing access to the YWCA archives, may account for why little has been written about it, and reinforces the importance of doing so here. Its absence from literature on exile issues underlines Tony Kushner's observation in *Second Chance*: 'time passes [...]. The history of the refugee domestics is thus one particularly at risk from present neglect and future obscurity'.[123] The YWCA's

---

120   The course could no longer be held in Seaford for security reasons; it transferred to Richmond for refugees already in Britain.

121   MRC, YWCA, MSS.243/92/3, CRTF letter, D. E. Brown, Secretary to Overseas Committee, to Curwen, 8 May 1940.

122   *Ibid.*, Alexander Maxwell, Home Office, to Curwen, 7 September 1940.

123   Tony Kushner, 'Domestic Service', in Werner E. Mosse, ed., *Second Chance. Two Centuries of German-Speaking Jews in the United Kingdom* (Tubingen: Mohr Siebeck, 1991), 553–78 (here 554–5).

contribution is difficult to evaluate, and best viewed qualitatively rather than quantitatively, for despite its best endeavours, it is seen to have largely failed in its avowed objectives of helping refugees from Czechoslovakia, due to circumstances beyond its control. Yet there was a real need for the training course. The British YWCA's own International Employment Department had noted in November 1938 that Jewish women in particular were singularly unprepared for domestic work, reporting 'at least 90% failures' of some 150 placed.[124] Although these figures did not pertain specifically to Czechoslovak women, the general situation did. Natural disinclination aside, many women (Jewish and Christian), were indeed unprepared for the drastic social upheaval wrought by the war. As Gerda Mayer observed: 'my mother stands thoughtfully in the middle of the room, gently swashing the broom to and fro, as if uncertain what to do with so esoteric a device'. Yet '[a]mong other things she is thinking of going to England on a domestic permit'.[125] Even with relevant domestic training or experience, however, demands for orthodox domestics via the Central Office for Refugees Domestic Bureau, Toynbee Hall depot (East London),[126] could not have been met by these highly acculturated Jewish women from Czechoslovakia.

Tensions: Employees and refugee domestics

Overall, the domestic service experience was not a happy one for Czechoslovak women whatever their background, including those who came to Britain independently of the YWCA, BCRC or CRTF. Despite the

124 MRC, YWCA, MSS.243/92/1, Correspondence with Prague YWCA, British YWCA Central Club to Grenfell, 24 November 1938.
125 Mayer, *op. cit.*, 12–13.
126 IWM, Layton, box 1, Central Office for Refugees, Domestic Bureau, Position as at 13 December 1939, with Ruth Tomlinson letter to Layton, 16 December 1939.

Domestic Bureau's guidance in publications such as *Mistress and Maid*,[127] tensions inevitably arose between some employers and their unsuitable refugee employees when expectations clashed. Gratitude for a safe haven sometimes gave way to resentment at perceived mistreatment or exploitation. Problems also arose when the roles of mistress and maid were reversed in exile. This was the case for Susan Groag Bell's mother Edith, who in Opava (Troppau) 'breakfasted in bed. Afterwards [she] consulted the cook about the meals for the next two days' and would go to her dressmaker. Aged 38, she became a maid to a vicar's family in a Sussex village mostly inhabited by middle-class people. Mother and child slept in the maid's room and ate in the kitchen after Edith had served in the dining-room; nevertheless the employers had difficulty dealing with a servant 'who was so obviously their equal', and whose 'carriage and her manner, despite her maid's uniform, belied her office'.[128] Edith Sterne also arrived in Britain in early 1939, having been ordered by the Gestapo to leave Czechoslovakia by March or April that year.[129] Aged 28 and awaiting her husband, she had a law degree and, in her own words, 'the self-confidence of the well-educated'. 'The only thing I knew about housekeeping, though, was that one hung the bedding out of the window! The lady of the house was *not* delighted', she recalled, while another employer 'looked down on refugees'. The kindness of other people, Sterne's inner strength, and belief that her exile would be 'only for a short time', helped her to endure what she called 'the great culture gap', and the dull sight of identical 'rows and rows of council houses' in Sheffield.

These situations demanded sensitivity of employers, and resilience of the refugee domestics who endured tremendous changes and shifts in social standing, both during and post-WWII. Some interviewees had felt humiliated and offended by having to use the separate servants' entrance and toilet 'as if we were dirty'. While social stratification and the notion of 'the right sort' existed even in the ideologically egalitarian Czechoslovak

127 *Mistress and Maid. General Information for the Use of Domestic Refugees and Their Employees*, Domestic Bureau, Central Offices for Refugees (London: April 1940).
128 Susan Groag Bell, *Between Worlds. In Czechoslovakia, England and America* (New York, USA: Dutton, 1991), 13–14, 78; AI.
129 Edith Sterne, AI.

Republic, it was more pronounced in Britain, which still headed an empire – whereas Czechoslovakia had been part of one for centuries. A sense of superiority, together with natural reserve or 'British standoffishness' (and in some instances anti-Semitism), influenced an employer's acceptance or rejection and treatment of other races, particularly anyone of a lower social status like servants, foreigners (hence refugees) and Jews. Jewish refugee domestics represented all three groupings. 'Doing the Christian thing' and being kind to refugees did not therefore necessarily extend to befriending them. Moreover, refugee women and their personal histories were beyond the experience, hence comprehension, of most of their British employers and acquaintances. 'People in England did not think about it' Elizabeth Weiss observed, referring to the wider refugee predicament.[130] Her view was echoed by other refugees; 'sympathy' is not the same as 'understanding'. If, however, the 'opportunism and blatant self-interest' of British refugee policy regarding domestic service work cited by Kushner in *Second Chance*[131] was considered a negative feature, the British YWCA attempted to transform it into a positive element as far as possible in order to save lives.

Other means of entry into Britain

Nursing was another life-saving means of entering Britain and working legally (though like domestic service, the policy was seen as primarily meeting a need for nurses and trainees rather than helping refugees). Elizabeth Weiss arrived in London by train via Germany in June 1939 for this purpose, having queued at the British embassy in Prague several times to apply for a nursing (or domestic service) post. She first stayed with a Quaker family in Croydon, who 'thought that all refugees from Czechoslovakia were gypsies'. This not only highlights the general lack of knowledge about

---

130   Weiss, AI.
131   Kushner, *op. cit.*, 563.

Czechoslovakia, its people and culture, but also the misconceptions that abounded about them, and reinforces the social stratification discussed here. Weiss was not a gypsy but a German-speaking Catholic medical student, forcibly removed from Karlovy Vary in 1938 by 'apologetic Nazis who spoke fluent Czech', simply because her mother was thought to be a Communist. In England, at least, Weiss was no longer 'afraid of the door bell ringing'.[132]

The exiles were by no means all from the Sudetenland, nor did they come to Britain solely as nurses or domestic servants; some were professional people who had the means or could raise funds to travel independently, especially experienced doctors and dentists. A number of refugees had private means to pay a guarantor and/or friends and family member(s) in Britain whom they joined. Sent to safety by her parents, 16-year-old Zora Karas from Trenčin, Slovakia, arrived in 1938 with diamonds in the soles of her shoes[133] (though others arrived bereft of their financial resources blocked by banks or confiscated en route). Emigrés at that time were allowed to take only the equivalent of 10/- which was soon used up. Social Democrat Eve Road, who had helped refugees in Prague and 'never expected to become one herself', was remembered and in turn helped by Quaker Tessa Rowntree. Arriving in Britain just before the new entry visa requirement came into force on 1 April 1939, the 'penniless' Road joined her brother, who was being supported by the CRTF.[134]

Lives transformed

Life was far from easy for the new arrivals; neither a homogeneous unit associated with the 'nation state' model comprising one nation, one language, nor economic migrants, they were grateful to be alive; all had been

132   Weiss, AI.
133   Vera Sturgess (Karas), AI, PP re: mother, Zora Karas (Mayer).
134   Eve Road, AI.

at risk. Both Tschapek and Weiss recalled the suicides and attempted suicides in their escape groups, and few people could forget those who had failed to escape. Prospects for a peaceful life and fresh start were shattered, however, by Germany's invasion of Poland, obliging Britain to declare war on Germany: as Clausewitz argued, war is a continuation of politics by other means.[135] It radically shifted British policies concerning refugees, including internment and war effort contributions. The war and its outcome ultimately decided the fate of thousands of Czechoslovaks and their descendants: the trajectories of some of them are recorded in the following chapters.

135   Carl von Clausewitz, *On War* (London: Everyman, 1993), 99.

CHAPTER 2

Friendly Alien/Enemy Alien?
Internment and MI5 Scrutiny

The onset of WWII and subsequent developments caused major security concerns within parliament and British security agencies, due to the large number of resident foreign nationals of 'uncertain loyalties'. Were they friendly aliens (i.e. with the Allies) or enemy aliens? How to distinguish between them, and what measures should be taken regarding them, were fundamental but complex issues, as this chapter demonstrates with regard to refugees from Czechoslovakia. Reluctant to follow the WWI model of mass internment of aliens, the government initially pursued a more liberal policy, but which gradually became stringent. Firstly, the Emergency Powers (Defence) Act 1939 was promulgated prior to the declaration of war on 3 September 1939 in readiness for it, soon followed by The Defence (General) Regulations, 1939. Regulation 18B gave the Home Secretary wide powers regarding detention orders aiming to prevent people acting in a manner deemed prejudicial to public safety or the defence of the country, though distinctions at this juncture were still made between those perceived as victims of the enemy (e.g. Czechoslovakia) and suspects aiding it. As Peter and Leni Gillman note in *Collar the Lot*,[1] when Home Secretary, John Anderson, announced in the House of Commons on 4 September 1939 that refugees from Czechoslovakia would *not* be treated as enemy aliens, Hugh Dalton declared, 'This is reparation for Munich'.

---

[1]   Peter and Leni Gillman, '*Collar the Lot!' How Britain Interned and Expelled its Wartime Refugees* (London/Melbourne/New York: Quartet, 1980), 41–3.

Tribunals: Classification of refugees

Nonetheless, the policy entailed the creation of some 120 tribunals to classify enemy aliens according to the degree of risk they represented; they were defined in The Defence (General) Regulations, 1939, as 'a person who, not being either a British subject or a British protected person, possesses the nationality of a State at war with His Majesty',[2] with clear implications for anyone of German or Austrian origin.[3] Each tribunal was chaired by a legal advisor, given some Home Office guidelines, but advised not to apply measures too stringently when placing refugees in one of three categories from October 1939:

A. to be interned.
B. not to be interned but subject to restricted movement (no more than 5 miles from their place of residence without police authorisation).
C. no restrictions imposed.

Whereas, however, refugees summoned by the local police force could be accompanied by a friend, they could not be represented at tribunals by a lawyer; yet Home Office officials assisted tribunals on points of policy, and Ministry of Labour officials influenced decisions regarding work permits for aliens. Moreover, the process by which tribunals were confidentially informed about individual cases was significant not only in terms of decisions made at the time, but also in ascertaining why certain refugees (though not others) from Czechoslovakia were suddenly interned in May 1940; as Gillman notes, tribunals could accept information from a variety of sources. Those sources included letters and testimonials from relevant agencies or reputable British subjects, as well as information forwarded secretly by the Home Office, police, Special Branch or MI5. Consequently, refugees could be interned without ever knowing why, making decisions difficult to challenge. The system's openness to manipulation, if not outright abuse, resulted in some acrimonious accusations by divided and over-anxious

2   Institute of Advanced Legal Studies, series GA2-E 59–60, Statutory Rules and Orders 1939, vol. 1, 790.
3   Austria was then considered a supporter of Fascism, not a victim of it.

refugees, as will be reviewed in the latter part of this chapter, together with MI5 scrutiny of those refugees allowed to remain at liberty.

The definition of an enemy alien cited here was open to (mis)interpretation and, as shall be seen, over-simplification in some instances. Early on, the Home Office assumed a measure of loyalty to Britain from refugees who had fled Nazi oppression on racial, religious or political grounds and until May 1940 usually placed them in category C. Internment literature deals amply with the wider policy issues and diverse origins of internees, by for example, Yvonne Kapp and Margaret Mynatt, François Lafitte, David Cesarani and Tony Kushner and, more recently, Richard Dove.[4] To complement rather than duplicate existing literature, attention will be concentrated here on sources relating specifically to the situation for Czechoslovak women refugees, and other nationals who had sheltered in Czechoslovakia before fleeing to Britain.

Internment of refugees

Having hitherto been classed as friendly aliens, the sudden reversal in May 1940 of Britain's internment policy was a shock to Czechoslovak refugees, and to those who had previously sheltered in Czechoslovakia from Nazi oppression. Police were instructed to arrest all Austrian and German women classified as category B, and at a War Cabinet meeting on 21 June 1940, John Anderson, then Secretary of State for Home Affairs and Minister of Home Security, reported that 'enemy aliens were being locked up as fast as accommodation could be provided, and that the accommodation vacated by internees sent

---

4   Yvonne Kapp and Margaret Mynatt, *British Policy and the Refugees, 1933–1941* (London: Cass, 1997); François Lafitte, *The Internment of Aliens* (Penguin Special, Harmondsworth/New York: Allen Lane, 1940); David Cesarani and Tony Kushner, *The Internment of Aliens in Twentieth Century Britain* (London: Cass, 1993); Richard Dove, ed., '*Totally Un-English*'? *Britain's Internment of 'Enemy Aliens' In Two World Wars: Yearbook of the Research Centre for German and Austrian Exile Studies*, 7 (2005).

overseas would be filled at once'. A few 'reliable aliens' already interned would be released.[5] This contrasted sharply with British public sympathy for refugees from Czechoslovakia in autumn 1938, but as Paul Tabori observes in *The Anatomy of Exile*, 'blame must be tempered by the understanding of the fears aroused' given the fall of France and the Low Countries and 'innumerable tales of fifth-columnists'. All this left ill-armed Britain feeling that 'she could not take any risks [...] whatever discomfort or even suffering this caused',[6] in the belief that the country would be invaded. Thus, whilst the rationale regarding security measures was comprehensible, the procedures applied to refugees from Czechoslovakia were inconsistent and at times puzzling.

'The preparatory procedure at the different Tribunals has been in no sense uniform', stated Section II, CRTF Report on Activities for December 1939. 'In the provinces the local refugee committees [that helped care for some CRTF refugees] were sometimes given the lists of refugees who were to come up for hearings and sometimes they were not. Often they were given only twenty-four hours' notice that the refugee was to appear'. As at 31 December 1939, 463 CRTF refugees (not necessarily all Czechoslovaks) had yet to appear before a tribunal, and the results of 177 cases were still awaited. The classified results, however, of 1,070 refugees questioned by the tribunals and extrapolated below are indicative of the impending difficulties induced by the nationality issues raised in Chapter 1:

Under the heading 'Nationality – Austrians/Germans/Stateless'
– seventeen refugees registered with the Trust were classified as category A and interned [but no Czechs or Sudeten Germans at this stage].
– 205 Austrians, Germans and stateless refugees, however, were placed in category B [vs only twenty-seven Czechs and Sudeten Germans].
– while 777 Austrians, Germans and stateless refugees were placed in category C [compared with only forty-six Czechs and Sudeten Germans].[7]

5   The National Archives, London [TNA], CAB/65/7/69, War Cabinet 174 (40), Conclusions of Meeting, 21 June 1940, point 13.
6   Paul Tabori, *The Anatomy of Exile. A Semantic and Historical Study* (London: Harrap, 1972), 337.
7   Imperial War Museum [IWM], Stopford Papers, RJS 3/13–3/17, file 3/16, CRTF Report of Activities for December 1939, Tribunals, 1–4.

The implication is that CRTF Sudeten German refugees, despite their German roots, were adjudged anti-Fascists, while CRTF Reich German and Austrian refugees were not, despite having initially fled to Czechoslovakia for safety.

There is a paucity of published material specifically about the internment of refugees from Czechoslovakia, particularly those who were Czech-born, and ostensibly no cogent reason for the refugees' restricted movement or eventual internment. Potential security risks did, though, lie in inherent complications which are not always drawn out in more general works or those dealing with German-speaking refugees as a group, so they will be touched upon here. The interlinking complications were essentially three-fold: geographic, ethnic and political. As noted earlier, Czechoslovakia did not conform to the inter-war concept of the 'nation state' but comprised diverse regions and ethnic groups which, in the brief period since the state's inception in 1918 had not become a cohesive entity. Furthermore, under a central government in Prague the official language was Czech, but it was not the mother-tongue of all of Czechoslovakia's minorities, notably ethnic Germans, who mostly spoke little or no Czech at all.[8] This was to have serious consequences even for those loyal to Czechoslovakia, for the legacy of the former Habsburg Empire, its geographic spread and policy of Germanization, confounded language and national identity issues for both the refugees and the British authorities.

Of the three elements, it is difficult to ascertain whether ethnicity or politics caused British authorities greater concern, for not only were numerous refugees from Czechoslovakia ethnic Germans, Reich Germans or Austrians, they were also Communists. The 'Reds under the bed' syndrome is usually associated with the post-war 'Cold War' era, but ample documentary evidence shows that Britain's anxiety about Communism long preceded it. In a country still headed by a monarch (then King George VI), memories of revolution and the execution of his extended family members in Russia would have been readily rekindled. Official British mistrust of Communists (British and foreign), was heightened on the brink of war

---

8   Language Rights Law of the 1920 Constitution, regarding ethnic minorities.

by the August 1939 Non-Aggression Pact between Hitler and Stalin, and although the Pact was negated when Germany attacked the Soviet Union in June 1941, fear of the spread of Communism as a destabilizing international force persisted. As the Communists Yvonne Kapp and Margaret Mynatt wrote: 'If the word "Communist" evokes a violent reaction in some people, the words "foreign Communist" more than double the effect; one has no need to magnify the menace conjured up by those two words in order to excite the deepest prejudice'.[9]

Czech Refugee Trust Fund assistance

Unravelling these problems was no easy task for the British authorities, and the question of passports, linked as it was to wider identity and loyalty issues, became a crucial one, as the CRTF Report of Activities for December 1939 recorded:

> The work of the Enemy Alien Tribunals Department of the Trust has been especially complicated by uncertainty as to how the refugees had been registered by the police on the outbreak of war, and in consequence whether they would appear before the Friendly or Enemy Aliens Tribunals. Several hundred refugees believed by the Trust to be German or Austrian, have apparently been registered by the police as stateless, possibly because they were not in possession of passports issued by the Government of their own country, but only possessed Czech Interim Passports which were issued to refugees.[10]

These so-called 'stateless' refugees were 'all rated by the police as Friendly Aliens' and would be 'dealt with under Friendly Alien procedure', yet 'a small number of Czech refugees with valid Czech passports have been rated by the Enemy Alien Tribunals'. Although a 'much larger number were summoned' they were saved by information provided by the Trust,

---

9   Kapp and Mynatt, *op. cit.*, 61.
10   Stopford Papers, *op. cit.*, 3–4.

and their cases transferred to the appropriate friendly alien tribunal. The
report continued, Sudeten Germans nevertheless:

> constituted a quite special problem, because whilst it is clear that a Czech with a valid
> Czech passport is a Czech citizen and a Friendly Alien [contradicting the situation
> just described], the national status of a Sudeten German with a Czech passport does
> not seem absolutely clear, and the national status of a Sudeten German with a Czech
> Interim passport seems to be wholly obscure, since the Sudeten Germans have been
> and remain registered with the [British] police indiscriminately as Czech, German
> or Austrian citizens.[11]

The resultant confusion surrounding the nationality and passport issue
rendered many Czechoslovak Sudeten German refugees susceptible to
internment; this issue is reflected in the registration cards of women later
interned on the Isle of Man, and will be revisited.

Initially, the surprise turn of events was mitigated to some extent by
the CRTF, principally by the Communist Margaret Mynatt,[12] aided by
'skilled' helpers like Kate Thornycroft (later Field). A former refugee herself
(Mynatt subsequently held a British passport), she had known several of the
refugees personally before the war, and 'prepared all the material for all the
refugees who were to come up to the tribunal [...] giving every detail that
she could and explaining what they were doing, what they had been doing
when they'd come' for the lawyers, 'who were completely lost', commented
her friend and colleague, Yvonne Kapp: 'No other organization, who didn't
have a "Margaret" to do that, could possibly have produced such material. It
was quite unique'. Mynatt noted, however, that one of the questions posed
at the tribunals to test the men's allegiance to the Western Allied Powers,
was whether they would take up arms against the Soviet Union, and if they
said no they 'got a black mark', which reflected adversely on their wives too.
Despite every endeavour to vouch for refugees in the Trust's care and provide
favourable references from October 1939,[13] the exiles were summoned to

---

11   *Ibid.*
12   Charmian Brinson interview with Yvonne Kapp, 1997, private papers [PF].
13   TNA, HO 294/7, CRTF Outline of Events in the Period July 1939 (date of com-
      mencement) to 31 December 1941.

tribunals followed by a series of new tribunals to review category B cases, and
from 11 May 1940, German and Austrian refugees were targeted. Some 60
per cent of the Trust's German and Austrian refugees were interned, though
only around 1,020 (12 per cent) of the total number of refugees registered with
the Trust were interned (including some Czechoslovak men and women).

Many of the tribunal conclusions are widely considered to have been
hasty and arbitrary, due to insufficient knowledge, varying standards applied
and general misunderstandings, sometimes causing friendly/enemy aliens
to be miscast. Not considered the same security threat as men, however,
relatively few women in category C were interned. For example, Communist
Hedwig Huenigen was not interned, though from the Sudetenland, but
her brother-in-law Gerhard, born in territory then constituting part of
the Habsburg Empire, was classified as Austrian hence an enemy alien, by
British immigration officials unaware that the Czech Crown Lands had
regained their independence and national identity in 1918. Language difficulties compounded the problem. Arriving alone and unable to explain
his case to the authorities, the German-speaking Gerhard was subsequently
deported to an internment camp in Canada, to Hedwig's distress. She
expended considerable efforts to convince the British authorities that he
was a bona fide Czechoslovak citizen, and to arrange an eventual return to
Britain after his harrowing encounters with Nazi deportees.[14] Although the
Huenigens were loyal to Czechoslovakia and had made a point of speaking
Czech in addition to German, by December 1939 there were some 3,000
ethnic German Czechoslovak refugees who were mostly German-speaking
rather than Czech-speaking.[15] That Czechoslovak citizens could not speak
the official national language seemed unthinkable to British officials, arous-
ing suspicion regarding national and political allegiance.

Ultimately, however, the CRTF was virtually powerless to prevent the
internment of those in its care. Minute 543 of a Meeting of the Trustees on
21 May 1940 on the Position with Regard to Internment, Evacuation,[16] could

14   Hedy Fromings (Huenigen), AI, PP.
15   TNA, HO 294/7, CRTF, Consideration of Future Activities, undated but with
      CRTF correspondence dated September 1947.
16   CRTF, Minutes, Meeting of the Trustees, 21 May 1940.

record only that 'so far as it was known [...] 67 refugees in the Prohibited (Kent, Sussex and Essex) and 76 in the Unrestricted Areas had been interned', necessitating the closure of some sixteen hostels and the opening of new ones, such as Fortis Green hostel in London. Trustees were informed that 'friendly aliens were being moved out of the Restricted Areas as far as possible', and resolved that: 'chronic invalids who had suffered internment should be notified forthwith to the Home Secretary, and that [...] internees about to take examinations or to be emigrated should be notified, but that all other cases should be left to the individual employer or other interested individuals or bodies' to apply for exemption or release from internment.

Czechoslovak women outside the Trust's sphere also suddenly found their lives transformed in unexpected and unwelcome ways. Catholic Maria Ratzer from Mariánské Lázně had joined her husband just before the 1938 Munich Agreement, in 'one of the biggest transitions she made in her life'.[17] The Czechoslovak Baťa shoe factory estate in East Tilbury was far removed from her society and milieu at home, where Ratzer had danced in palaces and begun medical studies at the German University in Prague – 'the culture shock was immense'. Moreover, Germany's subsequent occupation in 1939 of rump Czechoslovakia in addition to the Sudetenland, rendered her a refugee '*sur place*', unable to return to her country of origin due to the changed circumstances. Britain's declaration of war on Germany compounded the situation, and as her husband was one of the few Sudeten Germans working for Baťa (UK), they had to move 'at one day's notice' from what had become a coastal security zone under the Aliens (Protected Areas) Order of April 1940, and re-settle elsewhere. Lieselotte Bedřiška Strossová arrived in Britain with her son on 16 June 1940, only to find herself sent to Holloway Prison on 15 July 1940. Having lost touch with her husband who had been serving in the Czechoslovak army in Agde, in France, she wrote to the Czechoslovak Consulate in London appealing for help.[18] The response is not known.

17   Maria Ratzer, 'Maria's Life – Remarks at the Celebration of Her Life – Stirling Hall, Pollokshields Burgh Hall', 1 August 2007, Peter Ratzer, PP.
18   School of Slavonic and East European Studies [SSEES], LIS 3/3/8, letter from Holloway Prison, 15 July 1940.

Isle of Man: Women internees

Soon after the CRTF's May meeting, *The Ramsey Courier* of 28 May 1940[19] announced the 'Arrival of the Aliens – First Batch to Land on the Island'. 'Some 3,500 women aliens are to be interned', the whole of Port Erin and Port St Mary being taken over for this purpose, and numbers were expected to rise to 'several thousands'. Although the 'Government Office state that the women will not be kept behind barbed wire, as will be the case with the male internees in the other three camps',[20] 'special precautions' would ensure internees did not leave the district. A 'barrier' was to be erected, and 'ordinary citizens' would not be allowed to enter except on 'specific business there'. The camp area included the bay, tennis courts, Rowany golf links and the open-air swimming pool, but while the prospective internees were being 'collared', the proprietors of boarding houses and hotels were preparing for those to be allocated to them and 'catered for much in the style of the ordinary seasonal traffic, although, of course, not on so lavish a scale'. The billeting allowance to proprietors, the newspaper added, was £1.1s per week (one guinea, hence the nick-name 'guinea pigs') per adult aged 18 and over, 10/6d for children aged 14 to 17, and 8/6d for younger children. An official Dietary[21] of items included kosher meat, to be issued daily. Despite the facilities, it was hardly a 'home from home' environment, and Jewish internees in particular worried about their easy capture and subsequent fate should Germany occupy more than the Channel Islands.[22] Some 4,000 women of diverse nationalities were ultimately interned on the Isle of Man (IoM). Details of their shared experiences as women are

19 Manx National Heritage Library [MNHL], MD 354, Account No. 6472, Returns: 1945 and Miscellaneous Papers.
20 TNA, HO 213/1053, Internment, however, noted high barbed wire fencing surrounding both parts of Rushen camp.
21 MNHL, IoM Government Circulars Relating to Aliens, Internees or Detainees 1939–45, Part 1, No. 2222, Billeting Claims, 7 June 1940, and No. 2280, Dietary, 12 July 1940.
22 Germany occupied the Channel Islands June 1940–May 1945.

related in personal narratives placed with the Imperial War Museum,[23] recorded in Home Office documents, and described by Manx National Heritage Curator Yvonne Cresswell,[24] while academics like Charmian Brinson have concentrated on German and Austrian exiles.[25] The focus in this study remains on Czechoslovak women and those with Czechoslovak connections, though their internment is approached from the perspective of closely intertwined national, gender and group dynamics.

Women and children internees from Czechoslovakia

No one chose to go the IoM. Everyone listed for internment was forcibly removed at little or no notice, usually by local police officers. Dawn raids were commonplace. With barely time to pack essentials, frightened and bewildered women and children were transported under escort by train to Liverpool, and thence by boat to the IoM from which escape was almost impossible. Anna Tschapek and her 10-year-old son, Walter,[26] were taken from their home to the station in a police van, and spat upon in Liverpool en route to the port by onlookers who believed them to be dangerous enemies. They were interned in Port Erin on 30 May 1940, and lodged in Bradda Glen. Anna's Alien's Registration Certificate issued on arrival in Britain on 24 July 1939 bore a hand-written entry stamped 21 October 1939 by Leeds City Police, stating that 'The holder of this Certificate is to be exempt from internment until further

23 IWM, sound archive, for example, Ruth Soldan, *et al.*, including 'Czech civilian wife of German political writer', accession no. 3964.
24 Yvonne M. Cresswell, ed., *Living With the Wire: Civilian Internment in the Isle of Man During the Two World Wars* (Douglas: Manx National Heritage, 1994).
25 Charmian Brinson, '"In the exile of Internment" or "Von Versuchen, aus einer Not eine Tugend zu machen" [concerning attempts to make a virtue out of necessity]: German-Speaking Women Interned by the British During the Second World War', in William Niven and James Jordan, *Politics and Culture in Twentieth-Century Germany* (New York/Suffolk: Camden House, 2003), 63–87.
26 Walter Tschapek, AI.

order'; but a 'further order' had not been anticipated. Anna's husband, Franz, who had just commenced employment in a Bradley factory, was interned in Onchan (a male IoM camp) two weeks before her. 'Why?' Walter still asked, for they were Czechoslovak citizens, albeit German-speaking ones, and opposed the Munich Agreement. Perhaps their Communist beliefs were expressed too strongly, or they could not answer appropriately due to their limited command of English. Perhaps they were simply unlucky, like the Czech-born women and children interned while awaiting visas for onward migration to the USA.

Whatever the reason, the outcome was that some non-political as well as political refugee women, together with their children aged under 16, were interned in Port Erin or Port St Mary (jointly known as Rushen Camp), as evidenced by the Women's Camp Nominal Roll, Port Erin, 1943–1944,[27] and the women's registration cards which have fortuitously survived, unlike most men's cards. A Manx National Heritage Library search found that the registration listings for women and children contained around 140 entries mentioning Czech connections in some way, and although many of the entries gave nationality as German or Austrian, the place of birth and/or last residence outside Britain was mostly in Czechoslovakia. A further search narrowed the number to some eighty-eight registration cards of refugee women with links to Czechoslovakia.[28] (Their names cannot be mentioned for reasons of confidentiality, but may be cross-referred with other sources such as lists in Margaret Layton's Papers cited in Chapter 1, and the Women's Camp Nominal Roll, which included older women born in Czechoslovakia – some with English names suggesting marriage to Englishmen and/or naturalization). What at first glance might seem merely a scant record of assorted dates, provided a wealth of valuable details which statistics alone could never do; but whilst they provided answers to some questions, they posed new ones too.

A breakdown and analysis of the data[29] serves to underpin the convergence of geographic, socio-political and historical issues discussed earlier

27   MNHL, HO 215/478 (284580) photocopy of TNA, HO 215/478 on internment.
28   MNHL, Female Czechoslovakian Isle of Man World War Two Internees, Collections Database, registration cards. The men's cards cannot be traced; efforts have been made to reconstruct listings.
29   MNHL, Collections Database, registration cards, *op. cit.*

in this study, by providing details, demonstrating discrepancies and inconsistencies in record-keeping, and highlighting continued confusion resulting from the Munich Agreement over attributed, adopted and enforced nationality, exemplified by the statement: 'German, previously Hungarian [in other cases Polish or Austrian] and Czechoslovak'. This was due partly to enforced nationality changes arising from Germany's annexation of Austria and the Sudetenland, with further territorial claims by, for example, Hungary, and partly due to intermarriage with ethnic or Reich Germans or Austrians, which could involve either or both a change in citizenship and relocation to another country – usually the husband's. The amount of information on individual cards varied; some did not indicate marital status, others did not mention occupation, yet more confused Czechoslovakia with Austria (presumably because the place of birth given had been part of the Austro-Hungarian Empire). Some Czechoslovak town names were misunderstood and incorrectly spelt by British officials, for example, Opara instead of Opava, Bino for Brno, and some towns were given by their German name, others by their Czech name, or like Stettin attributed to the wrong country due to border shifts at various times. What emerged most positively of all from this data is an insight to the background of the internees, and a more composite picture of them both as individuals and group members, than would otherwise be the case.

Of the eighty-eight cards, sixteen entries pertained to visitors, interesting in their own right but not included in the immediate discussion of seventy-two internees, whose lives bridged the nineteenth and twentieth centuries; their date of birth ranged from 1875 to 1915, the majority of women being born between 1903 and 1915. At least thirty women (possibly more given changed place names and difficulties in identifying villages or hamlets), were born within Czechoslovakia's inter-war geographic boundaries (regardless of Czech or German spellings), in places such as Visnove, Libova, Tachau and Opava. Seventeen of these women, designated according to their registration cards as Czech-born, had 'Applied for U. S. A. visa' but awaited the 'Green Card' under the American quota system for immigration. Surprisingly, they were mainly in the older age group, and only one woman had children (two) with her. Not surprising, however, given their age and the social norms of their era, was the fact that thirty-six of the total seventy-two women in question were married, fourteen of these being Czech-born, and two women had married fellow refugees in Britain, a hint of hope, perhaps, for a more settled future, showing that life in exile continued against the odds, despite one woman's husband being classed as stateless. The marital status (where given) of the remaining women is as follows: thirteen single (notably in the older age group which raises the question why did they not marry – work, war?), three divorced (two of whom were listed as Czech-born), and four widowed (three of whom were listed as Czech-born). The figures presented in this sample are not absolute; nevertheless, they are indicative of the (then) prevailing social and political trends and re-affirm that women, as well as men, escaped to Britain.

Variations in the type of passport held, when, where, and to whom issued, are likewise significant details,[30] testifying to the different periods of migration described in Chapter 1: Czecho-Slovakian passport, Czecho-Slovakian Stateless Passport, Czechoslovakian *Fremdenpass* [Alien's passport] and Czechoslovakian Document of Identity. Each one 'tells a story'. Details of Czech passports and identity cards issued to women whose last address was in Katowice or Cracow in Poland, for example, signify specific rescue efforts by Hermann Field.[31] Acting on behalf of the British Committee for Refugees from Czechoslovakia (BCRC), he carried money and vital documents to them following delays in immigration formalities which left over 200 refugees stranded in terrible conditions by May 1939. Of twenty-three women listed in the IoM registration cards as a 'Refugee from Nazi oppression', ten were listed as Czech-born, as was one of three women listed as a 'Refugee from Nazi oppression on political grounds'. Except in two instances, concerning a Jewish and a Catholic woman, the British authorities either did not consider religion noteworthy or abandoned such distinctions, for the records are incomplete, with only one woman classed as a 'Refugee from Nazi oppression on racial and political grounds', and only two women as a 'Refugee from Nazi oppression on racial grounds', one of whom was given as Czech-born. The sense of oppression

---

30   TNA, KV 2/2714, document 14a, 3, explains the visa problem.
31   Field's unpublished letters from Cracow to his mother in America describe the situation, Field family, PP.

and injustice felt by these interned women was immense. Mindful of the statistics cited in Chapter 1 regarding both political and racial refugees from Czechoslovakia, as well as Austrians and Germans who had initially sheltered there, it is clear that figures for the latter two classifications would have been much greater had the data been recorded consistently. Anna Tschapek's IoM card, for instance, does not denote that she was a political refugee. Why?

The inconsistency may have arisen simply from haste on the part of different officials and authorities dealing with hundreds of internees; another explanation is that fuller disclosure of personal information to the British authorities was neither required nor volunteered. Tensions rooted in political differences between interned Czech and ethnic German, Reich German and Austrian refugees forced to cohabitate in a very confined environment (together initially with some Nazis) might, however, have been intensified by societal divisions revealed by their occupations (where given). These ranged from two Czech cooks to a Czech instructress in jewellery manufacture and a Czech needlework teacher, a German factory worker from Czechoslovakia and a domestic servant, to a German and Austrian dress designer, plus a dressmaker, secretary, children's nurse and a photographer. There was also a Czech housewife, and three women (Czech, Austrian and German) reported as having no occupation, though whether they too were housewives or unemployed workers is not known. The correlation between this data and the women's lives during their internment is discussed below.

Life 'behind the barriers'

The disruption of any form of 'normal' life reconstructed in Britain was total, and any vestiges of renewed family life broken by separation, presenting women with challenges as great as, if not greater, than those arising on their arrival in Britain. On arrival the women had been self-respecting refugees, even if some people considered them inferior, and were acutely ashamed to then be detained like criminals, sometimes initially in Holloway

Prison; internment thus required much more adjustment than was ostensibly the case. Nevertheless, Yvonne Cresswell suggested, in many ways
life in Rushen Camp became a microcosm of society outside it; it might
even be said that the multi-dimensional social stratification and differences were accentuated by close confinement, hence were more evident
'behind the barriers' than outside them, and harder to contend with due
to lack of privacy to reflect and recover, coupled with too much time for
introspection.[32] For city dwellers from Prague, Vienna and Berlin, and the
more sophisticated women generally, the very location of the camp and
the sense of isolation from 'the real world' that it created, was a cause of
misery; even in 2009, a brochure for Balmoral Hotel described Port Erin
as a 'small, sleepy fishing village'. Moreover, radios were prohibited under
The Defence Regulations (Isle of Man) 1939, 12 June 1939, as was the use
of telephones and telegrams by enemy aliens or anyone acting on their
behalf,[33] though some internment accounts mention internees listening
to the news on their landlady's radio in the communal lounge.

From the perspective of distinct gender and group dynamics posited
by Cresswell, the women's experience of internment differed considerably
in a number of ways from the men's, not least because the men's Camp
Commandant was generally less strict than his female counterpart, Dame
Joanna Cruickshank. The men were allowed to elect 'house fathers' in their
respective living quarters (as in the CRTF hostels), and were largely self-
organizing if hierarchical, with school, university and the armed forces as
role models. Relieved of family duties as the traditional breadwinner and
home provider, they could revert, to some extent, to their single status and
'mental space', and artists had time for self-expression. In contrast, women
from Czechoslovakia during the 1930s and 1940s were, in the main, still the
traditional home-makers rather than professional career women: despite
outnumbering men in the homeland by 443,304 in 1930 due to WWI,
statistically they were under-represented as 'persons in leading positions' or

32   Discussion with Yvonne Cresswell, Curator, Social History, MNHL, and diverse
      testimonies.
33   MNHL, *op. cit.*, IoM Government Circulars relating to Aliens, Internees, Part 1, and
      Defence Regulations.

as 'employees in higher positions'.[34] As internees, many women were not only without their own home, but bereft of any personal domestic physical space which they had control over, and could identify with. With that role eliminated, the risk of becoming depressed and institutionalized increased. This also applied to the older unmarried women who lacked status or rank in society, especially away from the traditional multi-generational household, and those aged 40 or over were more prone to suicide than younger internees with children, who provided a reason for living. For these and further reasons considered here, internment may have impacted far more strongly on the women and children than on the men.

A mother would have been the key female in her own household, but as an internee with children in her care, she shouldered the full responsibility for them without her spouse's help. Fifteen children were listed in the sample of registration cards referred to here, including Walter Tschapek and an eight-month-old baby born on the IoM. Their presence and needs brought together mothers of children of different ages, while married women with husbands in other IoM camps or deported to other countries could similarly group and share their concerns. This effectively excluded bored and frustrated younger single women in an unnatural single-sex situation who, like some older women, were not necessarily favourably disposed to noisy children, particularly at close quarters. The conflicting needs and requirements of internees in extremely overcrowded conditions easily strained tolerance levels and relationships, as Walter recalled: he and his mother shared a room with an Austrian woman who wanted the window open at night, while his sickly mother preferred it to be closed.

Added to the age differential were religious and political differences previously alluded to, class and the alienating 'upstairs-downstairs' dynamic brought out in Chapter 1. Both cooks listed in the IoM registration cards were given as Czech, and had quite possibly been employed as domestic servants in the homeland by ethnic Germans or Austrians. Internees of a higher social standing would not normally have lived on equal terms in such close proximity with them, let alone shared a bed, which most women were obliged to

34   Czechoslovak Ministry of Foreign Affairs, Department of Information, Statistical Handbook of the Czechoslovak Republic [joint Czech/English] (London: 1942).

do owing to the extreme shortage of single beds reported by Dorothy Naftel (discussed below). Added to socio-political divisions among internees billeted together haphazardly compared with the CRTF's carefully organized group system and hostels, there were differences between internees and their respective landladies, which increased tensions in the billets. Moreover, as Cresswell commented, the known presence of Nazis, prostitutes and some lesbians would have worried mothers with impressionable young daughters. The question of 'the right sort' of person or acceptable company was therefore omni-present in the 'closed world' of the camp as well as outside it, but there were problems of a very practical nature too.

Complaints and remedies

On 13 June 1940, internees Gerda Doerfel (former assistant in the CRTF's London Medical Department), Gertrude Schimmitat, S. Stahl and Sabina Aldersberg wrote jointly to Heinz Schmidt, their German Salda Committee (i.e. Communist) group leader, describing the conditions and expressing the hope that the CRTF would get in touch.[35] 'We have not our clothes which we need very badly', they wrote, 'we have only a very few things here and [...] it is very difficult to manage with the children. We are only able to clean the clothes in cold water'. They went on to mention that three of the women were ill and needed 'extra nourishment' but did not have the money to pay for a doctor's visit, and reminded Schmidt that two of their children, aged 6 and 11, had had TB. 'We have to pay ourselves for soap, toothpaste, shoe repairs etc. It is impossible to manage without money', they stressed. The CRTF did indeed look into the matters, and confirmed the need for money in Financial Position of Refugees Who Are the Responsibility of the Trust, 'since '⅓ third to ½ the refugees are destitute' [sic].[36] It fur-

---

35   TNA, HO 294/223, letter, Port Erin internees to Schmidt, CRTF, 13 June 1940.
36   TNA, HO 294/17, CRTF undated note but evidently 1940.

ther reported its findings in General Conclusions and Some Suggestions, dated 20 September 1940 (also under other similar report titles).[37] 'The women are treated too much as naughty children', Inspector of Hostels Margaret Lloyd observed, and favoured the requisitioning of houses as in the men's camps over the boarding-house system, so that women, like the men, could organize their house and do their own cooking. 'This would help greatly in giving a much-needed outlet and occupation. The present enforced idleness is a source of difficulties'. Among other suggestions was the removal of Nazis and their sympathizers to a separate camp, mixed camps for refugee families, improved medical services including a full-time doctor experienced in gynaecology, facilities for schools, adult education and occupational activities, and a censored inter-camp mail system.

In time, all these suggestions were implemented. By late September 1940, steps had been taken to move known Nazi sympathizers into one part of the camp, and two subsequent reports that concurred with Lloyd's also noted how the problems and complaints had been addressed and remedied. The first, Report on Visit to the Women's Internment Camp in the Isle of Man, January 1941, was by Dorothy Naftel of the International Co-operative Women's Guild,[38] in support of twenty interned members of their respective national Co-operative and Trade Union Movements, whom she interviewed. Naftel's critical report highlighted the physical conditions and psychological hardships women internees experienced, and the effect of nervous tension on their health, in addition to more positive aspects like the Service Exchange Scheme, 'initiated by the internees themselves' whereby they received tokens for work carried out, which could then be exchanged for other goods or services they needed. Aided by government funds to purchase essential equipment, it was 'a real success' pending the introduction of limited paid work. Moreover, by 'fostering a spirit of self-help within a co-operatively run undertaking [the scheme] is a moral tonic to many women who have felt their dependence most

37   *Ibid.*, CRTF, Lloyd, report, Rushen Camp, Women, General Conclusions and Some Suggestions, 20 September 1940.
38   TNA, HO 215/55, Naftel, Report on Visit to the Women's Internment Camp in the Isle of Man, January 1941.

keenly'. Anna Tschapek, although chronically ill after drinking poisoned milk in Russia,[39] knitted items and contributed to the collective effort. Medical facilities improved vastly, as did amenities like a library, thanks to the British Council and Young Women's Christian Association (YWCA), and trips to the local cinema.[40]

Inspector C. R. Cuthbert of Scotland Yard, who replaced Dame Joanna Cruickshank as Commandant of Rushen Camp in May 1941, wrote the second report, Survey of the Women's Internment Camp and the Married Aliens Internment Camp at Port Erin and Port St Mary, Isle of Man, May 1940-September 1945; appended were photographs, a list of classes and a typical British weekly menu.[41] Porridge, cornflakes with milk, and tea (without lemon), replaced the customary central European breakfast of bread and/or rolls, cheese and/or salami and coffee, with dinner (currently called lunch) the main meal of the day (when fish was served frequently, Walter Tschapek recounted). If meals were meagre, repetitive and unappetizing in some billets, the range of subjects taught in the adults' schools was impressive. As in the men's camps, these schools were initiated by women internees of different nationalities who shared their considerable knowledge and skills, providing intellectual stimuli and therapeutic concerts and plays for fellow internees, effectively creating a temporary émigrée cultural centre. Activities comprised various language classes, art, music, dancing, shorthand, gymnastics and religious instruction, with pedagogy and English elocution proving the most popular. Handicrafts classes such as dressmaking, cutting and design (which link with occupations noted in the registration cards cited earlier), and glove-making (later extended to other handwork), provided the women with both an occupation other than assisting with dreary housework and the preparation of vegetables, and a means of obtaining goods for their own use. The women could eventually earn small sums of money by

39   Tschapek, AI.
40   TNA, HO 215/55, Internment report, January 1941, *op. cit.*
41   TNA, HO 213/1053, Cuthbert, Survey of the Women's Internment Camp and the Married Aliens Internment Camp at Port Erin and Port St Mary, Isle of Man, May 1940–September 1945 (completed 1947).

selling their handwork externally (also through projects like farm work), but conditions remained trying, as attested by photographs of women crocheting and others in a dressmaking class, wearing overcoats because of inadequate heating,[42] so internees gratefully accepted second-hand clothes from the Society of Friends (Quakers) and the YWCA. Above all, women duly set aside personal differences sufficiently to demonstrate their resourcefulness, and disinclination to be 'helpless victims'.

Pressure to ease regulations gradually took effect, though in the meantime they impacted severely on communication generally, and on family links in particular. Fraternization with locals was not permitted, and visitors were rare owing to travel costs, restrictions for aliens and the need for special permission to enter the IoM. Of the sixteen visitors mentioned earlier in the IoM registration cards, five women were married to Czechoslovak officers attached to the RAF, and one to a Czechoslovak army officer temporarily on the island (four wives were British-born). The remaining ten women with Czechoslovak connections (comprising three Czechoslovak passport-holders, three German passport-holders and others with various Czechoslovak identity cards and temporary passports), were visiting interned men. (Men were eventually allowed to visit their wives interned in other camps, but only once a month for two hours, and under close supervision).[43] Internees therefore relied on letters for contact with family and friends, and moral support, and it was not only the women who complained about their circumstances. 'It is the Czech and Jewish [men's] groups who are making most of the complaints' about being transferred to a camp with Fascists, Colonel Richard Baggallay wrote on 14 October 1941 from Alien Internment Camps HQ in Douglas, to John Moylan at the Home Office.[44] Peveril Camp Commandant, Ogden, wrote a fuller account of the problems to Moylan on 26 October 1941, including complaints of a more personal matter: 'Detainees who write or receive letters in a foreign language seem to be particularly unfortunate. I attach a record showing the times taken [up to twenty-seven days] for letters, written in Czech

42   *Ibid.*
43   *Ibid.*, 28
44   TNA, HO 215/248, Nazis and anti-Fascists, letter, 14 October 1941.

and posted in Cambridge, to reach the addressee', Herbert Werber, from his wife.[45]

Children were affected by internment too. Walter Tschapek saw his father only once for half an hour during their internment in separate camps, as the Married Aliens Internment Camp did not open in Port St Mary until May 1941 (by which time he and his parents had been released), and he remembered the ensuing sense of estrangement. In his father's enforced absence Walter, though aged only 10 or 11, took care of his ailing mother and even did the washing after attending what in his opinion was 'not a proper school', run by internee women (though Cuthbert commented favourably on the schools and kindergarten).[46] Like other children none too keen on learning French or the limited topics offered initially, Walter preferred exploring and climbing the rocks in what seemed a holiday haven, and greatly appreciated a parcel of toys sent by children in Glasgow.[47] Mothers, however, must have worried about their children's development and future, not knowing how long their internment would last. Their concerns were justified, for according to paediatrician Fred Martineau, 'The detention of children, whether newborn babies or adolescents, almost invariably causes them physical or emotional suffering'.[48] Conversely, however, the premise that a child's own psyche (like that of interned women) could, with innate confidence plus determination help overcome unfavourable environmental factors,[49] was substantiated by nine older children who passed the University of London Matriculation Examination whilst interned, Cuthbert noted. Walter's academic interests revived after his release from internment in April 1941; he duly gained a doctorate, and taught at the university in Halle, near Leipzig. He regretted the time spent in internment,

45   *Ibid.*, letter, Peveril Camp to Moylan, 26 October 1941, 3–4.
46   TNA, HO 213/1053, *op. cit.*, 25–7.
47   Tschapek, AI.
48   'Inside Yarl's Wood: Britain's Shame Over Child Detainees', *Independent on Sunday* (26 April 2009), 16, refers to the 'damning report by the Children's Commissioner for England', *The Arrest and Detention of Children Subject to Immigration Control* (2009).
49   'Unshakeable self-confidence is in the genes, claim scientists', *Daily Telegraph* (2 July 2009), 11.

but was not embittered, remembering instead the many kindnesses shown him, a view echoed by women with reference to Methodist Ministers Harry Johnson and Benson Harrison, and Sister Emmeline Cheshire, a Deaconess who worked with interned women.

Little appears to have survived of the women's own reflections on internment as portrayed in camp newsletters, but Cuthbert's private papers contain a file of revealing newspaper cuttings.[50] *The Isle of Man Weekly* of 5 October 1940 for instance, under the headline 'Journals of the Alien Camp', noted that like the men 'women internees at Port Erin have their own newspaper [...] which they have christened "The Awful Times"', and included extracts (though it has since been suggested that this was a spoof and never actually existed). Further insights came from *The Camp Tribune*, the first (and possibly only) edition of this journal dated 16 August 1941; happily it has survived.[51] The 'Port Erin Page' (spread over pages four and seven) humorously celebrated the women's departure from the camp and each other, rejoicing at being reunited with their respective husbands in the married aliens camp after 'one year of exclusive female company', an 'absolutely men-less fancy-dress ball last New Year's Eve', and 'hot-water-bottle-battles [due to shortages] in our "cosy" homes', noting also a proliferation of internee 'card-tealeaf-and-coffee-sediment fortune-tellers [...] Does he love me still?' Typical of women in their new, more normal circumstances however, a fresh 'catastroph[e]' arose for them. 'No lipsticks'. 'Nothing in the Beauty line' available in the shop when they so wished to be feminine again. The newsletter's contents were not all so light-hearted. News of the war was included, and a piece on immigration to the USA, balanced nevertheless by an item on the camp theatre and a children's page.

Another newsletter, produced not on the IoM, but at 37 Museum Street, London WC1, was *Hamaccabi*. Mainly in English, the January 1941 issue included the Czechoslovak *Hamaccabi*, with four pages in Czech. Published by the Jewish Bar Kochba, editions were circulated

---

50   MNHL, Cuthbert papers, MS 11196 on women's internment.
51   MNHL, M 31545, newsletter, *Camp Tribune*, no. 1 (16 August 1941), 4, 7, Michael Corvin, ed., former editor of Hutchinson's *The Camp*, and Onchan's *Pioneer* camp journals.

by the Maccabi Aid Committee;[52] this copy may have been sent to an internee and circulated in the camp, possibly as a result of a play Jewish and non-Jewish internees performed in English in Port Erin at Christmas/Chanukah, which Naftel refers to in her report as the 'Jewish history of the Macabees' [*sic*]. It was, she observed, the aim of those responsible for general education in the camp to 'foster a spirit of toleration among the different racial groups', and teachers 'were doing their utmost to persuade internees to use English as much as possible'. The newsletter covered a variety of topics ranging from Jewish sports history to a piece by Lucy Borchardt entitled, 'Jewish Navigation in the Making', about her efforts to train and save young Jewish men in her Hamburg shipping company, their escape to Palestine and the company's subsequent activities there. Social and cultural activities were not overlooked. 'You are cordially invited to a Musical and Dancing Party' on 16 February in Freedman Hall, Golders Green Synagogue' (north London) read one item; internees must have read it *very* wistfully.[53]

Life for women remaining at liberty

Life at liberty did not necessarily detach refugee women from the problems of internment, despite the IoM's physical remoteness. Various groups and organizations felt conscience-bound to assist internees, particularly women and children, and reduce the damaging effects of internment by providing practical help like 'extra nutriment among youths under 20' registered with the Children's Movement, a grant for clothing and books from the German Emergency Committee, 'comforts' to destitute Jewish

---

52   MNHL, M 31546, newsletter, *Hamaccabi*, 2/2 (January 1941), published by Bar Kochba, London.

53   The last two newsletters were rendered all the more interesting as historical WWII printed material by their discovery in the IoM archives in July 2009, apparently the sole copies in the public domain.

women from the Jewish Refugees Committee, and a welfare grant from the Church of England Committee.[54] The success of many similar efforts, however, depended on refugee women, requiring their time, energy and commitment. The Refugee Teachers' Association newsletter of November 1940 compiled by the Sekretärin, B. Sonntag,[55] and addressed to 'Liebe Kollegen! Mili[í] [k]Kolegové!' in German and Czech, carried extracts in English from a grateful internee's response (undated) to the Association's £1 donation to the interned children: 'my colleagues give such fine proof of their solidarity with their interned friends [...]. The conscience we are not forgotten makes us easier this internment', wrote the unnamed woman when 6/- were sent to the kindergarten, the rest to the school. She also appealed for urgently needed books: 'Every help is a comfort to us. So far we have worked [organized] a school for about 100 children in a church-hall under extremely difficult conditions with scarcely a penny or a single book to begin with. At present we are having 3 weeks holidays as the teachers are too tired and run down to go on teaching under these conditions without a break'.

Considerable broader support for internees came via *Die Frau in Arbeit/Pracující žena*, given as the periodical of Working Refugee Women (singular in the main title), in joint German and Czech.[56] The December 1940 issue for instance, reported the huge response to an appeal by the 'Committee for a[n] Xmas to interned Refugees', which raised over £571. More soberly, a Czech section headed 'Naše solidarita' [Our solidarity] mentioned some fifty interned Czechoslovaks apparently registered by the authorities as Austrian (hence enemy aliens), while another section, 'Vánoce [Christmas] 1940' began 'Smutné vánoce v emigraci', expressing sadness over Christmas in exile, with everyone remembering dear ones at home. Heartfelt thanks were conveyed in German and Czech in the January/ February 1941 issue for the hundreds of parcels sent to excited internees,

---

54 TNA, HO 294/17, circular attached to Henry Bunbury's note, 14 October 1940, praising Lloyd's report on internment.

55 Based at Hamilton House, Mabledon Place, London WC1, Fromings, PP.

56 *Die Frau in Arbeit/Pracující žena*, no. 8 (December 1940), 2, 7, and nos 7/8 (January/ February 1941), 2.

parcels packed by many united German, Czech and English friends and
helpers who worked on despite the frequent air-raids. The goodwill was
reciprocated, as the piece 'Internierte für Coventry' noted, by men interned
in Sefton Camp (IoM). On hearing about the heavy bombing of Coventry,
they sent parcels of toys made in their camp, with a note expressing their
'sympathy for the distressed air raid victims', which Mayor J. A. Moseley
was 'happy' to receive.

Supporting internees and prisoners was a pertinent aspect of the
Czechoslovak Red Cross's (CRC) multi-faceted work (see Chapter 3). Here
again, it was predominantly women volunteers like Marga Tomášková (also
Tomasek) from Fortis Green CRTF hostel, who joined the organization.
Karol Gandl, writing from Liverpool Prison on 10 November 1940, was
grateful for a CRC parcel containing warm underwear.[57] Allowed to send
two letters per week, he reserved one for his wife. The role of refugee women
during the main internment period of 1940–1 became doubly important
when women remaining at liberty replaced interned men, taking on extra
responsibilities or obligations. Hedwig Huenigen, Matron of a CRTF hostel
for children (see Chapter 4), was one such woman. On 20 May 1940, Hugo
Ehrlich of the CRTF Beuer Group (i.e. Sudeten German Czechoslovak
Communists), wrote advising her in German of the Group's decision
that should some of its leadership be interned, she and Kaethe Beckmann
'should then carry on leading the Group'. Arrangements would be made
to move her children's hostel 'somewhere near London', and he urged her
to consider the matter.[58] Group leader MP Gustav Beuer, his brother Otto
(director of the Co-operative Society in Reichenberg (re-named Liberec),
plus Communist member of the Czechoslovak Senate Karl Kreibich, anti-
Fascist Trade Union official Anton Rubal and journalist Ludwig Freund,
were indeed subsequently imprisoned in various places, then interned
together in January 1941. Huenigen's activities and administrative work
consequently increased, and in addition to rescuing her deported relative
she helped to support the interned men by means of letters, parcels and
ingredients for cakes. The value of that support is clear from Otto Beuer's

57   SSEES, LIS 3/3/8, Gandl, letter, 10 November 1940.
58   Fromings (Huenigen), PP.

letter in English from Lingfield internment camp in Surrey,[59] thanking her for 'the splendid "*böhm. Buchteln*"' [colloquial: a Bohemian yeast cake]. 'It was like a breath from home. It's a wonderful feeling to know that there are friends outside who never stop to take care of us'. On conditions at the converted racecourse Beuer observed, 'Here it's hard enough, but you know nothing can break our spirit and we are trying to make the best of it'. He even joked about them opening a 'Café Rubal' in the camp and having 'with our Kreibich Karl a very "Reichenbergen Ris[o]to"'. Though removed from mainstream life, he was nonetheless well informed and aware that Huenigen was 'overburdened with work'. 'I hope that you have got some help in the meantime' he added, sending everyone 'hearty greetings'.

In February 1941 these men were moved to another converted race-course, near York, where Gustav Beuer, 'who had entered [Brixton] prison as a vigorous and absolutely healthy man, was the first to fall seriously ill' due to 'the privations of prison life' described in *Morrison's Prisoners*,[60] so seriously that Beuer's wife (Elizabeth?), was informed of his transfer to a hospital and given the requisite police permit to travel there from London. Gustav Beuer did not die, but needed long-term treatment. To his wife's distress, the conflicting interests and concerns of the authorities, particularly regarding Communists, were manifested in confusing instructions. On 18 March 1941, J. Pritchard of the Home Office B-3 Division, informed E. Beuer that her husband had been released, and requested the return of the police travel permit issued to her, only to write on 27 March that she was 'misinformed by this Department': her husband was still in hospital, hence a further permit 'valid for a series of visits' was enclosed. On the same day, Czechoslovak Foreign Secretary Jan Masaryk appealed to MP Herbert Morrison for his assistance, repeating that the 'Provisional Czechoslovak Government has no interest whatsoever in keeping Mr. Beuer interned'. Release was finally granted, albeit not without further pressure on the authorities.

---

59   *Ibid.*
60   *Morrison's Prisoners. The Story of the Czechoslovakian Anti-Fascist Fighters Interned in Britain* (London: National Council of Democratic Aid, around May 1941) 14–18.

Another woman who strove to secure her then fiancé's release from internment, was Esther Dunn (later Freistadt),[61] British until 1941 when she married one of the few Slovaks to enter Britain in 1938–9,[62] and became an alien under British law pertaining at the time. Typically, matters were complicated by nationality issues which affected her, too. Freistadt's expulsion order 'for ever' dated 2 January 1939, confused British authorities and incriminated him. One can see why: born in 1903 in Pressburg (Bratislava), 'citizen of Vienna', 'country Germany', religion 'Israelite'.[63] Like others with Austro-Hungarian and German links, he was caught up in the political mood of the moment and ensnared in the resultant developments: Czechoslovakia's post-Munich backlash against Germans (resumed in 1945), Germany's insistence that ethnic Germans be treated as Reich Germans and Slovakia's impending collaboration with Nazi Germany. He certainly did not wish to go to Germany. Freistadt, with his brother, Leo, therefore obtained visas by purporting to emigrate overseas, and on 28 August 1939 he registered with the BCRC (later the CRTF), spending some time at the training centre at Redbourne. With the outbreak of war, CRTF Director Henry Bunbury vouched for him on 27 September 1939 stating, 'We have no grounds for doubting [...] his sympathies with the British cause'.[64]

Despite these assurances, Freistadt was interned in Lingfield in 1940. MP Eleanor Rathbone took up the case in her capacity as Honorary Secretary of the Parliamentary Committee on Refugees, advising Esther on 4 December 1940 to pursue the supposed immigration aspect. Freistadt had been busy too. One route from internment was employment deemed essential or useful, subject to Labour Exchange permission – requested in December 1940 by G. E. Harrison and Sons Ltd in Norwich, needing a scrap metal sorter. Their joint efforts paid off. On 21 March 1941 (responding to her letter of 21 November 1940), Esther received formal Home Office

61   Berta Freistadt, AI, PP, re: mother Esther Freistadt (Dunn).
62   TNA, KV 2/2719, 'The number of Slovaks [...] does not exceed a few hundred', Bruce Lockhart informed Viscount Halifax, Foreign Office, 10 October 1940.
63   Freistadt, PP.
64   *Ibid.*

notification of her future husband's release,[65] but it masks the anxious and frustrating months endured by British-born wives (BBWs) of Czechoslovak men with complex backgrounds.

MI5 scrutiny

Since the WWII internment process was by no means a consistent one, most refugees from Czechoslovakia remained at liberty, albeit watched by MI5 and each other. The CRTF was well aware of political dissent among those in its care, and of British public opinion shifting against them. On 5 September 1939, Margaret Layton[66] had therefore written to all the group leaders urging them to ensure that everyone contributed to the British war effort, and to report to the Trust anyone who was acting suspiciously.[67] Knowing that some early non-urgent arrivals not personally known to CRTF group leaders had 'slipped through' the system, the group leaders' importance in identifying members of their respective political parties and establishing genuine refugee credentials, had increased with the outbreak of war. Additionally, the Trust's Standard General Rules for Hostels Under War Conditions, issued on 24 June 1940, stipulated at Section.4. that the refugees, most of whom were living in Trust Fund hostels, should not '"go about" in groups of more than three people, nor enter inns or hotels', and at Section 6 inveighed, outside the hostels 'English only should be spoken. All telephone conversations must be in English',[68] to avoid drawing

65 *Ibid.*
66 Following the BCRC's closure in 1939, its former Chief Executive Officer and Secretary, Margaret Layton, briefly transferred to the CRTF in July 1939 together with other BCRC staff members, until her marriage.
67 IWM, Private Papers of M D Layton [Layton], Documents 16055, box. no. 07/70/1–2, box 2, letter, 5 September 1939 and group leaders' responses.
68 TNA, HO 294/18, CRTF, Hostels, Standard General Rules for Hostels Under War Conditions, issued 24 June 1940.

adverse attention to themselves. This was not without good reason. On 29 June 1940, Margaret Lloyd reported on problems at Patterdale Hall to which some 'trouble-makers' had been sent from Margate, and stated that 'as in Cumberland and Westmorland generally [...] the existence of political refugees apart from racial refugees is mostly unknown'; 'villagers are full of fear and suspicion of strangers and rumour is rife'.[69] Hetty Bower, the English warden of Fortis Green hostel, north London, recounted how 'despite very little discord' generally, the local police came to the hostel four or five times as the result of telephone calls accusing 'the foreigners' of being 'spies [...] sending messages to the Luftwaffe', because the black-out blinds had been inadvertently drawn back, possibly by the children.[70]

Alleged Communist control: CRTF

More seriously, refugees who had not been interned were hindered from spying or assisting the enemy by the 1940 Aliens (Protected Areas) Order, which prevented them from residing in coastal or other designated areas for security reasons. Additional restrictions on bicycle, camera and radio ownership served the same purpose, notionally if not in reality. Nevertheless, certain refugees who remained at liberty were kept under surveillance, as evidenced by Home Office, Foreign Office and MI5 documents held at The National Archives in London, and it is interesting to note who was watching whom. This is well demonstrated by the following MI5 memorandum of 30 January 1940:

> In the middle of December [1939], M. I. 5 received from Scotland Yard a report alleging that the Communist Party of Great Britain had obtained for three of its members influential positions in the Czech Refugee Trust Fund, and that the Central

69   TNA, HO 294/18, CRTF, Dougan, Memo. 3 July 1940 and Lloyd Report on Patterdale Hall, 29 June 1940.
70   Esther (Hetty) Bower, AI.

Committee of the Communist Party was congratulating itself on this outstanding success [...]. The results so far obtained seem of sufficient importance to be brought to the attention of the Home Office.[71]

It went on to name Yvonne Kapp, Assistant to the Trust's Director, Margaret Mynatt, Head of the Tribunals Department (friendly aliens only), Bruce Hole, Legal Adviser, and George Musgrove, Assistant Accountant, while Kaethe Beckmann and another Beuer group member, a Mrs Markus, and Gerda Doerfel, Marie Schmidt, Eva Goldmann and a Mrs Michaelis, were named as known Communists employed by the Trust. The same MI5 file contains a summary of the letter dated 12 January 1940 from Josef Bělina, leader of the general Czech group, highlighting the profound animosity to Communism felt by some CRTF refugees.[72] He accused the Trust of treating Communists preferentially, and made strong allegations against several Czechoslovak refugees, including the German-speaking actress, Elizabeth Warnholtz, who worked for the BBC, Communist group leader Gustav Beuer, and Communist Youth Secretary, Otto Šling. 'The hostels are full of Communist posters and pamphlets', Bělina claimed. 'In some places contact is being made with English Communists, which had bad results for the Czechs, many being interned'. MI5 and the Home Office concurred. CRTF employee Kate Thornycroft, then head of the hospitality section responsible for placing refugees in hostels, and her future husband, Hermann Field, were therefore also vetted as possible Communists, though nothing detrimental was found against them.

Nonetheless, suspicion abounded. An earlier Special Branch report of 14 December 1939 regarding the CRTF,[73] named two other women, Margaret Meinhardt and Margaret Mander (they both transpired to be Mynatt, due to misspellings), who were reportedly involved in 'liaison work' with the aliens tribunals, with access to 'fairly comprehensive lists of anti-Communist refugees of all categories'. By following government

71 TNA, KV 2/2714, MI5 Memorandum re: Communists in CRTF, 30 January 1940, and attachments.
72 *Ibid.*, Summary of Letter from Josef Bělina, 12 January 1940.
73 *Ibid.*, Special Branch Report Re: the CRTF, 14 December 1939.

directives to notify tribunals 'whenever anything is known against an alien, whether the complaint is a provable fact or merely rumour', the report argued, these Party members 'are taking advantage [...] by alleging that anti-Communist refugees are Gestapo agents' (apparently discovered by some refugees who were allowed to read the statements). The matter did not rest there. Hostility was predominantly directed against three groups who were being denounced, according to Edith Wedderburn's letter of 23 June 1940 to Home Secretary John Anderson:[74] Catholics, refugees who had renounced Communist Party membership, and those who 'had been anti-Hitler, and had helped the Czech Republic'. A supporting document, The Case of Therese Klimpelova, concerned a supposedly known activist from a Karlsbad (Karlovy Vary) family of 'fanatical socialists and adherents of the Czech Republic of Masaryk and Benes', and a member of the CRTF Reitzner group. On arrival at Bloomsbury House (London) for a tribunal hearing, Klimpelova was allegedly physically attacked by Beatrice Wellington in the presence of Weddderburn, a British-born nursing sister who had helped refugees in Prague, plus other witnesses. Klimpelova was, the report stated: 'imprisoned at Holloway Gaol on 19 June 1940 on an order from H. O. Aliens [O]rder from 1920, 22a. She has been without interrogation for six months. On the charge sheet belonging to Miss Wellington she is denounced thus [...] "Doubtful financial transactions in Prague. Seen in Deutscheshaus haunt of Czech Fascists and Military"'. It was pointedly added in the report that: 'The Deutsches haus [sic] was the centre for the feeding of refugees after the Munich agreement, and did not become the centre for Czech Fascists until after March 15th 1939. Miss Klimpel left Prague and flew non-stop to Rotterdam January 6th 1939. See passport'.[75]

---

74   National Archives, Prague [NAP], MV–L, karton 175, sg. 2–16-10, Case of Therese Klimpelova, with Edith Wedderburn's letters, 23 June and 12 November 1940 to Home Secretary.

75   *Ibid.*

German and Communist agents

The issue thus returns to the secret references and recommendations to the tribunals mentioned earlier, and through them the opportunity for denunciations or pernicious accusations; but denunciations could be made in various circumstances by any CRTF group, and were taken seriously by the authorities. Four women given as Czech, Herta Kral, Irma Pick, Emilia Meyer(?) and Katerina [i.e. Kaethe] Beckmann, staff members at New Lodge, Windsor (then the Trust's HQ), had been vigilantly observing Irmgard Sattler, a domestic from Hamburg who had gained Czech citizenship by marriage.[76] On separate occasions she was 'seen in various departments where she had no right to be during the absence of the departmental staff'. Furthermore, Berkshire Constabulary reported on 11 November 1939, a 'Czech national' read part of a letter in German which Sattler asserted was 'a botanical report'. 'Such words as "frontier", "coast", "sea" and "river" are stated to have been contained therein and one phrase read "a---(certain named flower) may be found in a given direction from the river 2½ miles distant"'. Her letters, it was observed, were not posted locally, but a bicycle ride away. Moreover, 'Adverse reports have also been received from British officials of the Trust [...]. She is known to have spoken against the Czechs and the Jews, and is thought to be connected with a trouble-making publication [unspecified] circulating among the refugees'. In addition, Berkshire Constabulary noted, she had latterly joined the Wollenberg Group, 'originally known as the "Demokratische Fleuchtlingshilfe" [*sic*, Democratic Refugee Aid], and which is regarded with some suspicion' by the Trust on various counts. Otto Wollenburg 'apparently introduced into his Group those who were rejected from other Groups and he is thought to have included a number of political agents who passed as refugees'. Whether Sattler proved to be an agent is uncertain.

76   TNA, KV 2/2714, Berkshire Constabulary report, 11 November 1939, and associated correspondence.

The intriguing case of Sophia Alexandra Clapham-Kukralova, 'very strongly suspected of being a German agent',[77] was also anything but clear-cut. Reports confidently but variously described her as Czech-born and Georgian-born, unofficially adopted by Maxwell Clapham (which provided neither British citizenship nor right of entry into Britain). While the British National Archives online summary stated, 'Post-war interrogation of a German agent showed that these suspicions were well-founded', the case remained, like many others, inconclusive. On the other hand, errors were made where refugees had genuinely been advised or found it necessary to use false names. A note sent on 10 July 1939 to Margaret Layton, concerning Greta Kohn, affirmed that 'She could not receive the Gestapo permit to leave Prague. Miss Wellington gave her a paper bearing the name Marta Doleckova on which she travelled'.[78] Nevertheless, that some Czechoslovak refugees were also agents for whichever side they championed during WWII, is surely a given. There is compelling evidence that Communist agents infiltrated the 1948 cohort of refugees too, but attitudes towards them had hardened long beforehand. 'I must state quite frankly that the Czecho-Slovak émigrés in Britain contain many undesirable elements', Bruce Lockhart[79] wrote on 10 October 1940 in a secret communiqué from the Office of the British Representative with the Czecho-Slovak [sic] Provisional Government in London, to Viscount Halifax at the Foreign Office. Lockhart enclosed a copy of the sixteen-page 'pamphlet' *Czecho-Slovakia's Guilty Men*,[80] dismissed as a 'diatribe' which attacked the Czechoslovak government in exile and was, in his view, 'pacifist, pro-Russian, anti-Imperialist and anti-capitalist'. 'It certainly calls attention to the noxious activities of émigrés who hold Czecho-Slovak passports' he declared, adding oblique criticisms of the CRTF, and comparing the low number of Czechs 'by race' with those who simply possessed Czechoslovak documentation.

---

77   TNA, KV 2/3122, Sophia Alexandra Clapham-Kukralova, 1942–51, Resume attached to letter 20 February 1942, G. J. Jenkins, Defence Security Office, Egypt to David Petrie, War Office, London.

78   Layton, box 2, *op. cit.*, Wisconsin file, Note to Layton, 10 July 1939.

79   TNA, KV 2/2719, *op. cit.*, Lockhart to Halifax.

80   Anonymous author.

Release from internment

Professor Hugh Seton-Watson and his wife May were markedly more sympathetic to Communists and supporters than Lockhart.[81] Writing on 3 October 1940 from Balliol College, Oxford, to Elizabeth Allen at the CRTF, May mentioned that Hugh was serving on the new Interned Aliens Tribunal, dealing with applications for release from interned anti-Nazi aliens.[82] Having seen a (presumably confidential) list of internees, she gathered that 'they were mainly the German and Austrian "double refugees"', and requested that helpful details about them be passed to the Tribunal. 'There has been the most appalling and disgraceful muddle over the whole thing', May expostulated, blaming Colonel Blimp (a British cartoon character) in the War Office, and the Home Office. 'But they are genuinely anxious now to put things right as far as possible, and where the Tribunal can produce full and accurate details the H. O. people are almost pathetically grateful'. Hopeful regarding Wenzel Jaksch's Sudeten German Social Democratic Party supporters, May was considerably less optimistic regarding 'the Beuer people – I know there are wheels within wheels within wheels: – who apparently have been pounced on because they are Communists, and for that reason may be more difficult to rescue [...]. But they are certainly all violently anti-Nazi and so could come under the scope of the Tribunal'; hence, she requested that helpful details be provided about them too. She had a point there, for Lockhart's establishment image of villainous Communist revolutionaries could seem rather exaggerated when applied to perceived idealists nurturing apparently good intentions concerning the fate of their homeland. The underlying difficulty, however, lay in the diverse political pathways to that future, pathways which met or diverged as the war progressed, and preoccupation with post-war allegiances and territorial boundaries increased, as will be seen later.

81   TNA, KV 2/2719, letter, Seton-Watson to Allen, CRTF, 3 October 1940.
82   Home Office, White Paper, *Civilian Internees of Enemy Nationality. Categories of Persons Eligible for Release from Internment and Procedure to be Followed in Applying for Release*, Cmd. 6233 (London: October 1940).

In the meantime, the question of release from internment still occupied the minds both of those interned and those endeavouring to secure their release. 'Recognizing that this war is essentially a conflict of ideas; that the ideas and issues are not confined by national boundaries; and that all in sympathy with our ideas are potential allies', the Manchester Co-ordinating Council for Refugees and Aliens[83] signed a resolution on 27 January 1941, pressing the authorities for the speedy release of sympathetic aliens, and the separate consideration of nationals like Czechoslovaks from occupied countries with governments in Britain. Public opinion was turning against internment and favoured a change in government policy, urged by the National Council for Civil Liberties,[84] and the National Council for Democratic Aid.[85] MPs like Eleanor Rathbone furthered the cause in parliament, and after her visit to the new Married Aliens Internment Camp, the Camp Speaker printed his letter of 4 August 1941 to the MP in *Camp Tribune*,[86] regarding release, occupation and welfare matters to be followed up. Exceptionally, a few women had had their cases reviewed and were released early according to the IoM registration cards cited here:[87] a Czechoslovak woman born in 1906 and erroneously registered on the IoM as Austrian was 'Exempted internment [but] subject to special [unspecified] conditions' in September 1940, while a German woman who had been working in Czechoslovakia was released with her baby, and was also 'exempt internment, special restrictions' [unspecified], in December 1940. Some women continued to be detained, however. Another German woman who had resided in Czechoslovakia appealed in December 1940, but was interned from May 1940 to January 1944. Inexplicably, a woman who was born in Vienna in 1908, held a Czechoslovak passport, and was initially classed as a 1939 Jewish 'Refugee from Nazi oppression' with temporary

83   TNA, HO 294/5, Status of Aliens in Great Britain. Draft Note 1941, Manchester Co-ordinating Council for Refugees and Aliens, proposal signed 27 January 1941.
84   *The Internment and Treatment of Aliens*, National Council for Civil Liberties (London: May 1941).
85   *Morrison's Prisoners, op. cit.*
86   MNHL, *Camp Tribune, op. cit.*, 2.
87   MNHL, Collections Database – registration cards, *op. cit.*

landing rights, exempted from internment and special restrictions applicable to enemy aliens, was nevertheless interned in May 1940 and not released until April 1941.

The majority of women, however, were released by around May 1941. Anna Tschapek, born in 1902, appeared before the Home Office Aliens Advisory Committee in Douglas Court House on 13 February and 4 April 1941, and was released with her son on 29 April 1941.[88] On 30 April 1941 the Leeds City Police Alien Registration Office stamped her U. K. Aliens' Registration Certificate (not to be confused with the IoM registration card), adding: 'Exempted by the Secretary of State from internment and special restrictions'. On 7 May 1941 the office added a significant note: 'Nationality amended to Czech on production of Certificate of Citizenship granted at Czech Legation, London, on 3.4.1940'. Whilst release was cause for jubilation, shelter thereafter was cause for concern. Many women had lost their accommodation as well as jobs, particularly nurses or those in domestic service. One woman's 'Leaving IoM for ...' section on her card read simply: 'Central Bureau of Refugees, Domestic Bureau, 44 Bloomsbury Street, London WC1', and where the Czech-born women awaiting US visas lodged, is not indicated on their IoM cards.[89] Other women were more fortunate, though it is not always clear whether their address was a private home or a small hostel, and difficult to verify. CRTF hostels consequently had a vital role in refugee women's lives after internment, as well as prior to it. One woman and her child went to 'Czech hostel, Barrack Lane, Nottingham'. Another woman, plus the German Communist Emmy Koenen released in February 1941, left for 'Canterbury Hall, Cartwright Gardens, London WC1' (then a CRTF hostel), where Koenen was later questioned by men believed to have been British security personnel.[90] Internment, though, continued to impact on women's lives. Left-wing psychology student Marianne Lowe,[91] who had witnessed a

88 Tschapek, AI, PP.
89 MNHL, Collections Database – registration cards, *op. cit.*
90 Emmy Koenen, 'Exil in England', in *Beiträge zur Geschichte der Arbeiterbewegung*, 4 (1978), 540–63.
91 Marianne Lowe (Adler), AI, daughter Dorrit Maltby (Lowe).

desperate mother throw her baby overboard, arrived on a coal-ship evacu-ating Czechoslovak troops from France in 1940. Lowe married a stateless German in 1942 after his release from internment on the IoM, but he had no work, so she became the breadwinner working in a nursery. She also became stateless under the prevailing regulations.

With competing political interests and allegiances very much in mind, all sides keenly noted the activities of Czechoslovaks in Britain, including President Beneš, so the entire spectrum of refugee political groups, their respective publications (where applicable) and the Communist-inclined Czechoslovak-British Friendship Club in London, were under scrutiny throughout the war. The focus remained on Communist and Sudeten German activities, principally those of men who had previously been the political leaders of the era; but as shown, this involved women too. The situation is illustrated by *Sudeten Germans and Czechs. Condensed Report of the First National Conference of German Anti-Fascists from Czechoslovakia*, a conference organized by the Communist organ *Einheit*.[92] Former internees Franz and Anna Tschapek participated, speakers such as Gustav Beuer urged everyone to unite against the common enemy and support the British war effort, representatives of the Czechoslovak government in exile attended it, Jaksch boycotted it – and the British Foreign Office monitored it.[93]

Conclusion

It would be unwise to surmise that all security concerns were without foun-dation, especially during wartime. Nevertheless, observations noted in MI5 and other documents variously denoted as 'confidential', 'secret' or 'top secret', can today appear speculative, implausible or inaccurate. A Special

92 British Library [BL], *Sudeten Germans and Czechs. Condensed Report of the First National Conference of German Anti-Fascists from Czechoslovakia, at Beaver Hall, London, October 16th-17th 1943, Einheit* (1944), then at 189 Westbourne Grove, W11.
93 TNA, FO 371/34330, Foreign Office notes, 1943.

Branch letter of 11 January 1940 for example,[94] asserted that the BCRC was 'an organisation aiming at the reconstruction of Czechoslovakia' – absurdly far from the BCRC's role described in Chapter 1. Moreover, it had officially been superseded by the British-administered CRTF since July 1939, with new, very specific aims also cited in Chapter 1. The claim that 'Prominent Czechs like Dr Beneš and Jan Masaryk are associated with the organisation' is also inaccurate. Yes, certain prominent people such as Anežka Hodinová and other former MPs were associated with the Trust and women refugees in various ways, but not the men named, who remained aloof from both organizations. Furthermore, when taken collectively, documents from this period can create an overall impression that a disproportionate percentage of the CRTF local and/or refugee staff were Communist. Whilst it is not disputed that some undoubtedly were, this should be balanced by the fact that 'following the outbreak of the war the staff reached a peak of 210' (up from 170 in July 1939) to cope with the work;[95] it is highly improbable that all 210 were Communists, selected on political grounds. Despite these and other discrepancies, the Trust was obliged to dismiss Yvonne Kapp, her friend Margaret Mynatt and others, because they were found to be Communists, an ideology that was utterly unacceptable in an organization directly responsible to both the Home Office and the Treasury. Interviewee Hetty Bower commented that whilst she had empathized with Communist refugees in her hostel, she concealed her own connections with the British Communist Party until after the war.[96] It is therefore ironic that hard-line Communists in post-war Czechoslovakia and the USSR should describe the Trust as 'a hotbed of spies and imperialist agents'.[97]

The conflict of ideas cited here between Fascism, Communism and capitalism manifested itself in diverse ways at all levels, and permeated every aspect of the refugees' lives in Britain; internment and all that pertained to it was but one facet of their struggles in exile. Victor Cazalet

---

94 TNA, KV 2/2714, Special Branch letter, Jeffcot to Gill, 11 January 1940.
95 TNA, HO 294/5, History of the Trust, Introduction to the Fund, VII Administration.
96 Bower, AI.
97 Marian Šlingová, *Truth Will Prevail* (London: Merlin, 1968), 55.

called it 'totally un-English', a phrase adopted by Richard Dove as the title of the book he edited.[98] Edith Wedderburn presciently declared in her letter of 12 November 1940 to Home Secretary Herbert Morrison: 'Long after this generation has passed away, the outrageous treatment which we have accorded the political refugee, who came to us for sanctuary after the Munich Agreement, will be recorded by the historian, and not to our credit!'[99] Britain's socio-political history is inextricably enmeshed with Czechoslovakia's, but if internment temporarily dictated the direction of exiled women's lives in a negative manner, the experience perhaps strengthened the women's resolve 'to make the best of the situation' and themselves – perforce quite independently of their menfolk. After their release, the resilient women internees described here had opportunities to achieve even more, in ways they might never previously have imagined or thought possible and, as anti-Fascists, to prove their support for the British war effort, as discussed in the next chapter.

98 Dove, *op. cit.*, 12.
99 NAP, *op. cit.*

A Women's War in a Foreign Land: Helping the War Effort

While women in occupied Czechoslovakia, particularly those of German extraction, were obliged to help the German war effort, their refugee counterparts were duly called upon in Britain following its declaration of war against Germany in September 1939, notably after the release from internment of most refugees from Czechoslovakia in around May 1941. Refugee women joined British armed services and Czechoslovak units attached to them, or contributed to the war effort in other ways: they supported, complemented and even replaced men when necessary. Yet their wartime roles and achievements are almost entirely overlooked, eclipsed by works (worthy though they are), about men – Czechoslovak soldiers and airmen – by men, for example, Alan Griffin, Neil Rees and Alan Brown.[1] Lewis White's[2] *On All Fronts in World War II, Part 3* contained thirty-eight testimonies of Czechoslovak servicemen, none by a woman. This chapter is therefore devoted to the exiled women's contribution to the war effort: it endeavours to remedy the imbalance and, in doing so, draws attention to the barely known activities of the Czechoslovak Red Cross in wartime Britain.

1   Alan Griffin, *Leamington's Czech Patriots and the Heydrich Assassination* (Warwick, UK: Feldon Books, 2004); Neil Rees, *The Czech Connection. The Czechoslovak Government in Exile in London and Buckinghamshire During the Second World War* (Printed by Croxsons, Buckinghamshire: published by author, 2005); Alan Brown, *Flying for Freedom. The Allied Air Forces in the RAF 1939–45* (Stroud: History Press, 2012).

2   Lewis M. White, ed., *On All Fronts in World War II, Part III, East European Monographs*, No. DLVIII (New York: Columbia University Press/Boulder, 2000).

Joining the war effort

President Beneš initiated Czechoslovak involvement in the war effort by informing the reportedly grateful Prime Minister Neville Chamberlain by telegram that: 'We Czechoslovak citizens consider ourselves as being also at war with the German military forces and we shall march with your people until the final victory and the liberation of our fatherland'.[3] Beneš also strove to establish a government in exile in Britain, and when France fell to Germany in June 1940, he pressed for over 1,000 airmen[4] and 4,000 soldiers of the Free Czechoslovak Army formed in Agde to be evacuated to Britain. The airmen subsequently served in Czechoslovak units of the Royal Air Force (RAF), while the military section re-grouped as the Czechoslovak Independent Brigade Group (known as the Czechoslovak Brigade), and helped to defend Britain.[5] Shifts in British policy facilitating Czechoslovak participation in the war effort were formalized through three measures. Firstly, the Allied Forces (Application) Order, 1940,[6] recognized the Czechoslovak Republic as an Allied power. Secondly, the Medical Register (Temporary Registration) Order, 1941,[7] allowing qualified foreign practitioners to practise in Britain. Thirdly, the International Labour Force (Registration of Czechoslovak Nationals) Order, 1941[8] which, 'with a view

---

3   Edvard Beneš, *The Fall and Rise of a Nation: Czechoslovakia 1938–1941*, trans. Milan Hauner, ed. (New York: East European Monographs, Boulder/Columbia University Press, 2004), 47–8; School of Slavonic and East European Studies [SSEES] archives, Lisicky Collection, LIS 3/3/7, undated Memorandum re: Czechoslovak Army in Britain links with telegram 3 September 1939, and quotes Beneš's message.

4   Beneš, *op. cit.*, 74–5.

5   Figures vary slightly, see: Griffin, *op. cit.*, 2–3; Karel C. Machacek, *Escape to England* (The Book Guild, Sussex: 1988), 114, 127, of the 5,000–10,000 servicemen, nearly half stayed in France, most Slovaks returned to Slovakia [then independent].

6   Allied Forces (Application of 23 Geo. 5. c. 6) (No. 1) Order, 1940, No. 1818.

7   Medical Register (Temporary Registration) Order, 1941, No. 24.

8   International Labour Force (Registration of Czechoslovak Nationals) Order, 1941, No. 723.

to enabling the best use to be made of the services of Czechoslovak nationals in Great Britain in support of the war effort', authorized 'the engagement of such persons', and required them to register with a local Employment Exchange. It applied to men and women, the latter aged between 16 and 50 (but exempted officials and members of the Provisional Czechoslovak Government, diplomats and active servicemen/women). One of the war effort procedures is illustrated by Grete Reichl's letter of 1 September 1941 from the Aliens War Service Department, confirming that her application for a permit to engage in Auxiliary War Services had been granted.[9]

In the meantime, for its part, the British-administered Czech Refugee Trust Fund (CRTF) was anxious to avert public prejudice against refugees in its care. To forestall perceptions of refugees as disloyal or parasites, Margaret Layton wrote on 5 September 1939 to all the group leaders noted in Chapter 1, urging their respective members to participate in the war effort, and required to know how they proposed to do so.[10] Responses were swift, detailed, and positive. Men were generally keen to fight, age and health permitting, and both men and women expressed willingness to participate in civil defence work as well as industry. They also offered professional skills. As Gustav Beuer stated on 7 September 1939: 'Our group has at its disposal a number of men and women doctors, nurses, red-cross workers, who could be used at the front and behind the lines'.[11] Initially, however, the Communists viewed WWII as an 'imperialist war', which some Czechoslovaks politically to the left of Beneš did not then support. Nevertheless, the prevailing mood of patriotism regarding Czechoslovakia, and gratitude to the British host, was demonstrated in a variety of ways. Former MP Fritz Kessler wrote jointly with others on 18 September 1939, from the London Representative of the Sudeten German Refugees' office, in response to the Lord Mayor of London's

9   Grete Reichl (Bader), Kate Ottevanger, PP.
10   Imperial War Museum [IWM], Private Papers of M. D. Layton [Layton], Documents 16055, box. no. 07/70/1–2, box 2, letter, 5 September 1939 and group leaders' responses.
11   *Ibid.*, Beuer's reply, 7 September 1939.

appeal for the (British) Red Cross and victims of war fund.[12] Recalling how similar appeals in 1938 had 'given new hope and security to three thousands Sudeten German Social Democrats' [*sic*], they apologized that 'refugees have hardly much money to offer', but each of the 1,150 SGSD men and women in Britain contributed 6d. In the same vein, Karel Lisicky, Acting Head of the Czechoslovak Mission to London, offered 'to forgo part of the extra food rations' allocated to diplomats 'for the purposes of official entertainment',[13] after food rationing had come into force in January 1940, and women economized on both ingredients and time, as guided in women's journals. When the United Nations (UN) Forces Club called for helpers Mrs B, a married woman employed by the Czechoslovak Ministry of Foreign Affairs, volunteered though free only on Saturday afternoons and Sundays.[14]

Such limitations to refugee women's aspirations regarding the war effort were typical, for contributions were largely governed by factors such as age, gender, geographic location, time constraints, professional or vocational skills and proficiency in English and Czech or German (depending on particular situations or requirements), as well as supply and demand and evolving needs generally. In the absence of authoritative data, it is difficult either to quantify the women's contribution to the war effort, or to capture fully the impact of the war upon them. Nevertheless, it is noteworthy that CRTF Estimates of the Age and Sex Distribution of Persons Registered With the Trust As at January 1940,[15] show that women constituted some 42 per cent of the total 8,645 then registered.

12   The National Archives [TNA], HO 294/74, Arbeitskreis (General), letter, Kessler, London Representative, Sudeten German Refugees re:Lord Mayor of London's appeal, British Red Cross, 18 September 1939.

13   SSEES, LIS/3/2/4, Foreign Office reply, 29 May 1941.

14   National Archives, Prague [NAP], Československý červený kříž [Czechoslovak Red Cross in London collection] [CRC], fond/ref. ČSČK-L, 842/634, box 20, Correspondence 1941–5, UN Forces Club.

15   Senate House Library, Historic Collections, University of London [SHL], Papers of Margaret Mynatt and Yvonne Kapp, Kapp (1), MYK/box2/5 [formerly held by Germanic Studies Library: CRTF Kapp (1)], CRTF, Age and Sex Distribution of Persons Registered With the Trust, estimated figures, January 1940.

In the four largest groups, females were aged:

40–45 (648 vs 865 men)
30–35 (644 vs 687 men)
35–40 (591 vs 758 men)
25–30 (442 vs 353 men) respectively.

Only 370 women were aged 50 or over, in contrast to 962 men (probably the more established political leaders and activists) at risk. It can thus be ascertained that the majority of women were young enough to be actively involved in the war effort in some way, though traditionally they might also be married, with children and associated commitments well before the age of 30. By 1941, some 9,000 refugees were registered with the Trust,[16] increasing to 12,696 by 1945;[17] they included women, most of whom would have contributed to the war effort. Although some activities simultaneously served both British and Czechoslovak interests, in other instances contributions were less direct or focused on Czechoslovaks. The forms of war service undertaken were therefore as diverse as the women who offered their time, energy and allegiance and who are central to the topic.

Civilian service: Czechoslovak Red Cross

The Československý červený kříž [Czechoslovak Red Cross] (CRC) was an important and fundamental form of war service open to all Czechoslovak women. Its activities in Britain were both wide-ranging and far-reaching, though little has been written about them or the women involved; for

16   TNA, HO 294/19, Czech Refugee Trust Fund [CRTF] Hostels – Canterbury Hall, Report on the Proposed Closing of London Office of the Czech Refugee Trust Fund, Introduction, 15 February 1941.
17   TNA, HO 294/5, CRTF, Annual Report to 31 March 1955, S.II, Numbers of Refugees Assisted.

these reasons the CRC and its supporters constitute this chapter's core. Originally founded in Prague by presidential decree on 6 February 1919, the CRC was liquidated[18] by the Nazis on 5 August 1940.[19] All was not lost however, for the training and experience gained in the homeland in peacetime became manifestly invaluable in wartime Britain. Thus, the CRC was temporarily established in London on 1 September 1940, by a further presidential decree, with President Beneš as its patron.[20] He appointed his wife, Hana Beneš(ová), as Honorary (Acting) Chairman, a position in keeping with her former social work with women and role of Vice President of the National Board of the Czechoslovak Young Women's Christian Association (YWCA).[21] Beneš(ová) was eminently suited for the task, but there was another reason too. She and Alice Masaryk, first Chairman of the CRC and daughter of the first Czechoslovak President, had been imprisoned in Vienna in 1915 accused of treasonable activity after Tomáš Masaryk and Edvard Beneš went into exile, attempting to regain Czech and Slovak independence from the Habsburg Empire. Beneš(ová) therefore knew very well the needs of prisoners and political activists, and was familiar with difficulties for women arising from political dissent and war; she had lived through WWI.[22] As had been the case in Czechoslovakia, the CRC in Britain was closely linked to the Czechoslovak government; its formal structure consequently comprised a Delegates Assembly, representing the Ministry of National Defence and the Ministry of Social Welfare, the General Assembly, and the Executive Committee. In addition to the Secretariat, there were five sections: social service, medical, nursing, junior,

---

18   NAP, CRC, *op. cit.*, box 44, Propaganda tisku [Press and promotion], The Czechoslovak Red Cross. Brief outline prepared for the Czechoslovak Ministry of Foreign Affairs, London, 26 October 1943.

19   *Ibid.*, Commemorative leaflet, *Czechoslovak Red Cross in Great Britain. 25 Years. From September 1940 to December 1943.*

20   Dates differ slightly according to source.

21   Modern Records Centre [MRC], University of Warwick, MSS.243, Papers of the Young Women's Christian Association (YWCA, UK archives), *To the Czechoslovak Republic on its Tenth Anniversary*, leaflet re: founding of Czechoslovak YWCA, 1920.

22   Gordon H. Skilling, *Mother and Daughter. Charlotte and Alice Masaryk* (Prague: Gender Studies o.p.s, 2001), 90–4.

and cultural.[23] The people who gathered around Benešová and made up the Secretariat or led committees, were mainly high-profile figures drawn from the military, such as General Ingr, Minister of Defence, or those with close government connections like Vice-Chairman Marina Pauliny and Mrs Drtinová, a minister's wife who became Chairman of the social services section. Max and Gillian Lobkowicz were also involved for a time with the cultural section, but as one former CRC volunteer wryly observed, 'Officers' wives were anxious to be seen in a good light – especially after the war; they were volunteers, but not like me!'[24]

In his own inimitable way however, Foreign Minister in exile, Jan Masaryk, set the tone in his weekly BBC broadcast to Czechoslovakia on 14 May 1941. The CRC had barely become fully operational when its headquarters at 7 Audley Square were destroyed during the Blitz of 10 May 1941. A purely factual report noted the damage sustained and what was salvaged,[25] while Masaryk's personal account animated the event, transforming the disaster into a tribute to the CRC and its helpers, stating:

> Thanks to these people of ours the majority of the supplies were saved. When I arrived at the scene [...] I found there almost all of the employees of the Czechoslovak Red Cross, men and women – dirty, tired, but un-wearying, hungry and thirsty in their feverish work. There were the most varied and excellent collaborators there

He went on to mention the Slovak wife of a member of the government,

> who [...] had brought food to our people there and had stayed to help them. From the cellar comes a lady with her arms full of clothes – a general's wife. Three-quarters of the stocks were rescued [...]. And Jews and Christians were doing rescue work and it never occurred to anyone that there were differences between them of race, religion, class or property. So it should be even when bombs are not falling, and so it was in the first Republic. Let us bear that in mind.[26]

23   NAP, CRC, Brief outline, *op. cit.*

24   CRC volunteer, AI.

25   NAP, CRC, 842/634, box 44, undated report in Czech re: bombing of CRC HQ, May 1941.

26   Later published in Jan Masaryk, *Speaking to My Country* (London: Lincolns-Prager, 1944), 71–3.

This extract is significant both in terms of morale-boosting, and the moral message that it conveyed. It was clearly propaganda, but the claims were not without foundation. In the same broadcast, for example, Masaryk provided a rare portrayal of Benešová as a role model for Czechoslovak women, 'mucking in' with others, in sharp contrast to her formal and more dignified duties. He described how, after a meeting, he passed Hyde Park and saw 'a number of ladies spreading out wet but rescued clothing on the grass, clothes received by our Red Cross from America and Canada. Among them Madame Benes. The wide surface of the perfect English lawn is covered with things prepared for our needy ones'.

There were many 'needy ones', and as the challenges of the war and the pressing needs created by it increased, the CRC become a patriotic rallying point, attracting women volunteers and young girls of diverse ages and backgrounds. The political spectrum ranged for instance, from Benešová herself, whose husband headed the Czechoslovak National Socialist party (not to be confused with the German or Austrian parties of that name, the CNS being ideologically closer to the Czechoslovak Social Democrats), to non-Communist Marion Jeary, the English wife of Jaroslav Knap, Director of the Czechoslovak Institute in London,[27] and Communists like Marga Tomášková (Tomasek) plus other women in Fortis Green CRTF hostel, London. Except for one young man in a 'reserved occupation', the men there had served in WWI and were mostly past military service age, like Tomášková's husband, Alois, who had volunteered to join the Czechoslovak army but was too old and therefore worked in a factory producing aeroplane engines, hostel warden Hetty Bower recalled.[28] Thus, while a number of men filled sandbags, dug trenches and acted as firemen, the CRC was very much the Czechoslovak women's role. Indeed, women predominated in the organization, and their contribution, whether in a skilled or unskilled capacity, was vital to the success of the CRC's activities both within the Czechoslovak community in exile, and in the host community in Britain throughout WWII.

With British citizens fully occupied supporting their own servicemen (and later servicewomen), much of the CRC's work concentrated on

27   Nadia de Vivo (Knapová), AI, PP.
28   Bower, AI.

improving the lives of active Czechoslovak service personnel, including the 6,000 troops and 1,500 civilians in Russia in early 1942, for whom Benešová sought aid.[29] By December 1943, fourteen consignments of food, medicines and 'comforts' had been packed and sent to them by the CRC, with the help of the English-Speaking Union in London.[30] Mrs A. Blackman's letter of 14 May 1942 responding to Benešová's appeal,[31] reflected the attitude of the day, commenting that 'We shall be very glad indeed if, with the supplies that come here from America, we are able again to help your gallant troops and civilians in Soviet Russia, as we know how anxious they are in America that their help should reach your people'. By 21 May 1942,[32] even knitting needles were en route, together with four sacks of ski suits and a case of fur coats, followed in June by women's clothing, doubtless welcomed by both the civilians and the (only) company of female volunteers serving in the Czechoslovak army in Russia. Czechoslovak service personnel in Britain were by no means neglected during this period; tangible efforts to cheer them were made simultaneously, indicating the vast amount of work the CRC undertook. Between September 1940 and December 1943,[33] as many as 3,835 food parcels were packed by volunteers, mostly women, and sent to the sick and wounded wherever they could be reached. 19,594 Christmas parcels and thousands of cigarettes were distributed as part of the welfare assistance programme. In addition, twelve ambulances were donated to various military units. Furthermore, as Pauliny informed Lt. Col. Sir Thomas Cook, MP (Welfare Officer to the Czechoslovak Forces in Britain), in correspondence June–July 1942,[34] military patients, particularly those in Leamington Spa where the Czechoslovak army was based,

29   NAP, CRC, box 20, Hana Benešová, appeal to English-Speaking Union, London, 9 May 1942.
30   NAP, CRC, *25 Years* leaflet, *op. cit.*
31   NAP, CRC, box 20, Correspondence 1941–5, correspondence, A. Blackman, Assistant Secretary, English-Speaking Union London, War Relief, and Benešová, 14 May 1942.
32   NAP, CRC, box 20, *op. cit.*, Blackman to Marina Pauliny, 21 May 1942.
33   NAP, CRC, *25 Years* leaflet, *op. cit.*, statistics.
34   NAP, CRC, box 20, *op. cit.*, correspondence, Pauliny and Thomas Cook, MP, June–July 1942.

benefited from visits by Mrs O. Hezká and Mrs K. Stránská[35] (possibly the mother of interviewee Anna Sonnek), who 'looked after the welfare of our men in hospitals'. The war inevitably took its toll. Czechoslovak airmen had participated in the Battle of Britain, and in 1942 arrangements were made for an airman to be examined and have a prosthetic limb fitted at Queen Mary's Hospital special unit in Roehampton (attended by the famous British pilot, Douglas Bader). Earlier, in 1941, an air force sergeant in Glamorgan had been 'beginning to get depressed with prolonged hospitalization', so the RAF hospital sought the CRC's help in finding a suitable place for him to convalesce in the company of his fellow countrymen.[36] The CRC's military needy increased in November 1943, with the arrival of a 'contingent of Czechoslovak soldiers from the Middle East who had fought in the Battle of Tobruk'.[37]

Although the needs of Czechoslovak service personnel were of utmost importance to the CRC and its volunteers, those of the sizeable Czechoslovak civilian population in Britain were not overlooked. 17,212 items of underwear and 10,743 items of general clothing were supplied to refugees in 1940–3 alone,[38] as well as 'medical aid, clothing and games' to children at Czechoslovak state boarding schools, opened by the Czechoslovak government in exile and highlighted in Chapter 4.[39] Yet valuable as such practical assistance was, it in no way represented the full extent of aid rendered, for the CRC paid considerable attention to concerns which related as much to the psychological, as to the physical welfare of the exiles. Since these needs overlapped, the care of women and young children featured strongly in the CRC's schedule. The wives, for instance, of Czechoslovak men serving in the British Auxiliary Military Pioneer Corps

35 Anna Sonnek (Stránská), AI.
36 NAP, CRC, box 44, Correspondence 1941, letter, RAF General Hospital, St Athan, Glamorgan, to CRC, September 1941.
37 NAP, CRC, box 20, *op. cit.*, correspondence, 24 November 1943, CRC to Wheeler, Czechoslovak Ministry of Social Welfare, Dudley House, Cadogan Gardens, SW3, requesting assistance for the Czechoslovak soldiers.
38 NAP, CRC, *25 Years* leaflet, *op. cit.*
39 *Ibid.*, CRC, Brief outline, *op. cit.*

in Newmarket and the surrounding region, came partly under the CRC's care, especially the pregnant women, on whose behalf representations were made to the County Medical Officer of Health, in Bury St Edmunds, on 21 November 1941.[40] 'In view of the fact that these women are exiles in a foreign land, without near relatives or close friends, the Czechoslovak Red Cross is trying within the scope of its limited means to provide special care for maternity cases', explained Drtinová, adding that such women were usually admitted to the maternity wards of general hospitals nearest to their place of residence 'on the same conditions as British underprivileged women'. Moreover, the CRC contributed £1–1s per week towards the cost of each confinement, and each woman received a special allowance of 10s per week for a nutritious diet for eight weeks. In addition, each woman received clothing for herself, a layette for the baby, and a contribution of £3 towards the cost of a cot and pram – no mean feat on a very limited budget. Thanks to the CRC's intervention, the women in question were accepted by the Alexandra Home in Bury St Edmunds, at a fee of six guineas, subject to a reduction following assessments in 'special cases', thereby reducing the soldiers' worries. Though hardly a mother figure, the CRC nevertheless aimed to be a benevolent and reassuring substitute for anxious young mothers, or mothers-to-be. Former volunteer Marie Řehulková,[41] recalled that one of the CRC's many projects was to translate into Czech and adapt a Canadian Welfare Council booklet on coping with a baby in the first critical year, targeting inexperienced women who had no-one to turn to or advise them.

Czechoslovak women were mostly totally unprepared for the vicissitudes of life in exile, and like their British counterparts experienced gender role swap, reversing the traditional male role of breadwinner or main family supporter while men were away during the war. The problems had been addressed but also compounded by Britain's Order in Council

40 *Ibid.*, CRC, box 20, *op. cit.*, letters, CRC and County Medical Officer, Bury St Edmunds, 21 and 25 November 1941.
41 Marie Řehulková, AI, PP, referred to Olga Lewiová-Dubská, *Vaše dítě: Dvanáct listů mamince [Our Children: the First Twelve Months]* (London: Czechoslovak Red Cross, 1942).

of 17 November 1939, permitting the employment of refugees in a wide range of work.[42] Whilst women were no longer restricted to being nurses or resident domestics, they usually lacked the extended family support and funds for child care facilities to benefit from this new freedom. The CRC therefore eased the situation by establishing a residential nursery in 1940, at 44 Lansdowne Crescent in London's Notting Hill Gate area, where a number of women worked in the shops, clubs such as the Czechoslovak-British Friendship Club or Rada československých žen (Council of Czechoslovak Women), at 155 Notting Hill Gate. Leaving mothers free to work, some thirty children aged 3 to 5 stayed at the nursery on week-days, cared for by a resident matron and four staff members. Hana Vodičková, who had studied at the Social Health College in Czechoslovakia and specialized in children, joined the staff after being dismissed without warning or pay (30/- per month) hence almost penniless, from King's College Hospital, London, in around June 1940.[43] 'It was a shock', Vodičková stated, 'being mistakenly treated as an enemy alien like the German nurses', but she remained proud of 'having learnt Cockney to speak to the patients'. She also recalled rushing to rescue the nursery children and take them down to the cellar for safety during air raids, about which she had nightmares even when in her nineties. As a schoolgirl, Nadia de Vivo, in addition to packing CRC parcels with her mother, helped at the nursery as part of her war effort contribution when home from Hinton Hall Czechoslovak school.[44] She observed that clothes and toys were provided for the children, who seemed to cope with alarms and confusing sentences like 'Das ist ein jablko isn't it?' [This is an apple isn't it?], mixing German, Czech and English. Long school holidays were problematic for lone refugee mothers with older children, especially for those working as resident domestics in houses where their children were generally unwelcome, or for whom there was inadequate accommodation. Audrey Eckersley, Director of the Junior Red Cross section of the British Red Cross Society, contacted Mrs Heřmanová at the CRC on

42   This Order was revoked by another in July 1940: Kapp and Mynatt, *op. cit.*, 80.
43   Hana Vodičková, AI.
44   Vivo, AI.

28 February 1944, regarding a scheme inaugurated in 1943 for children of Allied Nations 'to stay in the homes of Red Cross members for the holidays', but government restrictions 'upon all unnecessary travel' caused the postponement of further plans.[45] For other especially needy cases, Karla Pfeiferová of the CRC's Social Welfare Section[46] sought financial assistance from the Save the Children Fund, which had been involved with the Kindertransports from Czechoslovakia and was concerned about the detrimental effects of war on children's welfare. The sum provided for clothing and maintenance was not large, but every contribution helped. Eight families benefited from a grant of £5 sent by Miss Pittman-Davis of the Fund, then based at 25 Gordon Square, London WC1.

Other projects were also undertaken in co-operation with Allied and British institutions and individuals, for the CRC could undoubtedly not function in a vacuum, nor was its care and attention devoted exclusively to its own community. In *Leamington's Czech Patriots and the Heydrich Assassination*,[47] Alan Griffin noted how a field ambulance donated by Czechoslovaks in the USA, and presented by Benešová in November 1940, was soon used by the Czechoslovak army's ambulance unit on 15 November, not for its own purposes, but to provide all possible help following the bombing of Coventry. The composer and conductor (then Corporal) Vílem Tauský, was one of the men 'who turned out with the ambulance'. Soon afterwards he composed *Coventry*, performed by the Menges [string] Quartet at Myra Hess's National Art Gallery lunchtime concerts to entertain and uplift London's workers. Similarly, the volume of *Seven Czechoslovak Carols* arranged by Tauský and Sheila Lennox Robertson, English words by Mary Cochrane Vojáček, was compiled for the CRC and distributed as something that Czechoslovak refugees could

---

45 NAP, CRC, box 45, Holidays for children, letter, Eckersley to Heřmanová, 28 February 1944.
46 *Ibid.*, box 20, *op. cit.*, correspondence of Pfeiferová, CRC Social Welfare Section, May 1944. The SCF had helped refugees via links with the Inter Aid Committee.
47 Griffin, *op. cit.*, 16–17.

share and enjoy with their British hosts, providing some temporary relief from the war (see Figure 4).[48]

Figure 4. Front cover of *Czechoslovak Christmas Carols*, compiled for the Czechoslovak Red Cross, London, during WWII. Courtesy of Nadia de Vivo (Knap).

Barbara Perry cherished the copy given to her as a young girl by a soldier in Beneš's Presidential Guard at Aston Abbotts, the Buckinghamshire village to which the Beneš's had moved in November 1941 for security reasons. Perry's father headed the Home Guard and stored Molotov cocktails in his garden.[49]

48   Vivo, AI, PP.
49   Barbara Perry (Williams), AI.

CRC auxiliary nurses

By 1942, the results of joint efforts between the CRC and the British Red Cross Society to train Czechoslovak women as auxiliary nurses who could work in British hospitals and contribute to the war effort, were plainly evident. Throughout 1941–3, 584 women were trained; Marie Řehulková was in the third group to be trained.[50] Řehulková had arrived in Britain on 22 November 1938 as an au pair to improve her English with a family in Buckinghamshire, so Britain's entry into the war in 1939 was 'a great shock', effectively obliging her to remain in Britain for the duration of the war. Together with three friends, she went immediately to the Czechoslovak embassy in London to offer her services in any way required, but ultimately responded to a CRC advertisement in the weekly newspaper *Čechoslovak*, published in London, and commenced her training in a class of about thirty young women in February 1941. The training was organized by Mrs M. Rechtová, Chairman of the CRC's nursing section, who had been a head nurse at the Baťa hospital in Zlín, Czechoslovakia. Courses were held at the CRC's second premises at 35 Porchester Terrace, London W2, and included lectures by Czechoslovak doctors, Rechtová and an English nurse, but although the lectures were mostly in Czech, the examinations in First Aid and Home Nursing were conducted in English. Řehulková was awarded her British Red Cross certificates in May 1941. In her unpublished reminiscences she wrote: 'I passed my exams. collected my working uniform including summer and winter coat and especially the badge to be worn in the middle of the collar confirming my nursing qualifications' (see Figure 5).

50   Řehulková, AI.

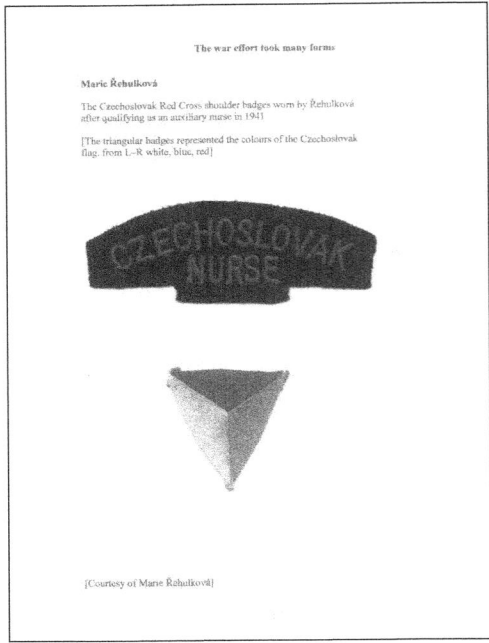

The war effort took many forms

Marie Řehulková

The Czechoslovak Red Cross shoulder badges worn by Řehulková after qualifying as an auxiliary nurse in 1941

[The triangular badges represented the colours of the Czechoslovak flag, from L.-R white, blue, red]

[Courtesy of Marie Řehulková]

Figure 5. Marie Řehulková's Czechoslovak Red Cross shoulder badges, London 1941.
Courtesy of interviewee.

An early assignment was in the German Hospital in Ritson Road, east London, where some Czechoslovak doctors were also employed.[51] They were greatly needed, for almost all the German staff had been interned on the Isle of Man as 'enemy aliens thought to be sympathetic to Germany'. In contrast, Řehulková's Certificate of Registration clearly stated on 21 February 1940, that she was a 'Czech refugee. Passed by Czech Tribunal'. She earned 5/- per day for all necessities (compared with the 2/6d Czechoslovak soldiers received per day plus a clothing allowance),[52] with no further expenses for food or accommodation. The fate of the hospital

51   Founded 1845, providing free medical care mostly for poor German-speaking immigrants; its role broadened later.
52   Griffin, *op. cit.*, 14.

remained uncertain however: Řehulková heard reports that an offer had been made to President Beneš's government to take over the administration of the hospital, but was declined as it was 'too big an undertaking and there were not enough qualified Czechoslovaks to run such a large establishment'. A longer assignment commenced in January 1942, at Putney's Royal Hospital (known as the Home for Incurables but renamed the Royal Hospital for Neuro-disability in 1995). Řehulková worked from 8 a.m. to 4 p.m., in a long ward with twenty mainly elderly patients, serving their food or feeding them if necessary, and generally caring for them. 'Language was not a problem', she commented, 'as there was little time to converse with the patients' though she spoke English fluently. When a patient told her that much as her wartime help was appreciated, he hoped she would return home after the war so as to not take an English person's job, she 'understood his point' without taking offence. Asked how hard the work was, she replied that she 'did not feel she worked too hard compared with girls on the Soviet front'. Most of her fellow nurses were Irish or Scots, but three other Czechoslovak nurses remained at the hospital until the end of the war. Řehulková, however, stopped working in 1943, when the Ward Sister considered it 'unsuitable for a woman six months pregnant to be working in a men's ward'. Like a number of her friends, Řehulková had married a Czechoslovak soldier in Britain, and received one of the 357 CRC layettes distributed to expectant mothers for their babies between September 1940 and December 1943.[53] 'Life goes on, despite all the horrors of the war', she observed. Rechtová and her colleagues continued to train nurses who could work in hospitals around the country, except in restricted coastal areas for security reasons,[54] though from 1942 lectures were at London's Hammersmith Hospital, Du Cane Road, W12. In her letter of 6 November 1942, Rechtova[55] informed K. C. Watt, Principal Matron of the Emergency Nursing Service at the Ministry of Health, Whitehall, that she was considering transferring some Czechoslovak auxiliary nurses

53   NAP, CRC, *25 Years* leaflet, *op. cit.*
54   TNA, HO 208/2, Home Office letter to CRTF 8 June 1940, 'Aliens – Protected Areas'.
55   NAP, CRC, box 20, *op. cit.*, letter, Rechtová to Watt, 6 November 1942.

to a Czechoslovak section due to be opened at Hammersmith Hospital, for 'sick Czechoslovak subjects, attended by Czechoslovak doctors'. (The number of qualified Czechoslovak doctors working in Britain increased after a group including Josephine Bruegel, then the only woman, graduated (by special arrangement) from the University of Oxford in July 1943; other women graduates followed).[56]

Fund-raising

In order to carry out and support the CRC's extensive work, a great deal of effort went into fund-raising, both in Britain and abroad, thereby saving the British government and public considerable expense regarding the welfare of Czechoslovaks in Britain. Fund-raising was essential, but the British Red Cross had asked the CRC 'to refrain from making public appeals among the British on behalf of the Czechoslovak Red Cross', as Pauliny diplomatically explained in her reply of 7 November 1942 to K. W. Lasch, British Council Education and Welfare Officer, Czechoslovak Depot at RAF St Athan.[57] Lasch's keen request for collection boxes to raise money during lectures on Czechoslovakia and gramophone recitals highlights the CRC's dilemma, for Pauliny added: 'The British Red Cross gives us such wholehearted moral and material support that we want to respect their request, all the more as this applies to all Allied Red Cross Societies'. The Ladies' Committee of Friends of Czechoslovakia in Liverpool received similar replies regarding their proposed fund-raising concert and membership subscriptions.[58] Nevertheless, support for the CRC's endeavours notably came not only from the Czechoslovak community but also from

56   See also Machacek, *op. cit.*, 166–8, 176–7.
57   NAP, CRC, box 44, Propaganda tisku [Press and information], letter, Pauliny to Lasch, 7 November 1942.
58   NAP, CRC, box 45, letter, Liverpool Ladies' Committee of Friends of Czechoslovakia to CRC, 25 March 1944.

the British public, and sometimes from surprising sources, institutions as well as individuals. The War Comforts Fund and Knitting Party of the Hammersmith (South) Conservative and Constitutional Association, was 'interested in knitting woollens for Czechoslovaks in the Czechoslovak Squadron of the RAF at Church Stanton' (and later for 310 Squadron in Exeter, plus 312 Squadron in Warmwell, Dorset), but required the wool.[59] Under regulations then in force, wool could only be purchased under license from the (British) Director of Voluntary Organisations, with the obligation to return to the London depot the equivalent weight of finished articles. Thus the group could not send knitted items direct to the squadrons, and Mrs Znamenáčková, Vice Chairman of the CRC's social section, had to confirm on 3 December 1942, that the CRC would indeed supply the wool. A special device for women at that time was the British 'Knitting Register [with needle gauge and measure] a handy help for the wartime knitter'. In a more personal and neighbourly way, Barbara Perry's family in Aston Abbotts also helped Czechoslovaks; Perry recounted how, as a young girl, she took money and woollen garments for Benešová's war effort work when Benešová lived in the so-called Abbey.[60] Strangers became linked by a shared goal.

Illustrating the diversity of war effort contributions to the CRC, valued help of another kind came from Jeary, who was not only very supportive of Knap's cultural work at the Czechoslovak Institute, but took great personal interest in her adoptive country. *The Czechoslovak National Anthem* was published with 'English words adapted by Marion Jeary. Music arranged by J. W. Sinclair', bearing the statement that 'The nett proceeds from the sale of these copies will be given to the Czechoslovak Red Cross Fund London': the price was 4d (see Figure 6).[61]

---

59   NAP, CRC, box 20, Hammersmith (South) Conservative and Constitutional Association, Knitting Party, and Znamenáčková, correspondence November-December 1942.
60   Perry, AI.
61   Vivo, AI, PP. Anthem published by Byroms, Liverpool, undated, probably around 1941.

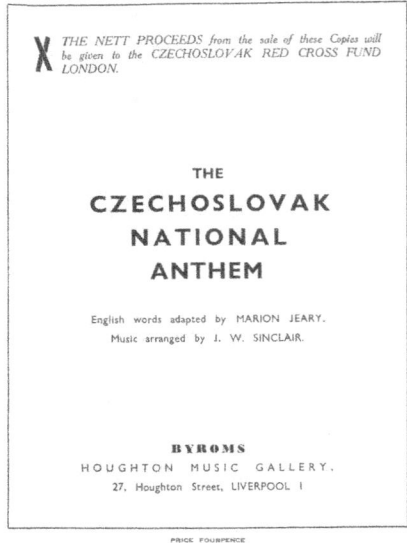

THE NETT PROCEEDS *from the sale of these Copies will be given to the* CZECHOSLOVAK RED CROSS FUND *LONDON.*

THE

CZECHOSLOVAK

NATIONAL

ANTHEM

English words adapted by MARION JEARY.
Music arranged by J. W. SINCLAIR.

BYROMS

HOUGHTON   MUSIC   GALLERY,
27, Houghton Street, LIVERPOOL 1

PRICE FOURPENCE

Figure 6. Front cover of Czechoslovak National Anthem: translated by Marian Jeary
(later Knap), proceeds to Czechoslovak Red Cross Fund, c.1941.
Courtesy of daughter, Nadia de Vivo (Knap).

G. Bodirsky, Czechoslovak Secretary to The New Europe Publishing Company in Bedford Row, London, wrote to the CRC on 3 February 1943, advising that it would soon be publishing Bedřich Smetana's *Evening Songs* (*Večerní písně*) in 'a special English-Czech edition', prepared and translated by the musician and singer J. Sliwinski, adding: 'It is Dr Sliwinski's and our desire, to dedicate 10% of the retail price (2/6 each copy) i.e. 3d for each copy sold, to the Czechoslovak Red Cross'.[62] The need for funds was always a pressing issue, and although some events did not induce immediate responses in this regard, they did publicize the CRC and its work. One such instance was a major military event at Harrods store in Knightsbridge in October 1941, which included films about the Czechoslovak army in

---

62   NAP, CRC, box 44, Culture, New Europe Publishing Co. to CRC, 3 February 1943.

France and Russia, and concerts.[63] Another CRC publicity opportunity arose thanks to the Women's Voluntary Service,[64] which arranged a display at its Broadway branch on 28 October (Czechoslovak Independence Day) in 1942.[65] A film about the CRC was also made in 1942 (for fund-raising purposes in the USA), possibly the one in which Marie Jana Korbel, better known as Madeleine Albright, acted as a child when living in Notting Hill Gate. In her autobiography, *Madam Secretary. A Memoir*, Albright described how 'The émigré community – with the help of the Red Cross – wanted to make a film about the plight of refugee children, and I was chosen to play the starring role. The film was done at a shelter not unlike the one in which we stayed'.[66]

Benešová's personal worldwide appeals were evidently heeded, in addition to her local ones. Through its counterpart in London, the Czechoslovak legation in Washington informed her on 29 December 1940 that the New York Red Cross was placing $13,000 dollars at her disposal.[67] Free Czechoslovaks emotionally linked though physically far removed from Nazi Europe, for example, in South Africa and India, fund-raised to provide additional financial and/or material support, thereby contributing to the war effort too, and women additionally knitted warm clothing. 'To bring hope and relief to thousands in times of anxiety and need' was the CRC's objective throughout its twenty-five years of service, celebrated in 1943,[68] and it undoubtedly played an important if 'unsung' role in Britain throughout WWII in challenging and difficult circumstances, touching and improving the lives of many people, thanks mainly to its willing women volunteers. Before leaving Britain after

---

63   NAP, CRC, box 45, Harrods Exhibition file, October 1941.

64   Later Royal (WRVS).

65   NAP, CRC, box 44, Propaganda tisku, *op. cit.*, letter, CRC to WVS HQ, 6 November 1942.

66   *Ibid.*, correspondence re: CRC film made by B. Bělohlávek and Otto Heller, 1942; Madeleine Albright, *Madam Secretary. A Memoir* (Basingstoke/Oxford: Pan Books/ Macmillan, 2004), 4, 9.

67   SSEES, LIS/3/2/4, letter, Czechoslovak Legation, Washington, to Benešová, CRC, 29 December 1940.

68   NAP, CRC, box 44, Propaganda tisku, *op. cit.*, in text of draft advertisement for *Cechoslovak*, thanking CRC supporters.

the end of the war, the CRC sent a special badge to nominated volunteers in appreciation of their sympathy and support: a letter regarding this was sent to Marga Tomášková at Fortis Green hostel. Her reply of 30 January 1945 has wider resonance, for she observed:

> All women [at the hostel] have contributed as far as their time allowed them to do so, taking in[to] account that they all have a full time occupation. Therefore we do not like to make distinctions because each one of them would have deserved recognition [...]. We will always gladly respond to any further call to our help and support your cause with the deepest conviction.[69]

The same sense of conviction motivated and sustained Hana Benešová, who had declared in May 1942, 'It is our sacred duty to help as best we can'.[70]

Other forms of service

Important though the CRC was, it was not the only form of war service open to Czechoslovak women. Elisabeth Tauber had already studied law for a year in Czechoslovakia, and received an offer from the University of Oxford to complete her studies there, but wanted to 'do something for the war instead', so worked for the Czechoslovak government in exile.[71] Kate/Katja Gould had come to Britain in 1937 to improve her English and become a journalist, and took a six-month secretarial course, adding English shorthand to her German shorthand, but was to use her skills in a very different way from that planned.[72] She became secretary to Fanny Grove at WIZO (Women's International Zionist Organization), working with women's activist Rebecca Sieff (daughter of Michael Marks, founder of the Marks and Spencer stores).

69   NAP, CRC, box 45, Odznaky [Badge], letter, Tomášková to CRC, 30 January 1945.
70   NAP, CRC, box 20, Correspondence 1941–5, *op. cit.*, letter, Benešová to Blackman, English-Speaking Union, 9 May 1942.
71   Elisabeth Tauber, AI.
72   Kate/Katja Gould, AI.

While Gould's English-German husband joined the Pioneer Corps, and her younger brother joined the Czechoslovak army in Britain, Gould worked in the Jewish Agency's publicity department (1943–6), in the same building as Chaim Weizmann, first President of the future state of Israel. Thus, Gould was present when the Agency held a conference at the end of the war, attended by men such as David Ben Gurion, Israel's first Prime Minister and 'father of the nation'. Gould commented, though, that during the war she spoke in English not German, even with her children. Elsewhere, many of the innumerable vacancies resulting from the conscription of British men under the September 1939 National Service (Armed Forces) Act were filled by refugee women, who responded to the host state's appeals. The caption accompanying an official Czechoslovak photograph stated: 'She trains for victory. A young woman from Czechoslovakia helps the British war effort by training in a government training centre. Her husband serves in the Czech army'.[73] Another photograph showed 'A factory in which aircraft components are being made' at a trading estate where 'Czechoslovaks have founded their own factories [...] engaged both on war production and making goods for Britain's export trade'.[74] Ironically, whereas Zora Flajsner was forced to work in Czechoslovakia for the German war effort,[75] Zora Karas and her mother worked for the British war effort as machinists in a London factory producing military uniforms, where 'other girls arrived in their [hair] rollers'. In this environment the educated and well dressed mother and daughter felt 'insecure at work and very alienated'. Despite the strained relationship caused by social differences between the refugees and co-workers, 'their strength of character and a genuine will to contribute to the war effort' helped the Karas's to persevere, and they later packed parachutes in another factory,[76] commented Zora's daughter, Vera Sturgess. Not least of all was Eva Frumin's contribution as a conductress on South Manchester buses, shocking passengers with

---

73   SSEES, CZE: MZV/ABCH/L 28 3 42–22, serial no. 47 37 series: 36 (no attribution, probably by Erich Auerbach who took a number of official photographs for the Czechoslovak government in exile).
74   *Ibid.*, CZE: MZV/ABCH/L 56 2 43–22, serial no. 46.
75   Zora Flajsner, AI.
76   Zora Karas, via daughter Vera Sturgess (Karas) AI.

her German accent. Born in Děčín in 1920, she had left the Sudetenland for Prague, then Liverpool in 1939, taking various domestic service posts. Her wry sense of humour is delightfully expressed in 'You my Passengers' by a Clippie, in *Lilliput Goes to War*.[77] Her surprising posts continued post-war, too, first working with the US army in Germany in the censorship section, then as a postwoman in Britain.

Yet for all their efforts, refugees were sometimes viewed with a degree of suspicion by the British public, as well as MI5, as has been discussed. The war years were therefore especially difficult for German-speaking refugees sometimes presumed to be Nazis, when the exact opposite was the case. Doubtless it was difficult for indigenous British citizens without knowledge of Czechoslovakia's history or ethnic composition, to grasp that some Czechoslovak citizens legitimately spoke German not Czech (probably indistinguishable from German to anyone unfamiliar with these languages). Consequently, two overlapping but paradoxical situations emerged during the war years: continued mistrust of foreigners and Germans or German-speakers in particular by some British people, while British defence and intelligence officials secretly channelled the linguistic expertise of refugees to Britain's advantage. Czechoslovak Valery Fuhrmann was employed by the British Foreign Office before transferring to 'top secret' station X (alias Bletchley Park) until after the war.[78] There she was entrusted with translating into English some German documents captured after the battle of El Alamein in 1942 and brought to London. Two women from Fortis Green hostel joined the BBC, including actress Elizabeth Warnholtz, who could usefully broadcast to women in Germany in standard German rather than a dialect.[79] Hostel residents displayed considerable resilience and resolve in testing times. For example, members of the hostel's choir like Pavel Seifter's German-born mother, wore brightly coloured Czechoslovak national costumes and sang to cheer people sheltering in London's overcrowded underground stations or

---

77   Eva Frumin, AI; '"You my Passengers" by a Clippie', in Kaye Webb, ed., *Lilliput Goes to War* (London: Hutchinson, 1985), 201–2.

78   Valery Fuhrmann, via daughter Dorrit Epstein (Fuhrmann) AI.

79   Bower, AI.

working in factories.[80] According to New Zealand-born Marian Šling(ová) who, with her husband Otto was associated with the hostel, the song and dance group proved to be 'a real service to the community'.[81]

Service in the armed forces

Although being identified as German-speakers could be problematic for the refugees concerned, their linguistic abilities played an invaluable if invisible role in the war effort. In a highly exceptional case, Fuhrmann's daughter, Dorrit Epstein, became the only known Czechoslovak in the Women's Royal Naval Service (WRNS), commissioned as an officer in 1943 (due only to her physicist husband's work for the navy, she maintained),[82] and was always referred to as 'the foreign WREN' (see Figure 7).

Figure 7. WREN Officer Dorrit Epstein, 1943. Courtesy of interviewee.

80   Pavel Seifter, AI.
81   Marian Šlingova, AI.
82   Epstein, AI, PP.

Secrecy was at the core of her land-based radio intelligence work 'codename Headaches!' in 'Y' service, intercepting German e-boat communications:[83] 'It was a fantastic job, very exciting'. Jewish Ruth Tosek reached Britain with her Sudeten German father in May 1939, and later wanted to go university, but being 'very patriotic for Czechoslovakia and Britain', decided to support the war effort instead and 'do her bit against Hitler' so, aged about 17, she joined the women's branch of the British air force, rapidly rising to sergeant.[84] As she spoke German without a foreign accent, she was soon placed in 'Y' service. Posted near the Kent coast, she sat with Austrian and Norwegian ground staff listening to German air force pilots' radio messages, noting down their orders regarding towns or cities to be bombed. These details were passed to officers who alerted radar personnel, enabling them to track the enemy aircraft. While radio communications between German pilots and their home station were temporarily blocked, Tosek posed as a German ground-staff operator, forwarding 'misinformation' to redirect pilots seaward or away from their true targets, thereby saving innumerable lives. This work continued until 'D-Day' (6 June 1944, the Allied invasion of German-held Normandy). The Jewish Czechoslovak Champion golfer Luisa Kramerová (later Lady Abrahams), who had come to Britain to play in a tournament with Henry Cotton just before war broke out, was in 'Y' service with Tosek, one rank higher than her, and became a major.[85]

Czechoslovak women were never conscripted, unlike their British counterparts who (subject to certain provisos), could be conscripted under the National Service (No. 2) Act, 18 December 1941. Nevertheless, 'it was fashionable' for single Czechoslovak women like those in Řehulková's circle of friends to volunteer and serve in Czechoslovak units attached to the Women's Auxiliary Air Force (WAAF) or Auxiliary Territorial Service (ATS), especially the WAAF, drawn by 'the glamour – they wore skirts not

83   E-boats were deployed especially in the North Sea and English Channel.
84   Ruth Tosek, AI.
85   'Lady Luisa Abrahams – a Truly Remarkable Life', interview with Ian Willoughby, Radio Prague, Czech Radio (23 January 2006), <http://www.radio.cz/en/article/75025>, accessed 31 May 2018.

trousers', but also by a sense of 'contributing to something worthwhile',[86] even though their pay in these services was a third of the men's. Elizabeth Weiss, who came to Britain under the nursing scheme, joined the WAAF,[87] as did Theresie Lowit from Karlovy Vary (see Figure 8).[88]

Figure 8. WAAF Corporal Theresie Schneider (later Lowit), showing 'Czechoslovakia' shoulder badge. Courtesy of interviewee.

With the help of the British Committee for Refugees from Czechoslovakia, she had joined her Social Democrat parents already in Britain (having been assisted by their party), and worked as a nursery maid 'to a kind Guildford family' that nonetheless treated her as a servant. 'Everyone wanted to join the war effort and do their bit', stated Lowit, but she was only seventeen-years-old and needed permission from the Czechoslovak embassy to join the WAAF, duly given in October 1941. Until 1945 Lowit was 'the only Czechoslovak girl' (marked out by the customary 'Czechoslovakia' badge sewn onto uniform sleeves) at fighter station RAF Colerne, in Wiltshire, but it did not trouble her because of the camaraderie: 'we were an absolute

86   Řehulková, AI.
87   Elizabeth Weiss, AI.
88   Theresie Lowit, AI.

team'. Corporal Lowit was later transferred to London, and demobilized in March 1946; her RAF Service and Release Book noted that she was awarded the (British) Defence Medal (see Figure 9).

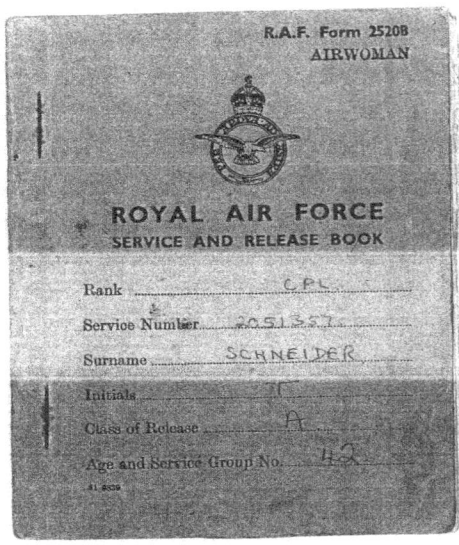

Figure 9. RAF Service Release Book, 1946. Courtesy of Theresie Schneider (later Lowit).

Although some Czechoslovak women spent time abroad during WWII, they were nonetheless involved in the British and Allied war effort before living permanently in Britain, like Kate Thompson.[89] In 1937 she had been studying horticulture and English in Britain for her Czechoslovak matriculation examinations, but WWII intervened. Thus, in 1939 she joined her parents in Jerusalem, moving with them first to Eritrea where she worked for the 'British occupation officer in charge of Eritrea', then to Egypt, working for the British navy as secretary to the Commander of the Levant, finally returning to Britain in 1945. Zionist LS, like other Jewish Czechoslovak women who had reached Palestine, joined the ATS

89   Kate Thompson, AI.

there, before marrying an Englishman and moving to Britain in 1946.[90] In contrast, Nina Dobosharevich,[91] a 'patriotic Volyn Czech' from Poland,[92] initially joined the Polish Home Army in 1939, but on reaching Palestine in October 1942 resigned and joined the Czechoslovak army in the Middle East,[93] which linked with Britain's ATS (see Figure 10).

Figure 10. Legionnaire Nina Dobosharevich, London, c.2005. Courtesy of interviewee.

The ATS was then actively recruiting in the region, and its support work had broadened. Dobosharevich could not only drive, she was proud to have been 'the first woman who did mechanics in the Czech unit' there. The post-Communist Czech government could finally acknowledge the part played by exiles,[94] and in May 2005 awarded her a medal for her war service.

90   Anonymity requested.
91   Nina Dobosharevich, AI.
92   See Lewis White, *op. cit.*, Volyn Czechs, 159–62.
93   General Andrej Gak was responsible for Czechoslovak recruitment in the Middle East.
94   Separate Czech and Slovak republics had been established by then.

Virtually housebound by then, the indomitable Dobosharevich joked, 'Where should I wear it, on my pyjamas?' then added it to her collection.

It would be incorrect, however, to claim that there was total una-nimity within the Czechoslovak community regarding the war effort. Tosek and other interviewees thought it 'very exciting, real comradeship', but also spoke of the anti-Semitism in the Czechoslovak RAF and army units.[95] Competing competencies created tensions at times between politi-cal groups, and some Communists adhered to the Comintern diktat, refus-ing to work in munitions factories or to fight – until Germany broke its non-aggression pact with the Soviet Union by attacking the country in June 1941, causing a major policy shift. This then raised the problem of which army to join – or not. The Czechoslovak army issued orders and instructions in Czech, which many German-speaking men from the Sudetenland did not understand, effectively excluding them. On the other hand, far from being glamorous, menial tasks were often assigned to male and female non-combatants in British army units, which could frustrate rather than fulfil the men's desire to serve actively. The various issues sometimes entailed complex conflicts of loyalties of a political, ethnic and national nature that impacted on relations and rebounded post-war, an aspect that is addressed in Chapter 6.

Sudeten Germans and Czechs, war effort conference

Efforts to counter such rifts and set aside unhappy experiences of intern-ment in the years 1940–1 are reflected in *Sudeten Germans and Czechs. Condensed Report of the First National Conference of German Anti-Fascists from Czechoslovakia, at the Beaver Hall, London, October 16th–17th 1943*.[96] The aim was to unite compatriots and foster good relations with British

95   Tosek's comments have been supported orally by other refugees, also a written tes-timony (anonymity requested).
96   Published by *Einheit* (1944), also subsequent conference proceedings.

and Czechoslovak authorities. A total of 477 'men, women and youth of all classes, professions, opinions and religious beliefs' attended, soldiers in the Czechoslovak army, members of the Czechoslovak government and representatives of various organizations, together with British trade unionists and journalists. Furthermore, 308 of the 403 Sudeten Germans contacted in large communities outside London, signed the conference appeal. 'We German-speaking Czechoslovak citizens wish to state loudly and clearly that we long to return to our home country and to win it back for us and our children, and that we recognise the obligations which have grown out of our loyalty to the Czechoslovak Republic [...] to do nothing is inexcusable', declared the eminent scientist Ernst Pringsheim in the opening speech. Communist MP Gustav Beuer stressed the need to fight alongside Czechs and persuade Czechoslovak German separatists not to support Hitler, while various speakers exhorted everyone to actively support the British war effort. According to Alfred Peres of the German Liberal Party, over 90 per cent of Sudeten German refugees from various political groups contributed to the host country as anti-Fascists, including women in the ATS and WAAF. The conference good-will messages were duly noted by both Czechoslovak and British authorities, and press reports reached the British public.[97] Moreover, a Sudeten German Committee was established to further promote and realize the objectives discussed; its representatives included Kaethe Beckmann, 'Women Organiser' and Marga Tomasek (Tomášková), 'Youth Organiser'. Hedwig Huenigen was prevented from attending the conference by some of the constraints mentioned early in the chapter. For such a politically committed and active woman, this was frustrating and disappointing. Private correspondence with Beckmann in the early war years to 1942[98] conveyed her fatigue and longing to be in London to participate more fully in political life, and contribute to the war effort by pursuing her true vocation in the women's movement, helping to organize activities and programmes at the Council of Czechoslovak Women in Great Britain (CCW) like her friend and fellow party activist from Reichenberg (now Liberec). In response, Beckmann emphasized the

97   TNA, FO 371/34330, MI5 notes.
98   Hedy Fromings (Huenigen), Hedwig's daughter, AI, PP.

value of Huenigen's war work as the devoted matron of a CRTF hostel for lone refugee children from Czechoslovakia and elsewhere, a commitment also gratefully acknowledged by the Trust in Chapter 4.

Czechoslovak youth

Individual and private recognition of women's war work, or Barbara Perry's praise for the Presidential Guards and pilots who 'were marvellous in helping Britain in the war' were valued, but did not aim to publicly acknowledge the war efforts of Czechoslovak women in general. Little attention has likewise been given to the contribution of Czechoslovak youth to the war effort, of which the following is but an indication. 'Young People Over School Age' played their part too, as the Refugee Children's Movement noted in its *Third Annual Report 1941–1942*: 'It is gratifying to report that refugee boys and girls are making a substantial and incalculably active and useful contribution to the war effort in a variety of forms'. Without specifying numbers or nationalities, it stated that some girls joined the ATS, initially working in the mess halls or as cleaners or drivers, but it was reportedly much more difficult for non-British girls to join the WAAF, so they joined the Women's Land Army replacing conscripted men on farms, or worked in the Fire Service as clerical workers, messengers or telephonists. Others preferred nursery nursing. Refugee student nurses studied topics such as anatomy, nutrition and hygiene for the National Society of Day Nurseries examination, receiving £52 per annum plus meals as trainees, then £120–£135 per annum once qualified. Demand for child care facilities rose as British mothers, like Czechoslovak ones, increasingly worked for the war effort instead of remaining at home. The opening in 1940–1 of the International Labour Board with special Labour Exchanges for Czechoslovak, German, Austrian and Polish nationals, was further noted, since it channelled young people into war industries, many of whom moved from the regions to Birmingham and London for training or higher pay.[99] *Einheit*, the Sudeten German anti-Fascist fortnightly published in London, also acknowledged the contribution of young people. The issue of 29 August 1942 devoted a page to *Die Jugend im Wareffort*, describing young people's war effort experiences – Anita in nursing, Peter in the Air Training Corps, and others in different factories.[100]

Impact of the war effort

Although WWII impacted heavily on the lives of British women and teenagers, they were at least in their own country, whereas for many women from Czechoslovakia it meant multiple additional adjustments in socio-economic terms. Refugee women had to adapt to a foreign language and the British way of life, and deal with animosity towards foreigners in addition to coping with the transition from housewife to employee, 'juggling' a job and/or war effort work while maintaining traditional supportive roles as wives and mothers. The physical and emotional demands could consequently be high, with added fears for family members and friends in the homeland, while British women feared for their menfolk fighting abroad. These factors, however, are notably moderated by other new experiences in the memories of some interviewees. Řehulková saw her soldier husband for only two days every six months, and had 'a definite feeling of freedom during the war', when 'married women started feeling more independent and had the security of an income'. Alexandra Kučerová,[101] who came to Britain aged 15, described her six years in the country as 'the happiest years of my life. I was young, healthy, met my husband who became the

---

99   TNA, HO 294/5: the RCM was then based in Bloomsbury House, Bloomsbury, like the CRTF.

100 'Die Jugend im Wareffort', vol. 3, no. 17, *Einheit* (29 August 1942), 13. The Priebsch-Closs Collection [formerly Germanic Studies Library], Senate House Library, University of London, editions from 1942 only.

101 Alexandra Kučerová, AI.

last commander of [Czechoslovak] 313 fighter squadron and won the Distinguished Flying Cross (DFC), and my daughter was born in Britain'. A narrow escape when working as a telephonist for the CRC at its Porchester Terrace premises, destroyed by a V1 'flying bomb' half an hour before she was due to start work in April 1945, did not alter her positive attitude.

The various Czechoslovak clubs and associations played a significant part in maintaining or raising refugees' spirits, but are dealt with separately in Chapter 5. Overall, caring, sharing and camaraderie are recurring elements of the war effort experience, which at times bonded diverse Czechoslovak citizens as well as Czechoslovaks and their British hosts, and ultimately informed and influenced long-term Anglo-Czechoslovak relations. Though not specifically citing Czechoslovaks, or recognizing the contribution made by Czechoslovak women individually or collectively (contrary to the focus here), a formal acknowledgement of refugees' war efforts appeared in a February 1942 League of Nations report which stated: 'Generally, the situation has so much improved that it is now almost a misnomer to describe this group as "refugees". The great majority are self-supporting and, with independent means of livelihood, they regard themselves as temporary exiles who are playing a useful part in the service of their own country and of the country of their adoption'.[102]

Indeed, some vocational training and skills gained or enhanced during the war were to be subsequently drawn upon not only on the women's return to Czechoslovakia, but when some (re-)migrated to Britain, enabling them to assimilate and contribute to Britain through their work. Though the term 'transferable skills' is much used in the twenty-first century, the practice has long preceded it, and constitutes an important aspect of Chapter 6. Well before the end of WWII, refugee women had moved beyond the stereotype of refugees as hopeless and helpless.

102   TNA, HO 294/6, League of Nations International Assistance to Refugees. Report by Herbert Emerson, High Commissioner for Refugees, C.25.M.25.1942.XII, Geneva: February 1942.

Mothers Without Their Children, Children Without Their Mothers

The forced separation of mothers and children, even for lifesaving reasons, is widely recognized by psychologists as mutually traumatic, especially where very young children are involved, and the experiences of those from Czechoslovakia (including ethnic Germans and some Reich German and Austrian refugees who had sheltered there) were no exception, as this chapter will demonstrate. Whilst acknowledging the body of medical and feminist literature on both trauma and motherhood, the approach adopted here remains a socio-historical one, so as to give the 'refugee voice' prominence rather than dwell on scholarly feminist arguments. This chapter therefore engages with the impact of some refugees' experiences, both positive and negative, regarding the importance of a mother figure or in some cases the inter-dependence of mother and child, which constituted a fundamental part of life in exile throughout the war years and beyond. Since 3,706,895 of the total number of 7,586,420 women in Czechoslovakia in 1930 were aged 15 to 44 (1930 Census),[1] and customarily married and bore children early, unlike today's trend, many of the refugee children would have spent their formative years or reached adulthood in wartime Britain. Children represented continuity, hope for the future and, as some mothers explained, gave women a reason to live. Given the traditionally close Central European family structure, women as mothers and their children's welfare and upbringing are inseparable topics.

---

1   Czechoslovak Ministry of Foreign Affairs, Department of Information, *Statistická Příručka Československé Republiky*, Československé Ministerstvo Zahraničních Věcí, Informační Oddělení, *Statistical Handbook of the Czechoslovak Republic* [joint Czech/English] (London: 1942), 12.

Forced separation

Forced separation occurred in various circumstances and at different times. Relatively few children accompanied their parent(s) in late 1938 or early 1939, for instance, partly because women accepting domestic service or nursing posts as a means of escape from Czechoslovakia were usually required to be child-free, and partly because the British Committee for Refugees from Czechoslovakia (BCRC) generally helped politically active men in most danger to escape first, leaving anxious wives and children at risk to follow at the earliest opportunity. For Hedwig Huenigen and her 12-year-old daughter Hedy,[2] and Anna Tschapek with her 10-year-old son Walter,[3] escape organized by the BCRC was not possible until after Hitler's invasion of rump Czechoslovakia during 14–15 March 1939. Following the fall of France in 1940, the wives and children of Czechoslovak government officials and servicemen who had gathered there were evacuated with them to Britain, but were separated once the servicemen regrouped. Some children, though, particularly Jewish ones, had been sent ahead to relatives, friends or even strangers in Britain while it was still possible, in the hope that families would soon be reunited in exile. When working in Prague with the BCRC, Trevor Chadwick had managed to send a few children to London by aeroplane, but the majority, 669 mostly Jewish children, came without their parents on Nicholas Winton's eight Kindertransports which departed from Prague's Wilson Station (thus were not directly part of the wider Kindertransport movement operating from Germany and Austria).[4] The first group escaped on 14 March 1939, just hours before Germany seized what remained of Czechoslovakia. The last Kindertransport of sixty-eight children left on 2 August 1939, with the 9-year-old future Lady Milena Grenfell-Baines, and her 3-year-old sister Eva, who both laughingly thought it a great adventure: 'it was the parents who were the heroes, saying good-bye'. Experiences and memories of them differed considerably though. One child was stripped

2   Hedy Fromings (Huenigen), AI, PP.
3   Walter Tschapek AI, PP.
4   Nicholas Winton, AI; Kindertansports occupied only part of a train.

naked by Nazis searching for hidden jewellery and money in her clothing, and Utta Klein's mother had packed so much food that Utta could not lift the rucksack which was inaccessibly placed with luggage, and she had to ask others for food during the long journey.[5] Another train, scheduled to leave on 1 September, the day Germany invaded Poland and the borders were closed, never left Prague. All 250 children were never heard of again and are presumed to be dead:[6] Hanuš Šnábl, who had escaped on an earlier Kindertransport, believed that his older brother, František, was with them, but never discovered František's fate.[7] Those who arrived safely mostly went to foster homes across Britain or, like the unhappy German and Czech-speaking Jewish Milena Roth, to her mother's English friend, Doris Campbell.[8] Consequently, both mothers and children endured the pain of separation, displacement, adjustment and, in some cases, rejection, their feelings variously concealed or conveyed in actions, words and letters over the years. On 3 July 1939, for example, Milena Roth's mother, Anna, wrote to Campbell, 'You as mother will make yourself an idea how I feel about sending away Milena, but I try to make myself persuaded that it is the right way'. Anna's anguish redoubled though; deprived of her daughter, she additionally risked losing her role and identity as a mother. Anna reluctantly submitted to the prospect of her only child addressing another woman (Campbell) as 'Mummy' rather than 'Aunty'; distressingly similar to the Czech 'mami' as Anna herself commented, it underlined her loss.[9] Milena, for her part, was later to write to her mother, 'I am dying with longing for you'.[10]

5   Milena Grenfell-Baines (Fleischmann), AI.
6   Winton AI; see also Muriel Emanuel and Vera Gissing, *Nicholas Winton and the Rescued Generation. The Story of 'Britain's Schindler'*, 3rd edn (London: Vallentine Mitchell, 2001).
7   Discussion, Hanuš Šnabl's widow Tanya.
8   Milena Roth, AI.
9   Milena Roth, *Lifesaving Letters. A Child's Flight From the Holocaust* (Seattle: University of Washington Press, 2004), 65–7.
10   Roth, AI.

Czech Refugee Trust Fund hostel for refugee children

How well the different factors regarding forced separation were ameliorated, depended to a large extent on the mothers' proximity to their child(ren) and the care and mothering they could provide, versus what the children received or lacked, which will be discussed initially within the framework of a children's hostel and the Czechoslovak state boarding schools in Britain. Two key elements in these contexts played a crucial part in the mothers' and children's lives: firstly, the transfer of affection (or otherwise) from an absent natural mother to a substitute mother figure for various periods of time, and the role, importance and influence of that person; secondly, in anticipation of post-war repatriation, the preservation of Czechoslovak national identity, language and culture within a foreign host community, whenever and wherever possible. This latter feature sometimes took a form of matrilineal nationalism, a notion described in the Introduction. As Halliday asserts with reference to another context but pertinent here too, the 'fusion of an image of maternity with national identity served its purposes' as nationalism 'seeks to mobilise women in support of its goals'[11] (in the present instance during and immediately after the Nazi occupation, but also later in exile during the Communist era). All these aspects obtained in the special hostel for lone refugee children established by the British Committee's successor, the Czech Refugee Trust Fund (CRTF). The children's hostel for boys and girls was opened in Broadstairs, then in Edmund Castle in Hayton (Cumbria), to which everyone was evacuated due to coastal bombing in 1940. Hedwig Huenigen was appointed as the hostel matron, but soon became known as 'Mutter Huenigen' (and remained so) to the children, separated from their true mothers because

---

11   Fred Halliday, *Rethinking International Relations* (London: Macmillan, 1994), 160–1; see also Iveta Jusova,'Matrilineal Nationalism in Božena Viková-Kunětická's Medrická,' Slavic Forum, University of Chicago, April 23–24, 1999, and 'Nineteenth-Century Theories of Race and Czech Nationalist Literature by Women.' SA/MLA Convention, *Race in Literary Histories*, Atlanta, GA, November 8–10, 2001.

they had arrived on the Kindertransports and awaited a foster home, or because they could not live with their parent(s) in Britain (see Figure 11).[12]

Figure 11. Hedwig 'Mutter' Huenigen, Matron of CRTF children's hostel.
Courtesy of daughter, Hedy Fromings (formerly Huenigen).

Refugee women in domestic service might only be allowed to have their child(ren) with them briefly during school holidays, if at all. Men like Ruth Tosek's father, whose wife could not follow him and died in Bergen-Belsen concentration camp, also found it difficult to keep their child(ren) with them and see to their needs, especially if working long hours (when allowed to work).

Thus, three groups of children were cared for at the hostel, totalling some forty to forty-five (figures fluctuated): eight to nine pre-school children, twelve to fourteen juniors aged 5 to 11, and teenagers from 12 to 16, the largest group, Hedy Fromings recalled. The majority were Jewish, and mostly German-speaking. Approximately half of those cared for were Czechoslovak nationals, including ethnic Germans and three Slovaks; one

12   Hedy Fromings (Huenigen), AI, PP.

was Hungarian, others were Reich German and Austrian refugees who had sheltered in Czechoslovakia. Those of school age attended Hayton Church of England village school, and Mutter Huenigen followed their progress carefully. Reports retained in her private papers reflect some of the problems encountered, 'Language and spelling difficulty' being the most common, where confused children switched from German and/or Czech/Slovak to English. Mathematics proved difficult too, 'the English [Imperial] measures being a drawback to these children' [accustomed to the European decimal system], sympathetic teachers wrote. Huenigen took her responsibilities seriously, reading about the problems of depressed and homeless children, and worried when some hostel children needed treatment for tuberculosis. In CVs prepared for the Trust Fund in 1940, she observed, 'Erika [...] needs a lot of love'; her German father, recently released from internment and without work, was unable to send any clothing for her. Slovak Franta needed substantial food and vitamins, while 'Mirjam [...] suffered a lot under the conditions of being a refugee [...] sometimes she is quite melancholic' (surnames withheld). Twice a refugee herself, Huenigen empathized, but was acutely conscious of the shortage of funds, medical and other resources, as well as the children's dislike of 'strange English food' like spam (except her daughter Hedy, who gained extra helpings). Huenigen worked constantly, including mending children's clothes, from 7 a.m. to 10 p.m. daily, mostly with only two or three refugee mothers as helpers. Nevertheless, in Hedy's words, 'she gave lone children, especially Jewish ones, extra loving care and attention, though a gentile herself', and resolutely gave Hedy no preferential treatment during her stay at the hostel. Many years later, Bobby (Boris) Marmour described Huenigen as kind, but firm.[13]

'Life in the hostel was very tightly structured. There was no time for mischief or to mope!' Hedy recounted.[14] The children had to help as much as possible, around the grounds, peeling potatoes, fetching firewood and feeding the chickens. Rotas for juniors and seniors included table duty, cleaning and washing up. It was not all work though: 'they tried to balance

13   Bobby Marmour, statement.
14   Fromings, AI.

our activities with hobbies, games, and our own concerts and plays, very lively!' The grounds provided ample space for play, and the teenagers held a dance every Saturday which locals joined in, and the English hostel warden, Mr Brown, obligingly played the piano. There were also outings to Carlisle, the public library, and gatherings in Keswick with compatriots working as foresters in the Lake District, or with young ethnic Germans from the Sudetenland going to join the Czechoslovak army in exile in Britain. Sport was popular, with teams competing locally, and some girls joined the local Girl Guide group, thereby making new friends. Nevertheless, those at home were not forgotten. It was deemed the duty of staff, teachers and helpers to make the children aware of why they were in Britain, where their parents were, and what was happening regarding 'the wicked events' of the war. 'One day we will go home', they were told, 'there will be victory'. Very small children did not entirely understand the meaning or implications of victory, Hedy recounted, but older exiles like her certainly did; they sat together and listened to the BBC radio news after doing their homework. There was also a 'wall newspaper' with news about the war attached to it, and children were encouraged to add their own items and essays. In their small community, children were sheltered but not cocooned. Adults and children alike knew about the deaths in Lidice, the Czech village razed to the ground in retribution for the assassination of Reinhard Heydrich, Deputy Reich Protector of Bohemia and Moravia, by Czechoslovak parachutists in May 1942, and observed the anniversaries.

News of relatives and friends in the homeland, however, was rare. *Notes for persons Wishing to Communicate With Friends in Enemy Countries, or Territory in the Occupation of the Enemy* set out the restrictions:[15] Hedy's letters were returned, though she eventually received two from an aunt.[16] Mutter Huenigen only discovered through a furtive message passed in 1942 by another woman in the Co-operative Movement, that her husband was alive 'but in F' (Flossenburg), a forced labour camp in Germany. Relieved by the news, Hedwig nevertheless worried about her husband and feared for her teenage son in Czechoslovakia, also a Czech patriot and anti-Fascist,

15   IWM, 84/38/1, Correspondence of Miss J. Brunner, file 1939–1942.
16   Fromings, AI, PP.

who had not been allowed to leave owing to his ethnic German origins, and his Communist father's politics.[17] Britain, in the meantime, was hardly the safe haven refugees had sought and expected, due to its declaration of war on Germany in September 1939. This had effectively prevented the arrival of many more refugees, including parents who had planned to join children sent ahead on the Kindertransports, but who subsequently lost contact with them, like the Roths. The situation reinforced the children's need for an 'anchor', a caring mother figure and a secure environment, especially when far from home. It was also important to the 8-year-old Tommy Freund and his mother, Helena (Lena), separated from economist and journalist Ludwig Freund (later Ludvík Frejka to appear 'more Czech' rather than Jewish). An intellectual and artistic but sick woman, she helped in the hostel as much as she could and, like her friend Hedwig, brought her child up alone in a foreign country.

In 1942 the hostel moved to Plas-yn-Green, in Denbigh, north Wales. By then, 'war effort' had long been added to the children's rota sheets, and various restrictions pertaining to refugees had eased, especially regarding employment, which allowed exile communities to contribute in various ways. With increased opportunities available, older hostel children like Ruth Tosek had joined the armed services, and 16-year-olds moved to adults' hostels, while younger lone children were gradually placed in foster homes. Mutter Huenigen's 'family' dwindled to six, so the hostel was closed on 12 December 1942. A CRTF employee, C. G. Willoughby, wrote to Huenigen concerning the matter and conveying the Trust's appreciation of the valuable work she had done. Treasured notes and hand-made cards from 'Huenigen's children' provide a more touching and personal testimony: they also indicate the profound impact of the children's upbringing in the hostel. Young children like Fritz wrote letters of thanks to 'Dear Mutter Huenigen', spelling chocolate in German and several English words phonetically, but always ending 'With much love'. Through them she learnt that 'Pitter [Peter] das not like it in London', and 'We are soon finisht with Schneider von Ulm' [sic], [Max Eyth's *The Taylor of Ulm*, about

17   Edmund Huenigen (junior) conscripted into German air force 1943.

eighteenth-century pioneer aviator Albrecht Berlinger], but older children showed their political awareness. Alfred drew a birthday card with a symbolic ship on the front, and some flowers inside, with the patriotic message, 'I hope that you are going to have your next birthday in Czechoslovakia'.

Another card, from Hans, was more pointed, bearing, in addition to a pretty flower and customary birthday wishes, drawings of the Czechoslovak, British and Soviet flags on one side, and on the other the entreaty 'Fight for FREEDOM!' [*sic*] (see Figure 12).

Figure 12. Patriotic birthday card for 'Mutter Huenigen'.
Courtesy of daughter, Hedy Fromings (formerly Huenigen).

Even a Christmas card from Shimmi and Susi depicted a castle with a Czechoslovak flag flying above it (probably representing Prague Castle, official residence of Czechoslovak presidents).[18] Mutter Huenigen had clearly

18   Fromings, PP.

made a strong impression, nurturing the hostel children in the diaspora, and helping to shape their identities as future citizens of the homeland.

Exile schools in Britain

There was no such mothering for children of diverse social, political and religious backgrounds in the co-educational Czechoslovak state boarding schools, opened by the Czechoslovak government in exile for Czechoslovak refugee children in Britain to prepare them for their ultimate repatriation, (re)integration and eventual contribution to the homeland. Nor were they the only schools with a strong nationalistic and/or linguistic orientation. Around twenty (mostly boarding) schools were founded worldwide by teachers exiled from Germany since 1933, largely following the 'German progressive educational reform tradition'. Among others in Britain, Hilde Lion, scientist and women's movement representative, founded Stoatley Rough School in Haslemere, Surrey, in 1934,[19] and with the Quakers' help in 1938, Minna Specht (instrumental in creating a temporary school on the Isle of Man when interned there from 1940 to 1941), transferred her school from Denmark to Wales, while near the end of the war, the Free German League of Culture [Freie Deutsche Kulturbund] established Theydon Bois School, near London, as discussed by Hildegard Feidel-Mertz in *Shofar* in 2004.[20] Such essentially German schools would have been important to German-speaking refugee parents from Czechoslovakia wishing to preserve their children's German or Austrian cultural identity, even though German was mostly neither spoken nor taught in them during WWII. Such was the case concerning Czechoslovak future poet Gerda Mayer (then Stein),

19   London School of Economics [LSE] Library (Archives), Stoatley Rough School
      Collection, 3/1, General Correspondence 1939–43; 3/3, General Correspondence,
      A–D, 1941–60, Part 3 'C' 1945–60, Czech students.
20   Hildegard Feidel-Mertz, 'Integration and Formation of Identity: Exile Schools in
      Great Britain', *Shofar*, 23/1 (2004), 71–84.

who attended Stoatley Rough School from 1942 to 1944, before doing 'landwork' in Worcestershire for the war effort.

Czechoslovak state boarding schools

Feidel-Mertz's publication does not include the Czechoslovak schools, with their focus on the Czech language, and lessons on Czechoslovak history and literature unobtainable at English schools. Czechoslovak schools were vital to parents who, not wanting the homeland to become a mere myth to their children, preferred the Czechoslovak system; they are therefore an important aspect of this chapter. The first Czechoslovak school opened in Camberley, Surrey, in September 1940 with around forty pupils and three or four teachers, but became unsafe when German bombers heading for London flew overhead, so in early 1941 the children were moved to Hinton Hall, near Whitchurch, in Shropshire. As more pupils joined the school, a separate primary–junior section was opened in 1942 at Maesfen Hall, in Malpas, Cheshire, then in autumn 1943 the secondary school section (widely known as 'gymnasium' in Europe) for pupils aged 11 to 18, moved from Hinton Hall to the larger erstwhile Abernant Lake Hotel, in Wales. On the whole, these pupils enjoyed a relatively privileged status compared with their compatriots at British state schools. Unlike Britain, however, boarding schools were neither a cultural nor social norm in Czechoslovakia, hence alien to many mothers, normally disinclined to relinquish parental control or to delegate maternal duties to those not employed by, or even known to, them. To a certain degree though, this is precisely what happened. Despite ambivalent attitudes to boarding schools, patriotic parents responded to President Beneš's call for all Czechoslovak children to attend these schools, in the belief that they were acting in their children's best interests, and enhancing their future prospects in Czechoslovakia. Eighty-six pupils (forty-four in the Secondary School, and forty-two in the Elementary School), were registered at Hinton Hall when it opened.

According to a breakdown listed in *Hinton Hall Annual Report 1941–42*,[21] the parents' professions ranged from Czechoslovak government employees (fifteen pupils), members of Czechoslovak/other Allied Armed Forces (eighteen pupils), teachers (one pupil), merchants (ten pupils), factory workers (eleven pupils), and 'private persons'[?] (twenty-eight). In their straitened circumstances, however, only 14 per cent of the parents paid the full fees themselves, and 17 per cent paid less than half, while 40 per cent of the pupils were supported entirely by the Czechoslovak Ministry of the Interior, 13 per cent by the Ministry of Defence, and 7 per cent by the Czech Refugee Trust Fund (incorrectly given as Czechoslovak Trust Fund). It further indicated that (at that juncture) the majority of pupils (fifty-nine) had both parents in Britain. Thirteen pupils had only one parent in Britain, and only thirteen pupils still had both parents in Czechoslovakia. Had further annual reports been published, these figures would have been updated.

Nonetheless, as with the children's hostel, obstacles to family reunion caused a number of children to attend the Czechoslovak schools of necessity, being unable to live with their mother or father due to lack of accommodation, the nature of employment, or because one or both parents were fully occupied by work and/or the war effort. Employees of Czechoslovak shoe manufacturer Baťa, in East Tilbury, and Czechoslovak refinery workers in Ireland, for instance, duly sent their children to the schools too. In Walter Tschapek's case, it was difficult for his chronically ill mother to take care of him, and although she depended upon his help in the absence of her husband (then a soldier) it was considered best for Walter to go to the Czechoslovak boarding school.[22] Whilst this was a wrench to Walter's mother and other parents, it was reassuring for them to know that their children were properly cared for, and being educated according to the Czechoslovak state system, replicated in every respect as far as possible in Britain. Children like Vera Gissing who had English foster parents, welcomed renewed contact with Czechoslovaks,[23] but such

---

21   *Hinton Hall Annual Report 1941–42* [dual Czech/English], 3, Nadia de Vivo (Knap), PP.
22   Tschapek, AI.
23   Gissing, AI.

was the perceived importance of these schools that children as young as 6-year-old Pavel Seifter, the future dissident and Czechoslovak Ambassador to London 1997–2003, were sent away to school by their mother or parents as late as 1944.[24] Eva Reich's mother, too, firmly decided that her daughter should benefit from the opportunity, and all that it implied in terms of Czechoslovak national identity; matrilineal nationalism was manifested yet again.[25] The ethos of these schools, though, contrasted strongly with the CRTF children's hostel and normal family life.

Nadia de Vivo recounted how 'We small children were sent running in relays naked to our evening bath which always ended with a jug of cold water being poured over us. We were encouraged with the words, "Nahý a tuhý" [naked and tough]'.[26] She and her older sister, Alena, both British-born, were sent by their Czechoslovak father to Hinton Hall for safety from the bombing of Liverpool, and to learn the Czech language and culture. 'The teachers and nurses who looked after us were Czechoslovak. Lessons were all in Czech and we soon learned the language. We were taught the history and geography of Czechoslovakia, Czech poems and songs, and we learned to dance the national dance, Beseda'. When Nadia moved to Maesfen Hall (junior section) she was chosen to present Hana Benes(ová) with flowers on the school's grand opening day. Teachers taught traditional Czech marionette plays, and embroidery using traditional Czechoslovak patterns of tulips, leaves and decorative apples, a skill carefully applied to a tablecloth for HRH Princess Elizabeth (later Queen Elizabeth II), in appreciation of two tubs of honey she had sent the school. Czechoslovak seasonal customs were observed too, and food was prepared the Czech way, subject to wartime food rationing and a restricted range of goods. While homesick Czechoslovak children living with English families might have yearned for familiar food, Nadia, whose mother was English, 'learnt to eat dumplings and cabbage prepared with vinegar [sauerkraut], and semolina

---

24   Seifter, AI.

25   National Archives, Prague [NAP], 1670 (1578), k.2, file 15, Sbírka Československé školy ve Velké Británii 1939–45 [Czechoslovak Schools in Great Britain 1939–45 Collection), Eva Reich (Schiffová), 'Recollections of Maesfen Hall'.

26   Vivo, AI, PP.

with cocoa sprinkled on it for supper'. Eva Reich was well accustomed to Czech food, however, and her mother worked as a housekeeper nearby, so could visit the school on her day off, bringing sweets and toys bought with what would have been meagre earnings. Nonetheless, Eva insisted that she bring enough for everyone, as she did not want to be singled out as 'having something others did not'.[27] Past and current political issues continued to impact on children's lives, even on the very young ones, and the Czechoslovak government's increasing engagement with the Soviet Union was reflected in school activities. As Nadia observed, 'towards the end of the war a certain Russian influence crept in.[28] We staged a children's opera called *The Wild Geese* which was Russian, and a Christmas play was about Czech partisans in a dug-out, waiting for the Russian troops to arrive' (and liberate the country). The ramifications of this development became apparent to parents only after the February 1948 Communist coup in Czechoslovakia; in the meantime, according to Nadia, 'Our teachers [at Maesfen Hall] were kind and dedicated. They managed to create a stimulating and profoundly Czech oasis in wartime Britain'.

Some of the approximately 140 older pupils at Abernant remembered their school days less favourably than Nadia de Vivo. Except for parting from his teenage sweetheart, Tschapek did not regret leaving Abernant, which he found 'restrictive and cliquey', maintaining also that the Kindertransport pupils formed an exclusive group within the school[29] (refuted by fellow pupil Milena Grenfell-Baines). Milena Roth thought the pupils precocious, and spent just one term there in 1943. It 'was a disaster from my point of view, and I didn't learn any Czech that anyone could notice', she wrote in *Lifesaving Letters*, though she was initially excited by the glamorous prospect of boarding school.[30] Aged 11, 'I couldn't adapt to what had become an alien environment again. Czechs seemed foreign now'. Her isolation consequently increased, for unlike Gissing,[31] whose foster mother had

27   Reich, *op. cit.*
28   Vivo, AI.
29   Tschapek, AI.
30   Roth, *op. cit.*, 162.
31   Verra Gissing, *Pearls of Childhood* (London: Robson Books, 1994), 41.

welcomed her with 'You shall be loved', Roth was extremely unhappy living with an English family; she felt rejected, and neither received any mothering nor could she temporarily transfer her affections to a mother figure. Despite this, Roth was relieved to return to it: 'I found everything Czech too painful to think about'. Marion Feigl commented that it took a while to adjust to Hinton Hall: as a Kindertransport girl, she too 'had been living in an all-English environment', and now was 'back in a little piece of Czechoslovakia, where everyone spoke Czech again'.[32] Moreover, 'I was probably not an ideal candidate for boarding school, since I had always been a bit shy, and, having been an only child, dependent on my parents'. 'The professors [teachers] at the school had their hands full caring for all of us children, so there really was no-one, to my knowledge, who could serve as a mother figure. I missed not having anyone who was there for me, in whom I could confide or turn [to] for advice'. Like Tschapek, she recalled that some children ran away, but 'as time passed I made two or three friends, and that made my stay at the school nicer'. 'Molly-coddling' was not encouraged. Confiding in her diary rather than worrying or complaining to her mother or father, Marion always wrote in English, reflecting the daily life, thoughts and feelings of an adolescent refugee girl – relationships, her yearning for letters from her family, and concern about her weight and clothes.[33] Marion also described the rush to complete her laundry, ironing and mending which pupils had to do for themselves, as well as her homework, school duties and generously mending a boy's clothes in the absence of a Mutter Huenigen figure. The pressure of schoolwork with the focus on Czech culture and language, was considerable for some pupils, especially for German-speaking ethnic German pupils whose identity was somewhat redefined (though whether according to deliberate policy or simply custom is uncertain). Susan Groag for example, was automatically listed as Groagová, with the typical 'ová' Slav ending to a female's surname. Although she spoke Czech very well in a short time, befriended and helped

32   Feigl, author's correspondence.
33   NAP, *op. cit.*, 1670 (1578), k.2, file 12, Deník Marion Feiglové 1943–4 [Diary of Marion Feiglové ...].

by Feigl and Fromings,[34] another pupil was kept down a year because of
her poor Czech.[35] The emotional and psychological pressures were considerable too, and not confined to adults. A sleepless night followed news
that Jews in Czechoslovakia would be deprived of ration cards and left to
starve, as nearly everyone had at least some Jewish relatives, Marion noted
on 14–15 February 1943.

Teachers ensured that political events and Czechoslovak anniversaries
were a prominent part of school life, recorded in both Hinton Hall's *Annual
Report 1941–42*, and Marion's diary 1943–4.[36] The former listed the commemoration of the birth of T. G. Masaryk, first President of the Czechoslovak
Republic, his successor's fifty-eighth birthday, and lectures marking the third
anniversary of Germany's occupation of Bohemia and Moravia. Writing
prodigiously about these and similar occasions, Marion's observations were
far more evocative than the listings: 'Today [15 March 1944] is a double
anniversary, a happy one and a sad one […], Daddy's birthday, and five years
ago today the Germans marched into Prague. In the third lesson we have a
kind of "remembrance" – everyone collects in the girls' study', and she went
on to mention the Czechoslovak flag displayed, reminders of the national
motto, 'Pravda vítězí' [Truth prevails], and the minute's silence. Also that
March, however, 'there was an air of excitement in the school', Marion
recorded in her diary, 'the allies [the Red Army] are only 48 kilometres
from Czechoslovakia!' A war map was drawn on the blackboard, showing
the front line in Poland, and its shift westward. Cultural events and activities were also linked to Czechoslovakia, such as Hedy Fromings' folk dance
group, a recital at the school by Czechoslovak pianist Líza Fuchsová, the
programme comprising principally Czechoslovak works, and an invitation
from the Manchester Czechoslovak Centre to a special *Halle Concert of
Czech Music*, films and talks.[37] To a contemporary reader, the curriculum
might be considered excessive. Alena Burton, however, saw these activities

34   Both pupils mentioned their friendship with Susan Groag Bell to this author.
35   Observation by Franci Drazil (Šmolka), AI.
36   Feigl, diary, *op. cit.*
37   *Hinton Hall Annual Report 1941–42*, op. cit., 'Some Excerpts from the School
      Chronicle', 5–7.

not as inculcation, but as a valuable extension of her father's promotion of Czech culture in Britain, primarily at the Czechoslovak Institute in London, of which he was Director: 'Czech school continued it' she believed.[38] For fellow pupil Marion, there was the occasional treat away from the intensity of school life, though this, too, was connected to Czechoslovakia. Referring to her uncle, Bedřich Feigl, she wrote on 5 April 1944, 'After he takes me to see his art exhibition at the Czechoslovak Institute, we go to shop for Susy's [Groagová] music, have tea in a charming little café, then see a very funny film called "French Without Tears"'.

School holidays were a problem without an extended family circle to help at such times, both for working refugee mothers and their children. The former mostly had very little time off, and even less money to entertain a child. For the latter, holidays could mean a nomadic existence. With Marion Feigl's parents already in America, her 1943 summer holiday was divided between two aunts, then a Mrs Wilks for whom Feigl had to carry a red handkerchief as identification and whose children were deemed 'fit company for her', a Mrs Symes, also in Manchester, and a Girl Guide camp near Peterborough, all of which Feigl apparently enjoyed.[39] Holiday reunions with parent(s), however, sometimes failed to meet expectations. Children not only grew quickly and changed, but in growing up away from home and having to be very independent at the Czechoslovak schools, they also risked growing apart from their parent(s), and were reprimanded for not writing and keeping in touch with them often enough. Tschapek was devoted to his mother, but felt estranged from the father he saw only briefly during his infrequent home leave from the Czechoslovak army, after being released from internment.[40] On one such occasion his father tried, with some embarrassment, to broach 'the facts of life', and was greatly relieved to find that the Abernant school doctor had already discussed them with the boys in class (the girls having been informed by the nurse). It was possibly a relief for some mothers too, aware of their children's transition from childhood to womanhood or manhood, and what that entailed. Thus, in

---

38   Alena Burton (Knapová), telephone discussion.
39   Feigl diary, *op. cit.*
40   Tschapek, AI.

addition to a formal education, the Czechoslovak schools served many purposes, among them (intentionally or otherwise), the provision of male role
models for boys, which lone mothers simply could not do. Ever observant,
Feigl wrote on 30 October 1943, 'After lunch help with the wiping in the
kitchen. Professor Türk is there too, wiping the dishes with his shirt sleeves
rolled up, singing lustily to himself'. This impressed her considerably, but
it also set an example for both girls and boys growing into adulthood and
sharing such domestic tasks, moving away from the traditional 'women's
work' distinction and attitude. What the girls did lack, though, was even
basic cookery lessons. 'Never having made tea for four before, [I] am at a
loss as to know how many spoonfuls of tea I am to put into the pot, and
put two and a half in', Feigl confided to her diary on 9 April 1944. Food
was too precious to experiment with, explained Gissing who, without her
mother, did not learn to cook until she was married,[41] whereas Grenfell-
Baines learnt from her mother,[42] who had ultimately reached Britain and
passed on to her invaluable practical life skills later put to use professionally.

The Moravian Church and the Fulneck School

Although the Czechoslovak state schools and CRTF hostels were the
most prominent organizations caring for refugees and their children from
Czechoslovakia, they were certainly not the sole ones. A counterpart to
such institutions, the much smaller Moravian Church, British Province,
contributed to the care of some Czechoslovak refugee children and women
too, though a former pupil of the Church's Fulneck (Girls') School, Libby
Dewhirst Mitchell, stated that this was virtually unknown.[43] Yet it not only
helped children to escape to Britain via the Kindertransports, met and accommodated them on arrival but, when requested by the parents of Tommy and

41   Gissing AI.
42   Grenfell-Baines, AI.
43   Mitchell, AI telephone discussion.

Eva Rayner (then Friedl), promised in 1938 to protect the children and not reveal their Jewish origins should Germany invade Britain, thereby dissociating parents from their children if necessary.[44] Historical persecution of the Moravian Brethren thus linked past and present forced displacement.[45] This section of the chapter may therefore complement David Stranack's book, *Schools at War*, in which their respective war effort and fund-raising activities are described, and Tony Sykes observes that 'In the true tradition of the Moravian Church the School welcomed these [refugee] strangers into its midst and provided them with a safe haven' as well as friends.[46]

Moravian Brethren members had first settled in Britain during the early 1700s to escape religious persecution in Europe, and an enduring aim of the boarding school they founded near Leeds in 1753 for their missionaries' children was, like that of the Quakers, to promote tolerance, Christian values and morals. It was fittingly named Fulneck (echoing Fulnek [*sic*] in Moravia, where Jan Amos Komenský [Comenius], educationalist and bishop, had headed the Moravian Brethren School from 1618 to 1621 before fleeing to the Low Countries). Contact, however, with what became Czechoslovakia continued through mission work. Church archives show that British adherents were concerned about and acutely aware of developments there during 1936–9, and with contributions from former Moravian school pupils, raised over £457 in 1936 to aid members in distress.[47] A

44 Rayner (Friedl), autobiographical note to Libby Dewhurst Mitchell, May 2001, for *Moravian Messenger* on the fiftieth commemoration of the Holocaust, and later letter to this author.

45 Ecumenical Council of Churches in the Czech Republic, *The Moravian Church (Unitas Fratrum)*, <http://www.ekumenickarada.cz/erceng/jedbrat.html> accessed 31 May 2018.
    Following Catholic Austria's 1620 White Mountain [bílá hora] victory over the Czechs, Nikolaus von Zinzendorf helped persecuted followers of Protestant Jan Hus [John Huss] from Moravia to settle in Saxony: known there as Moravian Brethren, they developed their missionary work under that name.

46 Tony Sykes, 'Fulneck Boys' School', in David Stranack, ed., *Schools at War* (Chichester: Phillimore and Co., 2005), 28–9 (here 29).

47 Moravian Church Archive and Library [MC], London, L1, General Directory (series iii) 1936–53, Czechoslovakia and England, February 1936–December 1937,

Minute (MIN 136) dated 14 October 1938, of the Provincial Board of the British Province of the Moravian Church, states that on the basis of information received concerning the flight of Moravian [Church] refugees and the difficulties of the Church in Czechoslovakia, an appeal would be issued to the Province for help for both individuals, and the Church [there] as a whole.[48] According to academic Seton-Watson, a 1930 census found that only 1,129,758 of Czechoslovakia's total population of 14,479,565 were Protestants, of whom merely 233,868 people were Bohemian Brethren members.[49] The Moravian Church (as it became known abroad) had therefore always been 'a small denomination in Britain, with no more than a few thousand members at that time [1938], so there was not a lot of scope to assist on any large scale,' Church Archivist Lorraine Parsons explained.[50]

It is therefore noteworthy that the Fulneck Congregation was willing to support an adult refugee as well as children, and on 31 January 1939 the Board offered free accommodation in the Choir House (MIN 164).[51] By 20 March 1939 (MIN 174), Miss D had offered to accommodate a woman doctor S, while two sisters (not related to S), could be accommodated in Fulneck; then on 3 April 1939 Brother (later Bishop) Shawe reported that the Yorkshire Congregations were willing to support Mrs N's parents in Fulneck (MIN 177).[52] Replying to MHW, an adherent in Ashfield, Wales, on 22 February 1939, the Church assured her that it was ready to take in refugees, and though government regulations made arrangements 'exceedingly slow', expected to have three or four children in its schools.[53]

---

correspondence, and List of cheques received on behalf of Czechoslovakia during 1936.

48   MC, Minutes of the Provincial Board of the British Province of the Moravian Church, Minute Book, P. B. 39, 9 April 1937–26 June 1940.

49   R. W. Seton-Watson, *25 Years of Czechoslovakia* (London: New Europe Publishing Co., 1945), 63.

50   MC, Archivist, email to author.

51   MC, Minute Book P. B. 39, *op. cit.*

52   *Ibid.*

53   MC, L1, General Directory (series iii) 1936–53, Czechoslovakia, England and America, January 1938-December 1947, Church correspondence and funds, 22 February 1939.

Fulneck School accepted some nine Czechoslovak boys overall.[54] MIN 150 of the Provincial Board recorded on 2 December 1938, that a concession regarding the fees of two Jewish boys whose father was a doctor in Prague, had been agreed at £20 each per term until they reached the age of 14, with the proviso that if they were registered, 'they should conform to the rules and regulations of the school as they affect religious teaching and worship'. This was quite the opposite from the Czechoslovak schools, where pupils received religious instruction from visiting representatives of the different faiths and churches if required by their respective parent(s) or guardian(s), but where several pupils were registered as being of no faith, particularly Jewish pupils with Communist parents. Following on from MIN 161, but dated 23 January 1939, another entry noted that the Fulneck Women's Missionary Circle wished to assist a Czech refugee boy by collecting money towards his maintenance at the Boys' School. The Board welcomed the proposal and was prepared to co-operate by reducing the fees, adding the practical suggestion that the Fulneck members could then arrange for a home and support during the holidays.[55] Former pupil Tony Sykes observed that similar help was given to eight girls who arrived at various times early in the war.[56] The Provincial Board's MIN 159 of 16 January 1939, confirmed agreement that the Headmistress of Tytherton Girls' School, near Chippenham, Wiltshire, could reduce the fees to £15 or as a minimum to £12 per term for refugee children.[57] Further help was arranged on 31 January 1939: according to MIN 164, Sister D was willing to take care of a girl if a scholarship was granted to meet a day-girl's fees at Fulneck; £15 per annum was duly granted. DN from Prague was recommended as a suitable entrant at reduced fees to Fulneck Girls' School,

---

54   Fulneck Boys' School Archives [FBSA], Details of Czech Boys Who Came to F. B. S. Immediately Before or During the 1939–45 War, Extracted From the Fulneck Boys' School Register, compiled by Robin Hutton, retired FBS history master Fulneck was not then co-educational, brothers and sisters met on Sundays.

55   MC, Minute Book, P. B. 39, *op. cit.*

56   FBSA, 'The Direct Effect of the Occupation of Europe on Fulneck', extract from talk to Fulneck History Society, 2005, by Tony Sykes, 'old boy' and Treasurer of Fulneck Former Pupils.

57   MC, Minute Book, P. B. 39, *op. cit.*

and one free place was offered at the Boys' School. Moreover, as a result of Brother Shawe's visit to Germany and Czechoslovakia, about which he reported on 20 March 1939, the Board accepted four more children aged 9 to 12, including Jewish Jan (known as John) and Vera Karlik (MIN 174). Minute 186, dated 5 May 1939, added that although money for the Karliks had been deposited, the Board was prepared to accept them free of charge if necessary. A suitable home with Mrs N for both term time and holidays was subsequently organized. John later enjoyed the hospitality of school friends during holidays,[58] and Libby Dewhirst Mitchell spoke affectionately of Vera, her 'best friend at school, who came to stay at Christmas'.[59]

By caring for these children, sometimes at reduced rates, the Moravian Church was of immense help to anxious refugee parents in Britain or elsewhere with limited resources owing to the war. Alexandra Kučerová arrived in Britain in 1939, and while her father worked in the office of President Beneš, she spent two years at Fulneck Girls' School before taking a secretarial course at Pitman's College, and joining the Czechoslovak Red Cross as a switchboard operator.[60] The boys' parents included a lone woman secretary employed by the Czech government in exile in London, military and government officials, as well as a writer, a bank manager, and a wholesale draper.[61] Following the evacuation from France to Britain of Czechoslovak military personnel in 1940, the sons of two officers were entrusted to Fulneck School at agreed fees (MIN 13, 11 September 1940).[62] One or two children were later transferred to the Czechoslovak state boarding schools, opened at the instigation of Rev. Dr Bohumil Vančura, a Minister of the Moravian Church in Prague who had fled to Britain after helping Jews;[63] nevertheless, approaches to the Moravian

---

58   Karlik, autobiographical email to Libby Dewhurst Mitchell, passed to this author with his prior permission.
59   Mitchell, AI, *op. cit.*
60   Kučerová, telephone AI.
61   FBSA, Fulneck Boys' School Register (extract), *op. cit.*
62   MC, Minutes of the Provincial Board of the British Province of the Moravian Church, Minute Book, P. B. 40, 27 June 1940–24 April 1946.
63   MC, L1, General Directory (series iii), Czechoslovakia, England and America, January 1938-December 1947, letter, Tytherton School to a Miss C. A. Z., 14 October 1940, noted Vančura was 'a kind of under-secretary in the Dept. of Education and Youth

Church do not appear to have been made haphazardly, but rather in the belief that it would respond sympathetically according to its religious principles and ties with Czechoslovakia, a view based on earlier experiences. 'I do not know who recommended Fulneck School to my parents but it was because of the Czech connection and the best thing they ever did', wrote Eva Rayner, who initially joined the school with her brother Tommy on a scholarship basis: 'At one point they [the parents] had planned to send us to Canada but after the sinking of [a] ship with children aboard they changed their minds [...]. We owe a great deal to Fulneck for looking after us'.[64] Another Jewish family, the Karliks, had already begun attending the Moravian Church in Prague sometime during the 1930s. John stated, 'I remember Vera and me being christened there. My parents became very friendly with the minister, a Mr Vančura, who then contacted Brother Shawe when the situation grew grave in March 1939', and together they facilitated the children's escape in June via the Kindertransports. In some instances the Church's care extended beyond the war years. On 29 January 1946, the CRTF wrote to Brother Shawe regarding the Karlik children, citing the Guardianship (Refugee Children) Act 1944 'empowering the Home Secretary to appoint a guardian for all refugee children' in Britain (e.g. CRTF registered children),[65] but added that this did not interfere with care at Fulneck School (hitherto acting as a guardian).[66] John felt 'very privileged and grateful' to the Church, and described how, despite his lack of English, 'everybody from the Headmaster (Tubby Taylor) down was very kind',[67] doubtless gratifying to the mother who had placed her trust in the Church on her children's behalf, though it meant being a mother bereft of children for an indefinite period, or possibly even permanently.

Welfare' under the Czechoslovak Government (in exile in London), and had made extensive plans for a Czechoslovak boarding school.

64   Rayner, *op. cit.*
65   Legal guardianship terminated when a refugee child was claimed by his or her parent(s), adopted, reached twenty-one or on marriage.
66   MC, L1, General Directory (series iii), Czechoslovakia, England and America, January 1938–December 1947, letter, CRTF to Brother Shawe, 29 January 1946
67   Karlik, *op. cit.*

Reluctant substitute mothers

While mothers without their children struggled to overcome their loss, some substitute mothers struggled to fulfil their additional responsibilities. For a mother to decline to save a foreign friend's child from imminent danger, for instance, would have been morally difficult, even for a seemingly non-maternal woman like Doris Campbell who ultimately 'took in' Milena Roth; but 'that a Jewish mother might refuse to help her brother's children was unthinkable!' Dorrit Epstein declared.[68] Thus her penniless[69] divorced mother, Valery Fuhrmann, a descendent of the Platzek family and of a Chief Rabbi of Moravia, became a reluctant substitute mother to her nieces, Elsa and Zuzana, aged 11 and 8 respectively.[70] She was helped by the MacKinnons, a prominent British Quaker family whose daughters Fuhrmann had become friends with during inter-war skiing trips in Austria.[71] Visas had been obtained for Fuhrmann and Epstein, and the MacKinnons then acted as guarantors for both girls, who arrived from Brno via Prague, thence on a Nicholas Winton Kindertransport in 1939. 'Rich children like Elsa and Zuzana wore tailored coats and matching hats, and had smart suit-cases, while the poor children had shabby ones', Epstein recalled. 'Still, they were a pitiful sight with their brown labels, clutching a teddy bear with one ear missing and a doll with one hand missing, and they cried all the way from Liverpool Street Station to our room, then the whole week they spent in London'. It was a tense and inauspicious start, and as in Milena Roth's case, the situation left an indelible mark, impacting on both children and carers.

Fuhrmann was obliged to rent an additional room, for which she sought financial assistance from the British Committee for Refugees from

68   Epstein (Fuhrmann), also re: mother, Valery Fuhrmann (Turkle), AI, PP.
69   Regardless of their financial position, émigrés were severely restricted, usually limited to £10 on leaving Czechoslovakia (after paying various taxes to the Nazi authorities).
70   Names have been changed.
71   Aline MacKinnon accompanied children on some Kindertransports from Prague.

Czechoslovakia.[72] A proud woman accustomed to comfort, according to her daughter, she hated begging and had 'little jobs', but resorted to the Jewish Refugees Committee which sent her nieces to boarding schools in the country, particularly once the London Blitz had begun. It was a miserable time. The girls only spoke German, and returned from the first school with lice in their hair: following Fuhrmann's complaints, they were sent 'to a better one', then to another in Wales,[73] though one headmistress, Epstein claimed, stole most of the food parcels sent by the girls' wealthy uncle in the USA. These schools, Epstein asserted, 'were all third-rate but needed money, so accepted refugees'. Fuhrmann, however, was unable to choose a school as she had no funds, and additional expenditure on train fares, shoes and gymslips accrued rapidly, increasing her financial worries since money could not be transferred from Czechoslovakia at that juncture. Nor would she risk sending the girls on a dangerous Atlantic crossing to America, despite their uncle's willingness to receive them. School holidays were therefore problematic, as ever, though some 'Welsh spinsters' helped out, and after Epstein's marriage in 1941, the girls spent time in her marital home, reading, painting and enjoying the then countrified Hillingdon, to which Epstein and her husband had moved after their London mews home was bombed. With a room of their own, a cat and local girls to play with, there was some pleasure in the girls' lives. Nevertheless, 'they felt so different from other children', Epstein recounted, and they did not appear to have joined any clubs or the Girl Guides. 'Whereas Zuzana was easy to get on with, Elsa was difficult, hostile and would not talk', nor would she communicate with the child psychologist to whom she was taken. 'The problem was aggravated by my mother, who didn't know how to deal with the girls'. Indeed, Epstein described Fuhrmann as 'negative, not warm and loving or tactile, and clinically depressed. She was very bad with children, including her own child'. Always critical, Fuhrmann constantly undermined her own daughter. As a substitute mother, she coolly corrected spelling mistakes and returned Elsa's letters to her. When Epstein's first husband

72   Possibly the Czech Refugee Trust Fund as the exact date of the girls' arrival in 1939 is uncertain.
73   Not the Czechoslovak school in Wales.

died in 1943, the children were devastated.[74] 'They had effectively lost
their parents at Prague railway station, then they lost a caring uncle, and
they lost me to the navy'. Epstein felt guilty about leaving them, for 'the
children had escaped briefly' from Fuhrmann 'who did not show love for
them', but as a busy 21-year-old woman Epstein did not feel ready to care
for them fully either, and felt impelled to join the British war effort. Thus
the burden of responsibility shifted back to Fuhrmann, and to Elsa, who
never forgot her father's last words to her: 'you hold on to Zuzana, you're
responsible'.

 'The poor children', as Epstein called them, 'had a very unhappy time;
they were too unhappy and disturbed to rebel', and remained trapped in
this situation until the end of the war, when they could finally join their
uncle in America and, in Zuzana's case, 'enjoy a luxury life and belated
childhood'. The dilemmas Fuhrmann had to contend with, however, were
not over. The allegedly lesbian headmistress of the girls' school 'had a crush
on Zuzana, and wanted her to live with her, saying she'd never forgive her
if she left'. Zuzana did leave, but was unable to cope with such emotional
pressures, and threatened to jump overboard en route to America (though
did not do so), while Elsa, who had started the first year of a nursing course
in London, refused to leave, only going to the USA after completing the
course in early 1950. In addition, Fuhrmann had the immensely difficult
task of informing her nieces of their mother's death in Treblinka extermi-
nation camp, which heightened the girls' resentment of the fact that their
unloving substitute mother was alive, while their own beloved mother
had been far away and in danger. Profound suppressed resentment fes-
tered on both sides of the Atlantic, some of it evidenced by documents
found when the uncle in America died, but though his nieces 'shared the
same experiences, their reactions were very different', Epstein remarked.
Zuzana, the younger girl, told her husband and children about her life,
but Elsa 'never spoke of being Jewish, nor of her time in England; she was
traumatized and in total denial'. In London, Epstein's mother had been
'very resentful regarding the girls; it was not in her nature to be loving'

---

74   South African physicist Leonard Klatzow who developed infra-red technology.

and her own daughter had been 'delegated to a nanny'. Fuhrmann perhaps felt 'cornered' and stressed by the strain of extra unfamiliar maternal duties she could not readily perform, and though not responsible for the girls' misery, Epstein still felt keenly their accusation that she had abandoned them for the Women's Royal Naval Service (WRNS). The purpose here, however, is not to apportion blame, but to highlight the pain endured by all concerned in such circumstances during WWII.

Mothers, daughters and family relationships

The experiences of natural parents from Czechoslovakia pre-war and throughout WWII, the separate or joint views of mothers and fathers and their relationship with their offspring, could impact strongly on children, influencing both the direction of their lives and their sense of identity. Some interviewees have accepted this as inevitable, others made distinct choices, as will be discussed more fully in the following chapters, but for children still under parental care or guardianship, where most major decisions were made for them, there was sometimes no immediate 'opt out' opportunity, especially concerning the all-important issue of education. In an ironic reversal of pathways, for example, while awaiting repatriation after the Czechoslovak school in Wales closed in 1945, Hedy Fromings, daughter of the committed Communist Mutter Huenigen, briefly attended the Haberdashers' Aske's Public Girls' School, readily adapting to the 'English manners' expected of her,[75] while Social Democrat Edith Sterne[76] was later to decline on principle as too elitist, a free place for her daughter Kate, at a girls' public day school. Nevertheless, when interviewed, Sterne expressed her regret at being unable to give Kate the carefree life-style and comforts that she had enjoyed in Czechoslovakia, a sentiment echoed by other

75 Fromings AI.
76 Sterne (Bader) and daughter, Kate Ottevanger (Sterne), AI and PP.

mothers. Mothers naturally wanted to do their best for their children, each according to her own understanding, shaped by upbringing and inherited values – or a reaction against them; thus mother and daughter relationships are especially relevant within the context of this study, for hard decisions had to be made by women who might consequently feel guilty about some perceived failing on their part, or be reproached by their child(ren). Such circumstances could either engender special closeness, as in the cases of Hedy and Kate, or give rise to irreconcilable antipathy towards the mother, as acknowledged by Berta Freistadt.[77] The issue of silence re-emerges, this time as strained marital relations between Freistadt's Irish/Scottish mother and Slovak refugee father, whose experiences were occasionally relayed to Freistadt via her mother, and woven years later into Freistadt's poetry, as illustrated by the following stanzas extracted from *Stop the Train*:

> ... Rows on a Sunday morning
> About mother Russia and the communist plot ...
> voices raised about the child ...
> ...she would get up ... and tell them to stop ...
> Then the silence
> ... on a good day the piano played.
> And he would banish us both ...
> the mother, the young girl ...
> 'Don't disturb your father,' she said ...[78]

Freistadt's novel, *Mass Dreams*, with its all-women communities, expulsions and strange maternal relationships, also evoked images of her difficult childhood.[79] As a teacher, she also taught creative writing, encouraging people to freely express themselves.

77   Freistadt, AI, PP.
78   Berta Freistadt, 'Stop the Train', *The Journal of Holocaust Education*, 8/1 (1999), 76–88.
79   Berta Freistadt, *Mass Dreams* (London: BookForce UK), 2007.

Which faith?

The contentious question of faith could also affect relationships between parents, carers and children, sometimes in a divisive manner. Berta Freistadt empathized with her father, resenting her Christian maternal family's rejection of his Jewish and foreign background, and her own alienation on account of her lesbian sexual orientation. She fought hard for 'patrilineal Jews' like her to be accepted as Jewish by the rabbinical authorities. This was in direct contrast to Eva Rayner, who whilst at Fulneck was confirmed into the Moravian Church. Ostensibly, it was a major decision and turning point in her life – of a kind strongly disapproved of by the then Chief Rabbi of Britain, Joseph H. Hertz, who complained to the CRTF a number of times about the lack of appropriate Jewish instruction afforded to refugee children in its care. Yet as was so widely the case in inter-war Czechoslovakia, Eva and her brother 'had not been brought up in any religion and did not go to Synagogue. Religion had never been an issue. I remember my father saying it was a disadvantage to be Jewish', she wrote. Consequently, she was not particularly aware of being Jewish until she came to England.[80] Indeed, Walter Tschapek reported that he had never seen orthodox Jews until his Channel crossing to Britain with Polish Jews, such was the degree of Jewish acculturation in the homeland, compared with the high ratio of orthodox Jews in Poland, or even Britain.[81] Edith Sterne's daughter was twelve before she discovered that she was Jewish, and then only accidentally. Wishing to protect Kate, her parents had perhaps heeded a moving farewell letter written in German on 20 April 1942. It was addressed to Kate's parents, Edith and Franz, and Aunt Grete [Bader later Reichl, see Chapter 3] by their Mutti [Mummy] just before she left Prague for Terezín; she expressed her profound love and advised:

> Do not be weighed down by tradition and too much religion. Remember that we were sacrificed because we were Jewish, and what we experienced others will tell you.

80   Rayner, *op. cit.*
81   Tschapek, AI.

So those who want to live here [Czechoslovakia] should accept the religion of the
land, so that future generations do not have to undergo these sufferings again. That
is what my experiences have taught me […].[82]

For Sterne's daughter the discovery was a shock, but reading *The Diary of
Anne Frank*, written by a girl when of a similar age to her, and with whom
she could identify, helped Kate to accept her 'new' Jewish identity.[83] Whilst
not markedly religious, she subsequently developed an active interest in
the Holocaust and Czechoslovak affairs. This situation resonates with
Ruth's post-war account in *You'd Prefer Me Not to Mention It. The Lives of
Four Jewish Daughters of Refugees*; though not specifically Czechoslovak,
Ruth's parents also wanted her to be 'integrated' and 'normal', and not to
constantly 'carry this legacy [the Holocaust] around' with her.[84]

Deaths

If the mothers and fathers had a great deal to cope with in exile, so at times
did their children. Children typically had to cope with their mother's
sickness, depression and, as both Hetty Bower, Fortis Green CRTF hostel
warden[85] and the CRTF noted, 'headaches'. Additionally, in some cases the
father's lack of fulfilment, with frustration leading to anger and moodiness,
was exacerbated by a lack of communication on the grounds that children
should not be burdened with adults' problems, and in any case would not
understand them. At times the role of carer was reversed, and young sons
or daughters had to care for their parent(s), as Walter Tschapek had done
when interned with his chronically sick mother. Care, however, did not

82   Sterne, AI, PP.
83   Frank's diary appeared in numerous editions after WWII.
84   Jewish Women's History Group, 'Ruth's piece', in *You'd Prefer Me Not to Mention
      It … The Lives of Four Jewish Daughters of Refugees* (London: Calverts North Star
      Press, 1983), 14–21.
85   Bower, AI.

prevent some of the deaths that occurred in the Czechoslovak civilian community, even in the relative safety of Britain.

Bower recalled the tragic deaths of three small children (another interviewee stated the figure was higher), attracted by poisonous berries which they had eaten, and the devastating effect on their mothers. Mothering, after all, was intensely private, whereas motherhood was very public, and the evident loss of a child entailed the loss of identity as a mother, not just as a woman, academic Gill Rye observed.[86] The local doctor, himself a Jewish refugee, consequently advised the grieving mothers to have more children as soon as possible.[87] Such advice is usual, but within the Holocaust context it also conveys overtones of 'replacement' children acting as 'substitutes' for lost relatives. Eva Reich recorded in her 'Recollections of Maesfen Hall' (Czechoslovak school), that two boys drowned while walking or skating on a pond as the ice was too thin to support their weight and broke, painful reminders to the mothers (if then still alive and contactable), of the premature mortality they had endeavoured to evade. Not for them or the hostel mothers the pride and satisfaction of watching their children grow and achieve something in their lives, nor would the dynamic of a mother's power or persuasion versus her daughter's or son's emphasis on differentiation in the relationship, that is, empathy versus ambivalence as Rye posited, ever be tested in these instances.

In sharp contrast to the pupils, Heda Franks from Brno 'lost her childhood' during three years in Terezín, caring for her mother there from the age of 14. Franks hated being 'touched up' by male supervisors to ensure that she had not stolen anything from the greenhouses where she worked, but her covert efforts helped to save her mother's life. Many mothers,

---

86   Gill Rye, *Narratives of Mothering. Women's Writing in Contemporary France* (Newark: University of Delaware, 2009), suggested universal connotations; book launch presentation, former Institute of Germanic and Romance Studies, University of London, February 2010.

87   See also Jean Owen, and Naomi Segal, eds, *On Replacement: Cultural, Social and Psychological Representations* (London: Palgrave, 2018), especially Chapter 1, p. 21; Dina Wardi, *Memorial Candles: Children of the Holocaust* (London: Routledge, 1992).

she recounted, committed suicide. Like other German-speaking Jewish citizens with memories of Terezín, Franks' mother thought that post-war Czechoslovakia 'was not the right place to bring her daughter up', and 'though not very maternal, did her duty' as in the past. They had arrived in Britain in September 1946, mutually dependent, and reliant upon Heda's aunt. Heda adjusted very quickly, attending evening classes for English and shorthand, whereas her mother was unable to adapt or settle, highlighting the older generation's difficulties. In the absence of any substantial lasting help from her sister, she moved to a boarding house, grew increasingly depressed, took tablets and had a breakdown, before being murdered there by another resident in 1972. Having been widowed and always told what to do by a domineering mother, Heda's mother had difficulty coping with life in a foreign country, and only stayed in Britain for her daughter's sake. Remembering all this, Heda resolved to be most loving towards her daughter and grandchild(ren).[88]

Refugee mothers expected their children to outlive them after WWII ended, and enjoy a happier, more settled life than theirs had been as exiles, but for some women personal tragedies continued with the death of young adult children, for whom sacrifices had been made. Returning home from college, Anna Sonnek's only son, John, was hit and killed by a car on 26 September 1966.[89] Having already lost her husband Josef soon after WWII, Winifred Plocka then lost her son Václav in 1985, all the more poignant since he was the first child to be born and taken to Lidice village following its destruction in 1942, when most of the children had been killed.[90] Gerta Vrbová's elder daughter, Helena, committed suicide on 9 May 1982, when working in Papua New Guinea. 'The pain of losing you does not go away', Vrbová wrote in a dedication to Helena twenty-eight years later, still wondering how she might have prevented the desperate measure. 'Bruised' by the Holocaust, Vrbová feared her experiences and her husband's had affected their children. 'I should have explained to you

88   Heda Franks, AI, PP.
89   Sonnek, AI.
90   Plocka (New, then Horáková), AI.

[Helena] how important you were' to the family; 'it was you and your birth that helped me to live and do something useful with my life'.[91]

Memories of mother

The importance of women as mothers can remain in the minds of their children, even (or perhaps especially) when they themselves have children or deal with them as teachers, like Rabbi Bernd Koschland, who suggested that the memory of one's mother could be important to sons as well as to daughters. Five generations back, his maternal ancestors were from Koschlanie [Kožlany], President Beneš's birthplace, but moved to Fürth, Germany, in the nineteenth century: thus, he and later his sister were sponsored by the B'nai B'rith Care Committee for Refugee Children. Aged 8, he arrived in Southampton on the SS *Manhattan* from Hamburg in April 1939, and was placed not in a CRTF hostel, but in one for some sixty boys aged 8 to 16, then with a non-Jewish family in Margate, and later evacuated from the coastal region. British children were likewise displaced by evacuation, but had the advantage of being in their own country, and speaking their own language. Eventually, due largely to his sister's efforts on his behalf, he moved to Tylers Green hostel, near High Wycombe, Buckinghamshire, for orthodox Jewish boys, where he felt happier and more settled from 1941 to 1947.[92] The early days in Britain were hard without a caring Mutter Huenigen figure or sympathetic Marion Feigl to darn socks and sew buttons onto clothes. The boys were taught to do these things for themselves and become self-reliant; useful but difficult for a small boy. Koschland missed his mother, and cherished the few letters he had from her until Britain declared war on Germany, when he was told by an older boy that he should destroy them because they were written in

---

91   Gerta Vrbová, *Betrayed Generation. Shattered Hopes and Disillusion in Post War Czechoslovakia* (Kings Lynn, UK: Zuza Books, 2010), 12.

92   The hostel moved to London after WWII.

German. Devastating as this was, Bernd did so, and has regretted it ever since. Together with old photographs, they were his last tangible links to the memory of his mother. As a mature adult, he wished that he had parents to visit or telephone and to care for, like his friends.[93] His sentiments were endorsed by former psychiatric social worker Milena Roth. Writing in February 2010 about a meeting of a therapeutic group in Britain called Fugitive Children, which included hidden as well as refugee children, Roth recounted that 'I got a chink of memory, that it really WAS unbearable for ME [*sic*]. We all agreed that we suffer from a lifetime of homesickness, and the loss of a mother is a never-resolved grieving'.[94]

93   Koschland, AI.
94   Roth (now Milenka Jackson), correspondence with author, 2009–10.

CHAPTER 5

Identity, Culture and Social Cohesion: 'Home Away from Home'

Although the terms 'culture', 'leisure' and 'social life' as used here may evoke images of Czechoslovak women refugees in Britain with 'time on their hands', from mid-1941 this was far from being the case. Unlike 1938–9 when employment restrictions prevailed, and 1940–1 when a small number of these women were interned, most women were fully occupied with work, the war effort and, for some, childcare. Late twentieth-century notions of a balanced work and leisure life-style were hardly applicable in war-torn Britain, when 'free time' was often bound up with an aspect of the war effort. Nevertheless, women did have some free time; but while detailed works exist in English about Austrian and German cultural life in exile,[1] there is a paucity of published literature about the parallel activities of women refugees from Czechoslovakia. It has left unanswered questions as to how, when and where they spent their free time, whether they interacted with British citizens socially, and to what extent their leisure and social life reflected their ethnic, religious or cultural identity and political loyalties. Various factors account for this: Czechoslovaks in Britain constituted a minority group outnumbered by refugees from neighbouring states, and the focus on President Beneš, soldiers and airmen, has virtually excluded women. In post-war Czechoslovakia, the Communist clampdown on publications pertaining to the 'Imperialist West' meant that Bořivoj Srba's *Múzy v exilu* [*Muses in Exile*], was not published until 2003, well after the fall

---

1   See, for example, Marietta Bearman and Charmian Brinson, *et al.*, *Out of Austria: The Austrian Centre in London in World War II* (London: Tauris Academic Studies, 2008); Charmian Brinson and Richard Dove, *Politics By Other Means: The Free German League of Culture in London, 1939–1946* (London: Vallentine Mitchell, 2010).

of Communism in 1989.[2] Moreover, it is in Czech, and concentrates on the performing arts. Time and the plethora of Czechoslovak clubs with confusingly similar and sometimes misquoted names, compounded by the closure or relocation due to bombing or the changing needs of organizations, and the destruction or loss of their archives, have often left only fragmentary evidence of their former existence. To attain a degree of cohesion the material is presented here under sub-sections, and by indicating what was available, it is hoped to provide some insight into this neglected facet of exile life, taking women's activities beyond their daily routines, and placing them as supporters and/or participants in the broader context of cross-cultural developments in Britain.

Émigré associations

Addressing the questions posed here, Czechoslovak refugees in Britain widely held to, and were sustained by, their central European concept of 'culture' as an all-embracing term linking artistic creativity, intellectual activities, etiquette and social customs. Culture was also an emotive political tool in WWII, bound up with the dilemma of integration, versus the patriotic desire of both preserving a Czechoslovak national identity in an alien environment,[3] and actively promoting it. Paradoxically, however, the arts could also divide Czech and German-speaking compatriots, and those of diverse political allegiances, rather than unite them by transcending differences. Slovak-speakers were a tiny minority in Britain and could understand Czech which is very similar, so could join in activities. Nevertheless, the various associations and émigré publications in Czech, German and/or English were extremely important to the refugees, collectively serving a three-fold function. Firstly, they enabled

2   Bořivoj Srba, *Múzy v exilu* [*Muses in Exile*, cultural activities in London 1939–45] (Brno: Masarykova univerzita v Brné, 2003), English summary, 854–8.
3   Numerous works exist on identity issues; for definitions adopted here see Hewitt and Kitreab in Alan D. DeSantis, 'Caught Between Two Worlds: Bakhtin's Dialogism in the Exile Experience', *Journal of Refugee Studies*, 14/1 (2001), 1–19 (here 3).

refugees to recreate (partly at least), a cultural life enjoyed in the homeland and in their mother-tongue, helping to counter the stresses of war by providing a vital source of information, moral support and camaraderie – a 'home away from home'. Secondly, they showed British citizens, including British wives of Czechoslovak men, that Czechoslovaks possessed a 'national' history and culture, while giving exiled Czechoslovak artists, writers and musicians an opportunity to display their talent; and thirdly, they helped to imbue children and young people with an awareness and appreciation of their culture prior to repatriation – an essential step in the transmission of cultural memory on a generational basis. Commemorative events held by various groups or societies were especially significant in exile, as indeed they still are today via the British Czech and Slovak Association, the Catholic Velehrad and Brookwood military cemetery, and women continue to play a full part in them.

Early Czechoslovak clubs and women's groups became, in effect, refuges, places where émigré(e)s could 'be themselves' and speak Czech, Slovak or German without being marked out as foreigners. They would not be criticized for speaking English badly or with a foreign accent, or condemned as socially inferior for holding a knife as one would a dessert spoon (widely accepted in Czechoslovakia), nor would the Continental way of knitting (entailing clutching the needles in one's palms instead of holding them like dessert spoons 'the English way') be considered strange. By WWII, London was already the hub of Czechoslovak expatriate social and cultural life. Successor to yet earlier entities, the Klub československé kolonie [Czechoslovak Colony Club] was established in 1919 at 26 Gloucester Avenue in north London; it provided general club facilities, primarily accommodating the British Legion Czechoslovak Branch (WWI legionnaires who had settled in Britain) and the Sokol movement (discussed here later). These associations formed the nucleus of a burgeoning Czechoslovak community, but the building was bombed in 1941. New premises at 1–2 Bedford Place, WC1,[4] were officially opened on 11 September 1941, but as the Československý národní dům [Czechoslovak National House], signifying a shift of focus. Although the core associations

4   Two interviewees mentioned club facilities in Cavendish Square, W1; in February 1940, the CRTF had offices at no. 9, possibly including recreation room(s) for refugees.

transferred to the refurbished premises, a café, space for dances and small-scale performances and relatively cheap short-term accommodation rendered the non-partisan National House a convivial venue for a new generation of Czechoslovak servicemen/women, and civilian refugees needing a 'home from home'. As at March 1942, the Colony Club's funds stood at £1,000, and 264 men plus 118 women were registered members,[5] though many more enjoyed the National House facilities.

Joint Czechoslovak Cultural Commission

London was the refugees' preferred place of residence according to the Czech Refugee Trust Fund (CRTF), and where many of the 1938–9 cohorts of refugees under the Trust's care were concentrated. They did not all necessarily feel 'at home' at the established clubs of that period, however, nor indeed speak Czech (a prerequisite for membership of the Czechoslovak Colony Club since its meetings were and still are conducted entirely in Czech), and the urge to develop their own cultural activities was manifest. Seeing 'the need of coordinating some sort of inner unifying activities', a Joint Czechoslovak Cultural Commission (JCCC) was formed in spring 1939,[6] comprising the Czechoslovak Group of refugees and representatives of German and Austrian refugee groups who had sheltered in Czechoslovakia. On the basis of 'pre-Munich cooperation' the JCCC organized small theatre performances and recitals, expenses being met by the Czechoslovak Group, individuals, and collections at a few public performances. Not content with this, the JCCC's ambitious development plan included 'contact work' ultimately with all (presumably CRTF) refugee hostels in Britain, providing mimeographed literary and educational material, visiting lecturers, and experienced men and women to help organize local activities and prepare and circulate suitable

---

5   *Věstník* [*Bulletin*], 'Působnost československé kolonie v Londýně' [item on Czechoslovak Colony Club], 1–2 (October 1942), 18.

6   Presumably still under the auspices of the BCRC, succeeded by CRTF in July 1939.

material in English. The JCCC also sought to improve what it called 'dispersed efforts – run amateurishly' by establishing a small cultural centre for Czechoslovak refugees, with club and rehearsal rooms, an office and a library. In addition, it hoped to expand projects that had already been initiated, such as a Czechoslovak workshop where arts and crafts training using old and modern Czechoslovak patterns would be applied to woodwork, lino cutting, and embroidery 'copying the national costumes' (see e.g. Figure 4). Ongoing projects featured a Czechoslovak choir of some twenty-five members, an orchestra, and the training of a group of actors for theatre and poetry recitals, which attracted professional actresses such as the German-speaking Elizabeth Warnholtz. A (weekly?) budget of 79/- (see Introductory Notes regarding currency) was therefore requested for general expenses, a typewriter and a full-time secretary. To justify its claim, the JCCC declared: 'We believe that for the present conditions, there is nothing more necessary than keeping up the spirit of people and keeping different members of the community interested in each other and their common cause' (against Nazi Germany).[7] Signatories to the JCCC's appeal to the CRTF of 4 December 1939 included Communist MP Anežka Hodinová on behalf of the Trust's Czechoslovak Group, and Czechoslovak actor/director Ota Ornest on behalf of the JCCC.[8]

Despite the idealism intimated here, dissent rapidly permeated Czechoslovak social and cultural spheres in Britain, especially among political refugees. Amidst such friction the Czechoslovak Cultural Commission (CCC) determined its early tentative programmes, as follows:[9]

> 6 December 1939
> Participation in the United Charities Christmas Fair, Mayfair Hotel, with Czech dances, folksongs and other entertainment. Tickets 1/-
> 15 December
> Saint Nicholas Evening with a real Czech St. Nicholas, Engel and Dewil [sic], Music Program and Dance, Eolia Building, Old Bond Street

7   Letter from 5 Mecklenburgh Square, WC1 to CRTF in Windsor.
8   Imperial War Museum [IWM], Private Papers of M D Layton [Layton], Documents 16055, box no. 07/70/1–2, box 1, letter, JCCC to CRTF, 4 December 1939.
9   IWM, Layton, *op. cit.*, three documents, 4 December 1939, re: CCC.

24 December
International Concert of Christmas Carols, Sadler's Wells [Theatre]
January 1940
Commemorative Evenings of [author] Karel Čapek held separately for Czechoslovaks
and for English public – details to be announced.

Significantly, these documents record projects, aspirations and attitudes of
the time. Most refugees had supposedly been in transit to other countries
immediately prior to WWII, yet the plans convey a sense of semi-permanency
in Britain caused by the war, as well as a firm resolve to maintain a satisfying
cultural life in exile for the duration. It seems unlikely though that much contact was made with London's East End Yiddish theatres or groups; as Jewish
interviewee Eve Road explained, 'Yiddish was looked down on and hardly
spoken in inter-war Czechoslovakia'.[10] Meanwhile, a Communist-orientated
Austrian Centre had opened in March 1939 at 124 and 126 Westbourne Terrace,
W2, with the (Czechoslovak) Communist Beuer Group nearby at 128, and its
Young Czechoslovakia group as well as the Young Austria group (then) based
at 132. Whilst this splintering of the Trust's national and political groups, and
a struggling cultural group with a Czech/German language divide may have
been regrettable to those concerned, the CRTF never purported to be, or ever
became, a key supporter of the arts: its primary concern was maintaining and
housing refugees in its care, not their cultural requirements. Thus, although
various projects were short-lived and others never realized due to insufficient
funds, they demonstrated a need, and paved the way for future plans.

Czechoslovak Institute

London was not only the émigré hub, but where the Czechoslovak government in exile was domiciled; this had a significant bearing on activities. Although there was no ostensible hierarchy of Czechoslovak-British

10   Eve Road, Author's interview [AI].

associations, the now hardly known Czechoslovak Institute (CI) was probably the most prominent and formal of them all. Its major events were attended by President Edvard Beneš, his wife Hana, British and Czechoslovak ministers and officials, MPs and senior Allied Forces personnel, from whom some Communist refugees initially distanced themselves, though serving Czechoslovak servicemen/women automatically became honorary members.[11] Acting as a showcase for Czechoslovak culture, the Institute combined elements of all three key cultural roles mentioned earlier, and generally fulfilled the JCCC's frustrated aspirations. Initially located at 18 Grosvenor Place, SW1, the CI was conveniently close to the Czechoslovak presidential offices at no. 9, and the Czechoslovak Legation at no. 8 (see Figure 13).

Figure 13. Czechoslovak Institute, 18 Grosvenor Place, SW1. Author's image.

11   *Naší Cestou* [*Our Journey*, guide, including clubs and societies in London], produced by *Naše Noviny* [*Our Newspaper*], August 1943, 78, both published for Czechoslovak armed forces in Britain.

Following the outbreak of WWII in September 1939, the British government had requested that the British Council provide facilities for the 'influx of foreign nationals', hence a 'Resident Foreigners Division' was established to organize programmes of cultural activities and English language classes. From July 1940 the Council additionally established several National Centres, commencing with the Polish Hearth Club at 55 Exhibition Road, SW7, followed by the Czechoslovak Institute.[12] A British-Czechoslovak Centre [Britsko-Československé centrum] already existed at 3 Clifton Gardens, W9, as a social and cultural centre to promote Anglo-Czechoslovak Friendship, but by May 1940 it sought to expand its cultural activities.[13] Thus, the Institute was officially opened on 21 January 1941, by Anthony Eden, Secretary of State for Foreign Affairs. With some 12,000 Czechoslovak refugees then sheltering in Britain, the CI became a cultural focal point, and co-ordinated the efforts of various organizations formed regionally.

Both the British Council and the CI's director, Jaroslav Knap, had long-term visions of post-war cultural exchanges, but for Knap there were more personal and immediate objectives, closer to 'heart and home', and patriotism and continuity in exile underpinned the CI's activities until 1945. An economics graduate, Knap had arrived in Britain pre-WWII to learn English but, in the words of his younger daughter, Nadia, initially 'devoted his spare time to the promotion of Czechoslovak culture in Liverpool', and worked on regardless of the bombs. 'It was a labour of love', her sister Alena added: he 'was a great patriot and a very good pianist'.[14] Knap's cultural endeavours were keenly supported by his 'Czechophile' English wife, Marion Jeary. An important partnership, they had forged links with the BC, Liverpool University, Silvermere refugee hostel, and Henry Wickham Steed, former Editor of *The Times* and supporter of the Friends of Czechoslovakia. The Knaps also translated the text of the

12   British Council, Allied Centres, <https://www.britishcouncil.org/organisation/history>, accessed 31 May 2018.

13   The National Archives, London [TNA], HO 294/72, British-Czechoslovak Centre letter to CRTF, 2 May 1940.

14   Nadia de Vivo (Knapová), AI, PP; Alena Burton (Knapová).

Czechoslovak national anthem into English, and wrote the English libretto for Bedřich Smetana's opera, *Hubička* [*The Kiss*], for its first British production performed by the Liverpool Opera Company, at Liverpool's David Lewis Theatre, on 8 and 9 December 1938.[15] The Knap's cultural work increased as more refugees arrived, and as with other groups, the BC allocated Czechoslovaks in Liverpool a 'National Room' as a base for their activities at the British Council House in Bassnett Street, in 1941.[16] On the strength of his work in Liverpool, Knap became director of the CI in London.

CI programmes

The Czechoslovak Institute's role and activities for men and women (and to a certain extent children) in London were essentially similar to those continuing in Liverpool, though on a grander scale, and with the means to develop them more fully; clubrooms and classrooms were available for English language classes sponsored by the British Council. Principally though, the CI became 'home' to various groups lacking one. Events took place virtually on a daily basis from 5.30 p.m. onwards, when people had generally finished work, with lectures, lantern shows of Czechoslovakia and popular bridge evenings for members and friends. A typically eclectic programme for October 1941 reflected links with various organizations, and the need to present a number of events in English in order to fulfil the Institute's objectives.[17] It included inter-Allied tea dances (tea included), admission 2/6, 1/- for members of the armed forces, and a concert with old English instruments and a soprano singer, at 2/6 for members, 7/7, 5/9 or 2/6 for non-members, which seems expensive. That some refugees in

15   Vivo, PP.
16   BC, Allied Centres, *op cit.*, national groups had a room each, access to English classes, library, shared areas.
17   TNA, HO 294/72, Czechoslovak Institute, October 1941, and programmes.

ented rooms pressed the CRTF to include cultural events when budgeting
their allowances, is a salient reminder of the central European belief in the
importance of being (or at least being seen as) 'a cultured person', a widely
used phrase in Czechoslovakia denoting someone well-educated, courte-
ous, and appreciative of the arts, even if a scientist like Renee Morton.[18]
By 1943, 'Informal English literature readings by Miss Baugh' were added,
courtesy of the BC, followed later in the year by Shakespeare readings. It
is not known how she dealt with his references to (landlocked) 'Bohemia.
The sea-coast' and 'the deserts of Bohemia', in Act III of *The Winter's Tale*,
or whether she carefully avoided that play!

CI exhibitions

Participation in these literary programmes clearly necessitated a good command of English. Conversely, visual programmes demanded no linguistic
skills, nor differentiated between Slav and German languages; the overriding
factor was Czechoslovak nationality. With the Institute's close connections
to British and Czechoslovak authorities, the emphasis on národ [nation] as
a rallying and unifying ideal in wartime, would have been entirely normal.
'There is no such thing as a common human culture', President Beneš wrote,
'only national ones'.[19] In addition to philatelic and other exhibitions such
as the Sokol movement (discussed here later, see Figure 14), Knap aimed
to introduce national artists to the British public, since few had exhibited
in pre-war Britain, and arranged an exhibition of drawings and engrav-
ings by Wenceslaus Hollar, renowned for his detailed studies of Prague's
buildings and people as well as London's before and after its 1666 Great
Fire, thereby linking Czechoslovakia and Britain.

18   Renee Morton (Stránská), AI.
19   Eduard Benes, *My War Memoirs* (London: Allen and Unwin, 1928), 494 [re: WWI].

If you are interested in Gymnastics and Sport, we invite you to visit the

CZECHOSLOVAK SOKOL EXHIBITION

held under the patronage of the Central Council of Recreative Physical Training

The Exhibition will be open on weekdays from 10.30 to 4.30. Sundays from 2 to 4.30 at the
CZECHOSLOVAK INSTITUTE, 18, GROSVENOR PLACE, S.W.1 (near Hyde Park Corner.)
Admission Free.   OCTOBER 23rd to NOVEMBER 4th inclusive.

Figure 14. Poster, Czechoslovak Sokol Exhibition, Czechoslovak Institute. Courtesy of
Nadia de Vivo (Knap).

President Edvard and Hana Beneš attended the opening on 8 April 1942
and on 23 April he accompanied HM Queen Elizabeth (later the Queen
Mother) during her visit.[20] While some contemporary artists preferred to
be associated with the Free German League of Culture, those exhibiting
at the CI included the Czech-/German-speaking Hella Guth, who had
studied both in Prague and at the School of Applied Arts in Vienna. Her
work ranged from woodcuts to illustrations for journals, posters and stage
sets, in addition to some cubist still life and portrait paintings. Her first
one-woman exhibition comprising drawings, watercolours, gouaches and

20   Vivo, AI.

several large surrealistic paintings, was held at the Institute in June 1943. Most of Guth's work, the Jewish Museum in Prague subsequently commented, 'was created in the difficult conditions of exile'. Sculptor, Mary Duras[ová] presented works in a joint exhibition with Vienna-based artist Marie-Louise von Motesiczky, in September 1944,[21] while in March 1944, Bedřich/Friedrich Feigl (also associated with the Free German League of Culture), had exhibited works featuring 'Czech national motifs in celebration of the imminent end to the war', though 'English motifs' with scenes of Regent's Park and figural compositions were shown too. Like many other émigré(e) artists of his era, Feigl's 'life and work […] disappeared from the Czech horizon' until the post-Communist 1990s.[22] It was not a situation that Knap and his wife either foresaw or would have wished.

CI music and Christmas

Music was particularly important to refugees, many of whom, like Edith Sterne,[23] played the piano, or the violin, like Eve Road,[24] who played for her own pleasure but captivated English children when working in a Cambridge nursery. It was therefore a major subject at the CI, though to what extent avant-garde Czechoslovak music, or any German music featured there is uncertain. Programmes indicate that Music Club meetings focused on works by national composers such as Zdeněk Fibich, but in keeping with the CI's 'Allied spirit' incorporated French and Russian music too. To this end a

21   Jutta Vinzent, *Identity and Image. Refugee Artists from Nazi Germany in Britain 1933–1945* (Weimar: VDG, Verlag und Datenbank fur Geisteswissenschaften, 2006), 161, Anglo-Sudeten Club, 156.

22   *Friedrich Feigl (1884–1965) Paintings, Drawings and Graphic Art*, Exhibition of the Jewish Museum in Prague, 1 November 2007–20 January 2008, Catalogue (Prague: 2007), 2, 60–1.

23   Edith Sterne, AI.

24   Road, AI.

concert on 12 October 1941 comprised pieces by Chopin, played by a Polish pianist, and some by Czech composer Smetana, played by Líza Fuchscvá.[25] As a schoolgirl Nadia de Vivo sometimes attended events: 'the concerts I remember were those of Liza Fuchsová and the violinist Mme Hladíková. The conductors Vilém Tauský (and later Rafael Kubelík) were also frequently at the Institute'.[26] While Czech and Slovak music doubtless pleased and comforted Czechoslovaks far from home, Knap also aimed to promote it. The CI therefore scheduled a British-Czechoslovak Carol Concert on 21 December 1941 with the Fleet Street Choir and the Czechoslovak Army Choir, followed the next day by French and Czechoslovak songs Tauský had arranged 'to Welcome Our French Friends'. These seasonal events were complemented by a children's party and a 'Christmas "At Home" for Czechoslovak Airmen and Soldiers'. Knap's wife, Marion, together with Czechoslovak ministers' wives and IC staff, helped with the catering for special receptions and events, and Vivo recalled 'the huge vánočka' [traditional plaited Christmas bread] baked in the large basement kitchen. This essential part of a Czechoslovak Christmas was a remarkable achievement given wartime rationing and the scarcity of vital ingredients – even a standard size vánočka required three eggs, sultanas and almonds. Whether baked with authentic ingredients or substitutes, the vánočka would have been *very* special, evoking personal memories of the homeland.

Lectures

Lectures continued, ranging from 'Lawrence of Arabia' by Foreign and Colonial Office official, Ronald Storrs, to 'Literature in Czechoslovakia today' by writer and BBC broadcaster Pavel Tigrid (just how current this was in wartime is unclear), but as the war progressed topics changed. Wickham

25   TNA, HO 294/72, Czechoslovak Institute programmes, *op. cit.*
26   Vivo, AI.

Steed's talk, 'After Victory – What?' on 3 December 1942 was chaired by Jan
Masaryk, then Minister for Foreign Affairs.[27] As if in answer to the ques-
tion, Frederick Gellner (interviewee Elizabeth Tauber's father, related to
Ernest Gellner known for his works on nationalism) delivered the paper 'The
State, the Individual, and the International Law' on 22 March 1943, under
the auspices of the Association of Czechoslovak Lawyers in Great Britain.[28]
Examining issues pertaining to nationalism and the protection of minorities in Europe, Gellner perhaps foresaw the problems that arose in post-war
Czechoslovakia – issues taken up in Chapter 6. In the meantime, lawyer and
journalist A. H. Hermann initiated a 'series of elementary lectures on Czech
history', targeting British-born wives (BBWs) of Czechoslovaks due to live in
post-war Czechoslovakia. Czech language classes or correspondence courses
at 30/- for twenty lessons with gramophone records at 6/- were organized,
while children and teenagers living with English families also needed to learn
or improve their Czech – crucial to their future prospects in Czechoslovakia.

Czechoslovak PEN Club

Links between the British PEN Club (BPC)[29] and the Czechoslovak
PEN Club (CPC), were strengthened by the onset of WWII.[30] The
British *P. E. N. News* of January 1939 accordingly announced an 'Informal
P. E. N. Party' on 7 February 1939 for 'Refugee authors from Czechoslovakia,

---

27 National Archives, Prague [NAP], 842/634, Československý červený křiž
    [Czechoslovak Red Cross Abroad, London 1939–45 collection] [CRC], karton/
    box 45, file: Přednášky i Manifestace [lectures and exhibitions].
28 *Ibid.*
29 Founded London, 1922, PEN stood for Poets, Essayists and Novelists; subsequently
    incorporated writers and journalists and supported imprisoned writers.
30 'Czech PEN club marks 85 years of promoting freedom of speech', Radio Prague,
    Czech Radio, <www.radio.cz/en/.../czech-pen-club-marks-85-years-of-promoting-
    freedom-of-speech>, accessed 31 May 2018.

Austria and Germany',[31] and its November 1940 edition announced the founding of 'A Czechoslovak centre of the P. E. N.' in London (at the CI), with President Beneš as its Honorary President, and former Prague PEN member, dramatist and Czech Brigade Medical Officer František Langer as its Chairman. Fellow Prague PEN member, Viktor Fischl, diplomat, writer and poet, became the Secretary. Under these high-profile patriotic refugees, the new 'centre' had 'the princip[al] aim of systematically propagating and cultivating Czechoslovak culture beyond the frontiers of their land', and to effect 'fruitful collaboration' with other groups of writers then living in Britain.[32] Whilst many women did men's work during WWII, established Czechoslovak men still held the senior CPC positions. Nonetheless, women were involved in the PEN and associated activities, predominating in catering or administrative 'assisting roles'. An occasion when women participated fully was *In Memory of Karel Čapek* (writer, playwright and former Prague PEN Chairman), held at the Rudolf Steiner Hall in London on 25 to 28 February 1940, attended by Jan Masaryk, Minister of Foreign Affairs; the net proceeds were 'used towards the Czechoslovak refugee work in England'.[33] The event preceded the CPC's formation in Britain, but shared some key aims, and was organized jointly by the Karel Čapek Committee, 'English' PEN Club ('English' being synonymous with 'British' in refugees' minds), and the Czechoslovak Cultural Centre. The proceedings are not only an example of Anglo-Czechoslovak co-operation, but significantly, in the light of difficulties described earlier, also of collaboration between Czech and ethnic German exiles, as verified by the printed programme. Produced by Ota Ornest, the event included the CCC's Dramatic Group, with actresses Elizabeth/Elspeth Warnholtz, Věra Langerová and Růžena Hlaváčková, joined by actors Ornest, Paul Demel and English counterparts Mary Ward and Henry Cuthbertson. Walter H. Susskind, pianist, composer and conductor played, then accompanied Swedish soprano Hella Toros in an excerpt from Dvořák's opera, *Rusalka*,

---

31 *P. E. N. News* [PEN], 101 (January 1939), *Announcement*, 3.
32 PEN, 114 (November 1940), 7.
33 *In Memory of Karel Čapek*, British PEN Club *et al.*, Programme, London 25–28 February 1940.

and the Czechoslovak Refugee Choir was conducted by Brother Bohumil
Vančura of the Moravian Brethren. Dances (whether folk or ballet is not
specified), were presented by Marie Hellerová, dancer and choreographer.

The BPC's November 1940 *Newsletter* highlighted supportive letters
and recommendations to internment tribunals, and a lament for the German,
Austrian then Czech PEN groups 'sadly depleted through the internment of
many members'.[34] Undeterred, the CPC held a party for BPC and International
PEN members on 19 February 1941 at its new base, the CI, with 'Music by
Czechoslovak musicians and short addresses by Czechoslovak and British
Authors' – and tea ('so English' taken with milk not lemon, a custom some
refugees adapted to and 'drank more tea than the English!').[35] The reception,
attended by Edvard and Hana Beneš(ová) merited a full account in March's
P. E. N. News, which concluded: 'the Czech Trio played, very beautifully […].
Altogether an impressive and enjoyable occasion'.[36] Following this success,
a 'Party' was held jointly by the CPC and Polish PEN Clubs at the Polish
Hearth Club, with another Czech Trio recital.[37] *P. E. N. News* reported in
June that CPC's Viktor Fischl had 'laid stress on the great bonds of sympathy
which unite the two Slav countries':[38] but politics are never static, and relations
between the two exile governments, if not directly between PEN members,
deteriorated as both countries claimed historically disputed areas. A later
joint effort was arranged by the 'English' and Czechoslovak PEN Clubs at
the Institute on 17 February 1942. A 'Reading by T. S. Eliot of his poem East
Coker', was followed by Libuše Pánková's translation into Czech, read by
Juraj Slávik (Czechoslovak Minister of the Interior in exile), to piano music
written and played by Tauský – with tea afterwards. Admission was 1/6 per
person.[39] The event launched a cross-cultural project, the *Evergreen Series*, translations of English poetry into Czech, edited by Pánková under the auspices of
the 'English' and Czech PEN Clubs. Priced 2/- per copy, translations would

34   PEN, 114, *op. cit.*, 7.
35   PEN, 115 (January 1941), *Announcements*.
36   PEN, 116 (March 1941), 4–7.
37   PEN, 117 (April 1941), 3.
38   PEN, 118 (June 1941), 9.
39   PEN, 121 (January-February 1942), front page, 3, 19.

be 'from different hands and each volume should contain a comment by an authority'. Planned volumes spanned selected works by Donne, Yeats, Auden, Cecil Day Lewis and English love poems. 'The P. E. N. in England broke new ground' with the programme, its March-April newsletter declared, 'and all the available space was occupied', the general view being that 'the experiment had been more than justified and ought to be followed by similar experiments'.[40] This and other programmes were manifestly fulfilling the CPC's aims in exile.

Play, *The Last Stone*

Possibly linked with PEN, Emil Synek's play *The Last Stone*, about the destruction of Lidice and treatment of its inhabitants in occupied Bohemia, opened on 12 September 1944, in London's Phoenix Theatre, in Charing Cross Road, after touring the provinces (see Figure 15).

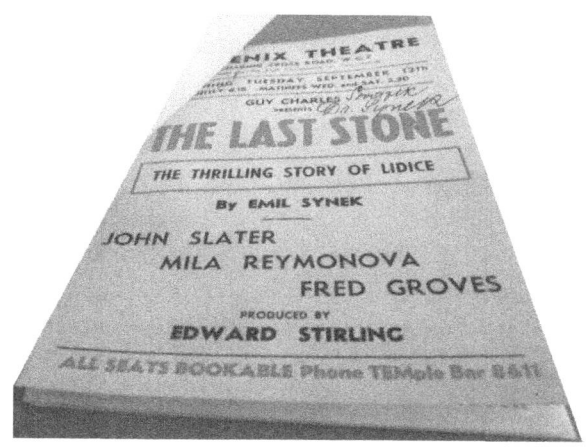

Figure 15. Phoenix Theatre poster for the play *The Last Stone*, courtesy of Devana Pavliková.

40   PEN, 122 (March-April 1942), 8, 11.

Produced by Edward Stirling of the English Players, it starred John Slater, Fred
Groves and Mila Reymonová. She had been, the *Birmingham Mail* of 9 August
observed, 'a great success in Bernard Shaw and Shakespearean plays in the
famous National Theatre in Prague',[41] and was 'also an accomplished violinist',
Tatler remarked;[42] but if the play moved Czechoslovaks, English reviewers,
whilst endeavouring to be kindly to the 'popular dramatist', were unenthusiastic.
'One suspects that something may have been lost in translation […] the play
seldom rises to the drama of its theme', stated *The Stage* on 14 September,[43]
though the *Evening News* found that 'Mila R[e]ymonová […] acts with much
emotional force and wins some decisive battles with the English language'.[44]

Women's groups, 1941 on

While Czechoslovak cultural and social organizations were established
entities in London, women's groups initially lagged behind. Small wom-
en's groups had certainly functioned concurrently with the Czechoslovak
Colony Club and early wartime cultural groups cited here; indeed, 'some of
the first organisations the refugees […] set up were the Clubs of Domestic
Workers'. These 'gave the girls [the] opportunity to break their isolation,
help each other and improve their education. The cultural programmes,
which were always of good standard, were well attended'. Moreover, it was
maintained, the clubs enabled women to 'realise the common interests
with their British fellow workers and showed them the way to the British
trade unions'.[45] Women's groups, however, were neither administratively

41 'Day by Day, The Play of Lidice', *Birmingham Mail* (9 August 1944).
42 'Mila Raymonova', *Tatler* (26 July 1944), 124.
43 'The Phoenix "The Last Stone"', *The Stage* (14 September 1944), 5.
44 'Lidice Horror on the Stage', *Evening News* (13 September 1944).
45 'Women and Their Organisations', *Frau in Arbeit/Pracující žena* [sic, joint German
    and Czech, English title given as *Women at Work*], 14 (August 1941), 11; special
    English edition.

nor ideologically united until Germany attacked the Soviet Union on 22 June 1941, shifting their political alliances. At that juncture, the two principal groups were Klub československých žen [Club of Czechoslovak Women, CCzW], formed in 1939, and Spolek československých žen (most confusingly similarly translated from the Czech as 'Club of Czechoslovak women', hence referred to here as 'Spolek/čž')[46] formed in 1941, but they were defined by their political outlook. CCzW was essentially Communist, pro-active, and enjoyed the support of Communist MP Anežka Hodinová, whereas Spolek/čž was apolitical, reputedly lacking the CCzW's drive and leadership, and was overshadowed by the former.[47] A middle way was found in late 1941 by the creation of Rada československých žen [Council of Czechoslovak Women in Great Britain, CCWGB], as an umbrella organization based at 155 Notting Hill Gate, W11 (see Figures 16 and 17); Marie Jurnečková, Social Democrat member of the Czechoslovak State Council in exile with special responsibility for women's movements and interests, became its Chairman.

Figure 16. Council of Czechoslovak Women in Great Britain (CCWGB), based at 155 Notting Hill Gate, W11 (just right of traffic lights). Author's image.

46 'Spolek' is synonymous with 'society' ('společnost') or 'group' ('skupina').
47 Srba, *op cit.*, 63–4.

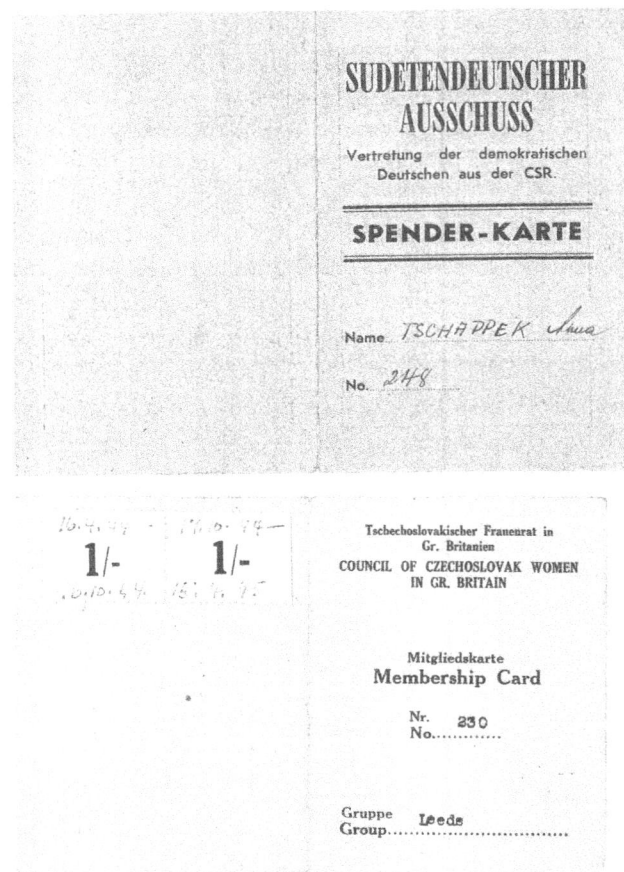

Figure 17. Anna Tschapek's Sudeten German Committee Representative Body of the Democratic Germans from Czechoslovakia, subscriber card No. 248, and CCWGB membership card, 1944– 1945, No. 230. Courtesy of son, Walter.

In different circumstances, President Beneš's wife, Hana, might conceivably have taken up the role. In wartime Britain, however, this could have been difficult, for the CCWGB appears to have been dominated by predominantly left-wing women inclined towards political activity or accustomed to such group activities in Czechoslovakia (e.g. the Co-operative Women's

Movement), and though anti-Fascist and broadly speaking patriotic, no supporters of Beneš's National Socialist Party[48] – at home or in exile.

London-based and regional groups: Young Czechoslovakia

Considerable attention was paid to constructive and instructive leisure activities for adolescents, young workers and students, willingly undertaken by men and women energetically preparing for the future, like Communist Youth Organizer Marga Tomášková from Fortis Green CRTF hostel, who would have led activities specifically for younger women and teenagers. Like Young Austria and Free German Youth, Mladé Československo [Young Czechoslovakia, YC] was a Communist-inspired organization keen to attract as wide a membership as possible, thus open to all young Czechoslovaks 'irrespective of nationality, political and religious allegiance'.[49] Based at 24 Clifton Gardens, W9, with over 1,000 members in 1939, and branches in Reigate, Boston Manor, Manchester, Liverpool, Sheffield and Glasgow, it was said to be the first mass social organization of Czechoslovaks in Britain.[50] Nonetheless, language could polarize refugees, even supporters of the same political party; an interviewee recalled how Czech-speaking Communists like her father went to one club, while German-speaking Communists went to another. Increasingly, YC propagated Communism and duly published its own newspaper, despite CRTF policy prohibiting political activity, and MI5 surveillance. Communist Youth Secretary, Ota Šling (also Otto Schling) circulated Communist literature, targeting young people in clubs and refugee hostels, sometimes accompanied by his equally committed New Zealand-born wife Marian, whom he had met in Britain

---

48   A democratic party not linked to Nazi Germany.
49   Marian Šlingová (Wilbraham, later Fagan), AI; see also Marian Šlingová, *Truth Will Prevail* (London: Merlin, 1968), 11–12.
50   Srba, *op. cit.*, 73–4.

through their youth work.[51] To idealist Communists it was a recruitment drive, raising political awareness and national consciousness, albeit in a contrasting way to that employed in the Czechoslovak state boarding schools in Britain. In both cases, the impulse to influence young people was strong, and the competing competences that co-existed in exile in Britain, would vigorously oppose each other in post-war Czechoslovakia.

Much of YC's attraction for young exiles was the social, cultural, amateur theatrical and sporting activities organized for them, coupled with practical help regarding adult education and work, and general members would not necessarily have been aware of the Communist influence in YC's leadership. From around 1941, YC operated partly from 19 Pembridge Villas, W11, in conjunction with the Czechoslovak-British Friendship Club (CBFC), the formal opening of which Hedwig Huenigen attended on 23 September 1941.[52] YC amateur productions were held in the (former) small Mercury Theatre in Ladbroke Road, W11, but YC's activities in Pembridge Villas 'were mostly political; Czech Communists held meetings and were instructed there', Ruth Tosek recounted, citing the Šlings.[53] Tosek's Jewish Social Democrat father had been politically active in Czechoslovakia and duly worked as a cashier at the club, but as a teenager she found politics boring so did not join the meetings, and was serving in the WAAF hence away much of the time. Other women though, were linked with the club; MP Hodinová spoke there, and Communist women's group activist (and former children's hostel 'Mutter') Huenigen, briefly worked there when it opened as a hostel, Dům československé mládeže (House of Czechoslovak Youth) in 1943.

51   Šlingová, AI.
52   Fromings, AI, PP.
53   Ruth Tosek, AI.

Czechoslovak-British Friendship Club and Friends of Czechoslovakia

Huenigen later became the Catering Manageress at the new Czechoslovak-British Friendship Club nearby at 27 Palace Court, Bayswater, 'where civilians and soldiers could meet, relax, dance or enjoy Czech cuisine, especially meat and dumplings', her daughter Hedy recalled.[54] The founding of the CBFC was prompted by Czechoslovaks, but is sometimes confused with Friends of Czechoslovakia groups, formed regionally by generous British people aiding arrivals in around 1939 and in the early war years. The objectives and activities of the two entities were strikingly similar though: to help Czechoslovak refugees, foster Anglo-Czechoslovak relations through social and cultural activities, and to fund-raise, underpinned in the CBFC's case by the provision of meeting places for Czechoslovaks, regardless of their ethnicity or political inclination. Yet again, however, political anomalies occurred. Despite the patronage of Barnett Stross, Labour MP for Stoke-on-Trent, and Wickham Steed's non-Communist active support of the CBFC, YC's use of the premises as a base for its London and regional groups attracted Communists, reinforcing the view that the CBFC was a Communist-inspired organization. BBW Rosemary Kavan described the characteristics of such clubs thus: a place where 'Members entertained their friends, polemicized, studied, played chess, wrote letters [...]. A newspaper was treated with respect [...]. There, conversation was [...] a morsel chewed voraciously to the core [...]. The Club was, in short, a microcosm of Czech intellectual life'.[55]

Whilst some secular and semi-political organizations remained London-centric, others proliferated regionally, like the CBFC branch in Red Oaks CRTF hostel, in Theydon Bois, Essex.[56] In Leeds, in 1944, Slovak Communist Mikuláš Teich and his Viennese wife, Alice (who had

54 Fromings AI.
55 Rosemary Kavan, *Love and Freedom* (London: Grafton Books, 1989), 4–5.
56 Peggy Kain, *Prague Winter* (Essex: REMprint, 1999), 55–6.

sheltered in Czechoslovakia until 30 September 1938),[57] were active in the
student movement and the CBFC branch. As far as they remembered,
there was no membership fee; both organizations were supported by a
British Council stipend, the Leeds CBFC being a 'minuscule replica of
the one which existed in Bayswater', Alice commented. Initially, various
clubs had often served the émigré population of a particular locale as a
whole, joining Czechs and Slovaks, Austrians, Germans, Hungarians and
Poles, but national groups gradually formed clubs of their own. There were
some thirty members of the Leeds CBFC, a mix of Jews and Christians,
Communists and Social Democrats, and two functions were to provide a
social milieu for émigré(e)s, especially at weekends, and to organize cultural
programmes, alternating weekly lectures given by refugee or local speakers. Around twenty-five people would attend, providing contact with local
inhabitants Mikuláš Teich described as 'sympathetic but not informed'.[58]

'Outreach'

'Outreach', an objective of the CRTF's Joint Czechoslovak Cultural
Commission in 1939 precisely to counter the lack of information regarding Czechoslovakia, and to generally assist refugees in the regions, also
became a feature of small Anglo-Czechoslovak associations that had opened
across Britain by 1941–2; the Scottish Czechoslovak Society, Aberdeen
Branch at 193 Union Street for instance and the Newcastle upon Tyne
Klub československé kolonie [Czechoslovak Colony Club], which required
pamphlets for 'našim anglickým přátelům' [our English friends].[59] A photograph headed 'Czechs collect in Leeds' in the *Yorkshire Evening News* of
5 August 1944, also comes under the category of outreach: 'Girls from the

---

57   Mikuláš, and Alice Teich(ová), AI.
58   Teich, AI.
59   National Archives [NAP], CRC, box 44, file: 25th Anniversary of Czechoslovak
     Red Cross.

National Children's Home at Bramhope, dressed in the national costume of Czechoslovakia, sold flags in Leeds to-day for the "Lidice Shall Live" campaign', drawing attention to the cause and country.[60] The growth and geographic spread of Anglo-Czechoslovak clubs is remarkable considering the size of the home country, and the relatively low number of its expatriates in Britain. The British Council, spurred perhaps by the Czechoslovak Institute's success in London, opened the Scottish-Czechoslovak House in Edinburgh on 5 November 1941, in the presence of President Beneš who 'greatly appreciated this initiative', aimed at 'understanding and association'. Organizations linked to the Scottish-Czechoslovak House included a Slavonic Society, students' union, the Centre for Scottish-Czechoslovak Christian Fellowship, and the Society of Friends of Czechoslovakia in Aberdeen.[61] Conversely, at the University of St Andrews which offered free places to Czechoslovaks, Renee Morton lived in her college and felt quite distant from both fellow nationals and local residents, being 'too busy studying and catching up' to participate in any clubs.[62] Having been an au pair 1938–9, worked at the David Eder WIZO-sponsored (Women's International Zionist Organization) farm in Kent,[63] then as a resident domestic for an Oxford Methodist Minister's family, Morton was finally doing what she had longed to do, and graduated in chemistry and physiology in 1944. She remembered always feeling 'a complete outsider at St Andrews – though not when with other scientists!' Balancing her scientific background with cultural interests, Morton made the most of her return to London, enjoying music, concerts and opera, as well as art exhibitions and museums, especially the British Museum, where she 'loved the Roman and Greek heads that were not equalled in Prague'.

60   'Czechs collect in Leeds', *Yorkshire Evening News* (5 August 1944).
61   *Edvard Beneš The War of 1939* [two addresses given in Scotland] (Prague: Edvard Beneš Society, 2005), 9–12.
62   Renee Morton, AI; a fellow student switched to medicine, a Social Democrat from the Sudetenland took a social arts degree.
63   Until designated a security area, the farm prepared young Jewish refugees including Czechoslovaks, Germans and Austrians, to be kibbutzniks in Palestine.

Masaryk Society

Masaryk Society members were equally keen on the arts and intellectual pursuits. The society's branches provided a focal point for refugees like Eve Road in Cambridge,[64] and others elsewhere outside London, such as Leeds, notably after University of London colleges and departments relocated to escape the Blitz. Founded as a student society at the School of Slavonic Studies (later School of Slavonic and East European Studies, SSEES),[65] it duly aimed to 'promote and encourage interest in Central and Eastern European society, politics and culture', and owes its name to Tomáš Garrigue Masaryk, lecturer in Slavonic History and Sociology when in exile in Britain prior to becoming President of the newly created Czechoslovakia in 1918. Wartime efforts to realize the society's aims, however, appear to have been on a modest scale compared with the CBFC, YC or Czechoslovak Institute, possibly lacking their financial support.

Religious groups

Whilst certain religious groups benefited from adequate, even ample financial support, they did not always provide the succour that adherents anticipated. Thus, amidst the fellowship, there was sadness and alienation on the part of some Czechoslovak Jewish refugees. Highly acculturated and not particularly religious, if at all, they 'did not fit in' a society where religious observance and social custom were an integral part of life, rather than something extraneous, reserved for weddings or Yom Kippur. Slovak refugee Charlotte Bushell, for example, when studying medicine at Leeds University during WWII, joined the Leeds Jewish Students Association

64   Road, AI.
65   The Society still exists.

(JSA), where the young men were 'mostly from indigenous families in the wealthy Jewish community' to which they turned for prospective wives.[66] 'Deep down', Bushell felt Jewish, yet at the club she 'always felt an outsider'. Bushell ultimately married in St Petersburg Square synagogue, London, a former JSA member, the son of her guardians' friends, but never shared his active interest in Judaism and Palestine, and the marriage was dissolved. While her sister Trude gives talks about the Holocaust, Charlotte, since their parents' death, has not opened 'the little blue prayer book' received from her maternal grandmother on leaving Czechoslovakia for Britain in December 1938, aged 14. More happily, Jewish Mikuláš and Alice Teich met in January 1940, in an Exeter Quaker club for refugees attended by some twenty-five predominantly Jewish members from Czechoslovakia, Germany, and Austria. Mikuláš was studying at the external college of the University of Exeter, and staying with a middle-class English-Jewish couple, while Alice worked as a secretary until Exeter was declared a security area in June 1940, and she moved to Nottingham.[67] Whilst there was no apparent pressure from the Quakers to convert, guilt and gratitude were complex, powerful emotions. They caused Social Democrat Eve Road, whose father was Jewish, to follow the Christian faith 'from respect for the Quakers' who had aided her escape from Czechoslovakia in 1939. Road felt that she 'ought to at least try to be a Christian', but in her later years reconsidered this, and was 'philosophical' when her son converted to Catholicism, then was ordained. She did not, though, become dislocated from her own sense of identity and place in history, nor reject it.

Although the majority of Czechoslovak Christian refugees were not very religious either, and most social or cultural associations were secular, religious entities provided additional social meeting points and pastoral care. Politics and religion intertwined, however, as is revealed by correspondence between Dorothy Andrew at Somerville College, University of Oxford and Jan Stránský, then Secretary to the Czechoslovak Prime Minister. Concerned, Andrew wrote to the ministry on 14 August 1940: 'so many of the refugees are Communists who do not represent the true

66   Charlotte Bushell, AI.
67   Teich, AI.

Czechoslovakia, and who add weight to the idea that the latter was an anti-Catholic state', continuing, 'Some of us Catholics here, feel very strongly that the need [to realize plans] is urgent, so much of the propaganda on behalf of Czechoslovakia is in anti-Catholic hands'. A note dated 27 August 1940 from the Czechoslovak PM's office at 114 Park Street, London W1, stating, 'The Prime Minister is very desirous of improving relations between Czechoslovaks and English Catholics', was reinforced by Stránský's letter of 25 February 1941 to Andrew, advising her that the Anglo-Czechoslovak Catholic Committee (ACCC) had been formed, and would issue a monthly bulletin and pamphlets on matters of Catholic interest, and welcomed her interest and help in the project.[68] Such literature would undoubtedly have been read by devout refugee women like Maria Stanzl in their free time, during and after the war.

Sokol

The Sokol [Falcon] movement, founded on the principle of a healthy body and mind through group gymnastics and sport, was banned in Czechoslovakia by the Nazis owing to its nationalistic foundations,[69] but furthered Anglo-Czechoslovak relations. Its London chapter, established in 1903, was reputed to be one of the oldest Czechoslovak émigré clubs in Britain,[70] and remained closely associated with the Czechoslovak National House, since 'Every Sokol branch outside the homeland became a national and social centre as well as a gymnastic training ground'.[71] Its membership

58   NAP, Ministerstvo vnitra [Ministry of the Interior, London], 1639, inv. č. 918, k1, file č. 21–1-22-2-1-32 (Am-Ant), sub-file 2–1/30/1, list 29.
59   Founded by Miroslav Tyrš and Jindřich Fügner, Prague, 1862, Sokol has chapters worldwide.
70   'Sokol mezi námi' [Sokol amongst us], *Věstník* (October 1942), 18.
71   Joan Roginson, AI, PP; 'Sokol in Great Britain', from Liverpool's Picton Hall Programme, 29 January 1944.

was augmented by chapters at Tilbury (Baťa factory), Czechoslovak RAF units, and from 1940 at Leamington Spa. The Leamington chapter, led by Bratr [Brother] Sergeant-Major Jan Koutný, comprised Czechoslovak soldiers evacuated from France. Quoting Joan Roginson, 'For a time they trained young local women in gymnastics at YWCA centres, colleges, and schools, then invited the local YWCA's keep fit group to take part in a demonstration in June 1941', at the Stoll Theatre, Kingsway, London, to piano music composed and played by Corporal Vilém Tauský (see Figure 18). 'It was great fun!' President Beneš and Jan Masaryk attended it, and the proceeds went to the Czechoslovak Red Cross.

Figure 18. Joan Roginson showing photographs of Leamington Sokol group, 2011. Courtesy of interviewee.

Roginson, known according to Sokol custom as Sestra Janka [Sister Joan], was 16 (not the requisite 17), but participated in the group until 1944, together with two Czechoslovaks of about her age Věra and Hana Steidlerová, and Brenda Adams who later married a Czechoslovak man. They were not charged a membership fee, and 'as one of Sokol's aims was to inform participants about Czechoslovakia', Roginson was presented with a copy of *Czechoslovakia Fights for Freedom*, published by the 1st Infantry

Battalion, as well as special coupons for 'a treasured navy blue pleated skirt and white blouse with a red trim, which the girls wore for Sokol events'.[72]

To prepare for the weekend events, they met and rehearsed once or twice a week in Leamington's Salisbury Hall, Bedford Street – quite different from Roginson's secretarial post at Sydney Flavell Company, which had switched from producing gas cookers to bomb cases and ammunition boxes. 'We lived for the present, the war seemed to go on and on, and people enjoyed the displays'. 'The girls', initially listed in programmes as the YWCA Club, gave a 'Display of Sokol Training' at Leamington College for Boys on 1 March 1941, 'In Aid of the Allied Services Club', then at Edgbaston Vicarage on 20 September 1941.

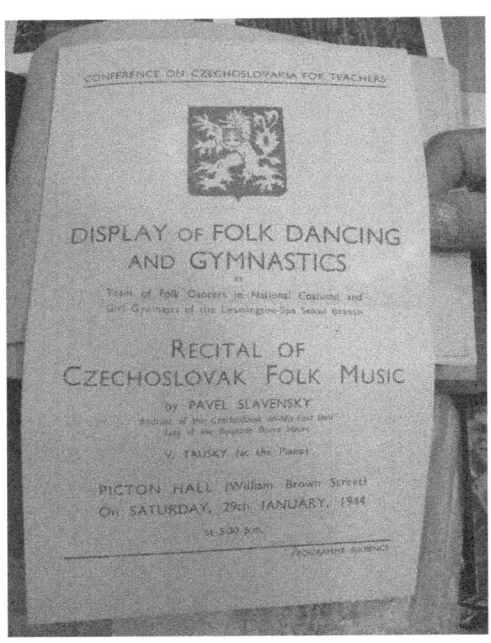

Figure 19. Poster, Picton Hall event, including the Leamington Sokol group.
Courtesy of Joan Roginson.

72   *Ibid.*, some 400 of the evacuated men were 'soldier-Sokols'.

A Conference on Czechoslovakia for Teachers, held at Picton Hall, Liverpool on 29 January 1944, included a 'Display of Folk Dancing and Gymnastics' (probably by the London Sokol Women's Team, which specialized in rhythmic exercises and national dances performed in national costume), and 'Leamington Spa Girls' Team' performed 'Sokol ball exercises' (see Figure 19). That the team's basic transport, food and when necessary accommodation expenses were all paid for was appreciated, but staying in a Liverpool 'hostel for fallen girls' with a cot by each bed caused some consternation – 'overcome by putting the balls in the cots like babies!'[73]

Further programmes included the 'Anniversary of the Czechoslovak Republic', attended by Czechoslovak Ambassador Maximilian Lobkowicz on 5 November 1944 in King's Hall, Belle Vue, Manchester, the last event for 'the girls' being in Leamington on 21 May 1945. 'In some twelve months they had travelled every other month to London, Tilbury, Liverpool and Manchester', and although the 'girls' group' continued after the Czechoslovak army had left Leamington, Roginson had already met her English future husband and 'gradually dropped Leamington'. Her future brother-in-law wrote anxiously from North Africa, 'don't marry a foreigner Joan', but in her opinion she would 'probably be too frightened about life in a foreign country' to do so. 'There were no romances with the [Sokol] Czechoslovak boys but lovely friendships, and you'd go dancing and to the cinema, or a dance at RAF Cosford, though the girls were shy at first and wondered what the Czechoslovak airmen would be like'. If some men's names have been forgotten, those of Jan Kubiš and Jozef Gabčík are well remembered. Stationed at Morton Paddox near Leamington, they 'came occasionally to exercise but were not part of the Sokol Squad', and 'the Sokol girls' knew that these men were going on a dangerous mission.[74] Only, however, after hearing news of Deputy Reich Protector Reinhard Heydrich's assassination in Prague in 1942 by Czechoslovak parachutists flown from Britain, and being told by Sokol members that 'Kubiš and Gabčík were not coming back', did Roginson realize what the mission

---

73 Programme note: UK Sokol funds came from compatriots in South Africa, Baťa and London Sokol.
74 Roginson, AI.

was – 'Operation Anthropoid'. Even in social activities, Czechoslovakia and the war remained omnipresent.

CRTF hostels and community activities

Sports, talks, debates, choirs and amateur theatricals or operettas were encouraged by the CRTF to keep the refugees' spirits up, and appear to have flourished in the more united Trust hostels where there was a common language, be it Czech or German, and shared political loyalties, as Marian Šlingová affirmed.[75] Fortis Green hostel had a sizeable choir which locals also joined, and its resident actress, Elizabeth Warnholtz, acted in Shakespeare's *A Midsummer Night's Dream* at an annual hostel garden-party, to which local English residents and dignitaries were invited (the CRTF provided a small 'social allowance' for such occasions). These were not formal events organized by the Trust or institutes of any kind, but by hostel wardens and residents, and depended on resourceful women, and men who were not serving in the armed forces.[76] Glenda Fraser, who grew up not in a hostel but in her parent's semi-detached house purchased just before the war in Berwick, Lancashire, described her resourceful mother Anna Hodbodová as 'not the stay at home housewife!'[77] Having arrived in Britain on a visit in 1935 and met her future husband, the 'very adventurous and enterprising' Hodbodová risked briefly returning to Czechoslovakia as late as 1938, trying to arrange the twinning of Berwick with Hradec Králové. During WWII when wool was rationed, she had a 'private arrangement' ordering knitting wool direct from Shetland, Scotland, and in the late 1940s when Glenda was still at nursery school, Hodbodová 'organized all thirty primary school children into a group and took them carol singing, singing Czech Christmas carols translated into English', for example, at homes for

75   Šling, *op. cit.*, 11, and AI.
76   Bower, AI, PP.
77   Glenda Fraser (Hodbodová), AI.

the elderly. Hodbodová had her own authentic Czech national costume, richly embroidered by hand, with large puffed sleeves, while the children wore colourful 'mini home-made' versions and thought it all tremendous fun. The church school was used for Sunday school and recreational purposes within the community, and Hodbodová taught children aged 5 to 10 Czech national dances to the music of 'two fragile 78rpm records of Česká beseda and Moravská beseda'. She also liked to attend meetings and talks relating to Czechoslovakia, at the International Club in Manchester.[78] The Hodbods knew several Czechoslovak families living in the area, including Czechoslovak school pupil Milena Grenfell-Baines (then Fleischmann), whose 'ebullient father Rudolf' dressed as Svatý Mikuláš (on 5 December, the eve of St Nicholas Day) for memorable children's parties. Rudolf is remembered too, for helping anti-Fascist German author Thomas Mann and his family gain Czechoslovak citizenship in 1936.

Remembrance

Remembrance and special anniversaries constituted an important aspect of life in exile during and after WWII as a moral and patriotic obligation to link with those at home, and to show respect for those who had suffered or died, rather than from any morbid sentiment, though 'communal grieving' in empathetic company for a shared reason could also be therapeutic and bonding, particularly while living in a British society that still adhered to a 'stiff upper lip' culture. Czechoslovak national events and figures, including women, were afforded considerable attention, but more personal anniversaries were observed too, both formally and informally on an institutional and individual basis, and involved a wide range of people. Independence Day on 28 October, celebrating the creation of Czechoslovakia in 1918, was the most significant occasion, all

---

78 In George Street, sponsored by the British Council.

the more so when observed in exile in October 1938 in the wake of the September Munich Agreement that commenced the dismemberment of the country. Ostensibly, the Dvořák Centenary celebrations of September-October 1941 were purely musical in nature, involving leading British musicians of the day like Adrian Boult and Malcom Sargent, who served on the Dvořák Festival Committee and conducted associated concerts at the Albert Hall and other London venues. Yet at a deeper level, 'the Czechoslovak nation' featured prominently and inseparably from each supremely patriotic programme. At the Czechoslovak Institute's opening event on 8 September, Otakar Kraus[79] sang the baritone part of Dvořák's *Biblical Songs*, and A. J. Patzaková, musicologist and member of the CI's Music Committee, opened the Exhibition of Dvořákiana she had organized. Indeed, women had a prominent role throughout these celebrations. Ever keen to promote Czech music, pianist Líza Fuchsová, and sopranos Růžena Herlingerová, Olly Riedová and Ludmila Clementisová variously performed in five of the six further programmes the CI arranged, and it was Patzaková who later collated and edited the booklet, *Antonín Dvořák 1841–1941 Centenary Celebrations*, with songs and translations.[80]

Paradoxically, whilst commemorations can be celebratory and uplifting, there may also be an underlying sense of loss, or yearning for what was in the past, as reflected in two commemorative booklets from this period. Bedřich Bělohlávek's 1941 eulogy, *Charlotte G.-Masaryk and the Czechoslovak Nation*, published in joint Czech/English by the Czechoslovak Red Cross in London, idealized her with phrases such as 'She gave to her husband's country more than any other woman' (she was American), referred to 'her heroism and service to truth', and commented on how she 'devoted special attention to the question of women' and their rights and 'endeavoured to influence her husband in this sphere' – presenting her almost as someone

79   Kraus sang (initially under a pseudonym) on the BBC radio, later at Covent Garden and Bayreuth.
80   A. J. Patzaková, ed., *Antonín Dvořák 1841–1941 Centenary Celebrations* (London: Czechoslovak Ministry of the Interior under the auspices of the British Council and Music Committee of the Czechoslovak Institute, 1941).

to be revered.[81] Františka Plamínková, 'A Great Patriot' executed by the Nazis, was similarly treated in the 1943 Council of Czechoslovak Women booklet, *In Memory of Františka Plamínková*.[82] Fellow Senate member Karla Pfeiferová contributed the piece 'Plamínková, the Embodiment of the Czechs' Struggle for Freedom', while MP Jurnečková's tribute, 'The Spirit of Our Women's Movement', stressed that Plamínková 'was the most outstanding personality within the Czechoslovak feminist movement after the First World War', pressing for equality with men in practice as well as in law. MP Hodinová described Plamínková as 'a source of undying strength and inspiration', but British contributors Margery Corbett Ashby, President of the International Alliance of Women, and Barbara Duncan Harris, JP, Chairman of the British Section of the Women's International League for Peace and Freedom, were also unequivocal in their accolades.

Retrospectively, the hyperbole employed in these extracts may seem excessive or overly emotive: viewed from a distance in terms of time, language styles and women's wartime experiences however, one cannot surmise that the sentiments expressed were other than genuine or deeply felt. To a lesser extent, the same principle applies to *The Spirit of Czechoslovakia*, 'a monthly bulletin of cultural and religious information'. Its 8 May 1943 issue was 'Dedicated to the Women of Czechoslovakia' for Mothers' Day (the second Sunday in May).[83] Greetings came from the Duchess of Atholl, MP Eleanor Rathbone, the Hon. Mrs Home Peel, JP and President of the National Council of Women of Great Britain and from Caroline Haslett, President of the British Federation of Business and Professional Women. Poems, however, like Hodinová's 'The Mother on the Battle Front', gave the issue a more personal element. Religion featured too, via Olive Wyon's 'The Spiritual Basis of the New Europe', offering hope for a better future through the Christian faith and way

---

81   Bedřich Bělohlávek, *Charlotte G.-Masaryk and the Czechoslovak Nation*, joint Czech/
      English (London: Czechoslovak Red Cross, 1941), 14, 11.
82   Council of Czechoslovak Women in Great Britain, *In Memory of Františka Plamínková
      Member of the Senate of the Czechoslovak Republic Executed by the Nazis* (London:
      1943), 2–8.
83   F. M. Hník, ed., *Spirit of Czechoslovakia*, IV/6 (8 May 1943), 46–52.

of life followed by mothers and their children, while 'The nation' and women's part in its preservation, re-appeared in Naomi Ripková's 'The Women of Czechoslovakia', praising their temperament, resolve and heroism as women and mothers – at home and in exile.

Hana Benešová's 'Mothers' Day 1943' though, went to the heart of the occasion, describing how it would be celebrated in the homeland. It was, she explained, on the YWCA's initiative that the occasion was adopted in Czechoslovakia after WWI, observed there with sprigs of apple-blossom worn as a symbol of motherhood and with flowers and decorated ginger-bread hearts which children gave their mothers. Moreover, 'Czechoslovak women now living in Great Britain will once again remember their mothers'. For most women living day to day without news of their mothers or even knowing where they were or whether alive or dead, this must have been an extraordinarily painful rather than joyful day, when they could neither give flowers nor place them (or stones if Jewish) on their mothers' graves, but Benešová's moderately sentimental piece was 'upbeat' and did not allow self-pity. That these publications appeared in English indicates a wish to attract British women readers and interact with them, as the journals could be widely circulated to British friends, associates and organizations. Furthermore, they were professionally printed, costly but presentable, and judging by the text probably produced with the assistance of a native English speaker. Yet *Spirit* cost only 3d, suggesting that these English-language publications were subsidized to promote Czechoslovakia. The left-wing *Die Frau's* [*The Woman*] perspective of Mothers' Day in 1944 diverged totally from the other publications with 'Zum Muttertag' [For Mothers' Day], a piece by 'Hedwig' (Huenigen) on the role of women from the Sudetenland, their importance as mothers, their problems and lives as citizens of Czechoslovakia.[84]

---

84   *Die Frau*, 42 (May 1944), 7.

Dances, marriage and citizenship

As a counter-balance to the sorrows and difficulties of wartime, social dances were immensely popular, and the most frequently cited leisure pursuit in refugees' interviews with this author; dances, with or without live music, were a way of relaxing and socializing both during and after WWII. For Czechoslovak women of marriageable age not in domestic service or isolated locations, there were opportunities to meet Czechoslovak men in Britain at the various clubs discussed earlier; other opportunities arose through paid or voluntary work, service in the Allied Armed Forces and associated social occasions. Civilians and military personnel alike gravitated to dances, especially those held in Czechoslovak clubs on festive occasions such as Christmas and *Silvestr* [New Year's Eve], when camaraderie meant an enormous amount to deracinated Czechoslovaks without family members in Britain. It was at such dances that many Czechoslovak couples first met. Alexandra Kučerová danced with her future husband Otmar on a small dance floor, to music played on a gramophone at the Czechoslovak National House in Bedford Square, where they could also enjoy a Czech meal. 'The six years in Britain [1939–45] were the happiest years of my life. I was young, healthy, met my husband who became the last commander of 313 fighter squadron and won the Distinguished Flying Cross [DFC], and my daughter was born in Britain!' she declared.[85] Marie Řehulková and her friends went to dances they knew would be attended by Czechoslovak soldiers when they were in London, but met her future husband in the Austrian club.[86] Dances were also opportunities for Czechoslovaks to meet compatriot servicemen/women outside their usual work environment. Ruth Tosek preferred RAF dances, as she found Czechoslovak airmen less anti-Semitic than the soldiers.[87] Conversely, local 'English' dances gave Czechoslovak servicemen/women the chance to meet British men and women, which led to a number of Anglo-Czechoslovak marriages, albeit against the advice of anxious British relatives and friends

85   Alexandra Kučerová, AI.
86   Marie Řehulková, AI.
87   Tosek, AI.

'to wait until after the war and see what Czechoslovakia was like', or 'not to have children until after the war', as in the case of 18-year-old Winifred New (later Horáková, now Plocka). She met Pilot Officer Josef (Pepík) Horák at dances in Watchfield in 1941, married him three months later, and gave birth to their son Václav in late 1942.[88]

If the decision to marry was sometimes speedy in wartime, permission from the British Home Office to do so where aliens were involved, was definitely not. A waiting period of some three months caused endless frustration, though doubtless it gave time for reconsideration about life with a foreigner. Nevertheless, while based in Warwickshire some seventy Czechoslovak soldiers reportedly married local women (1940–2).[89] In total, approximately 1,000 BBWs married Czechoslovak soldiers or airmen,[90] though two interviewees maintained that the divorce rate was high. There was definitely no fairy tale ending for one prospective BBW in Aston Abbotts, Buckinghamshire, to which the Beneš's had moved for security reasons. Villagers recounted how a soldier in the Presidential Guard had promised to marry a local woman, but after the war her fiancé disappeared without trace. She had (mis)understood him to be a count, in reality he was an accountant. He possibly married someone else; it is equally possible that following repatriation he became a political prisoner during the burgeoning Communist era, like so many men treated as traitors for having escaped to Britain and served in the armed forces. The unfortunate woman was devastated and eventually left the village: perhaps, though, she was spared the fate of BBWs trapped in Communist Czechoslovakia described in Chapter 6. As Rosemary Kavan commented, even in Britain 'marriage altered my status as well as my state [...]. I thus became immediately suspect and was required to report my movements regularly to the police'. 'Overnight', with no say in the matter, she had become both Czechoslovak and an alien under Czechoslovak and British law respectively.[91] Berta Freistadt's mother, Esther, met her Slovak husband

83   Winifred Plocka (nee New, later Horáková), AI.
89   Alan Griffin, *Leamington's Czech Patriots and the Heydrich Assassination* (Warwick, UK: Feldon Books, 2004), 30.
90   Kavan, *op. cit.*, 6.
91   *Ibid.*, 8.

when teaching refugees English under the auspices of the British Council in Brighton. Esther received extra rations 'for use at a wedding reception', though typically lost her British citizenship in 1941; on regaining it in 1942, she was still required to swear an oath of allegiance to King George VI.[92] In contrast, when nurse Hana Vodičková married a compatriot in Kensington Registry Office in August 1941, she retained her Czechoslovak nationality, and the Certificate of Marriage was witnessed by Hodinová-Spurná and her husband; in a foreign country without family members, the presence of friends on such occasions was paramount.[93]

Whilst any marriage entails adjustment, complex social and cultural demands confronted BBWs who, on marrying a Czechoslovak, acquired the feminine 'ová' ending to their new Slav (or German) name. BBWs were required to adapt to, if not readily adopt like Marion Knap (formerly Jeary), the culture of their husband, who usually expected his children to be brought up as Czechoslovaks in post-war Czechoslovakia. This necessitated good-will and compromise, especially when British customs conflicted with Czechoslovak ones. Seemingly minor cultural differences like celebrating Christmas on Christmas Eve not Christmas Day, eating carp instead of turkey, and an unfamiliar type of Christmas cake, could become divisive issues. The traditional British fruit cake with marzipan and white icing (or wartime substitutes) not only has no place in a Czechoslovak Christmas, but there is no special wedding cake at Czechoslovak weddings. When Plocka married Horák she borrowed coupons for her dress, and the top tier of her English wedding cake was perforce only cardboard. Later, when her husband joined Czechoslovak 311 Bomber Squadron in Thetford, Norfolk, she was the sole BBW, 'living far from civilization, and only met other wives at weekly luncheons in the officers' mess'.[94] Whereas BBW counterparts living in cities could go to Czechoslovak clubs, Plocka had to cope alone; whilst officially a 'Czechoslovak', in reality she knew little about her adoptive country and its culture, she stated. She did, however, occasionally accompany her husband on day visits to the Czechoslovak

92   Berta Freistad, AI, PP.
93   Hana Vodičková, AI.
94   Plocka, AI.

defence offices in London,[95] eating 'beautiful meals' in Czechoslovak club restaurants nearby (probably the CBFC or the Czech restaurant in Portsea Hall, 61–3 Edgware Road, near Marble Arch).[96]

First Lady

As the Czechoslovak President's wife, Hana Benešová was effectively First Lady of the Czechoslovak community in exile in Britain.[97] She does not appear to have been a member of any clubs, and when not working as Honorary Chairman of the Czechoslovak Red Cross in Britain or on official engagements, spent much of her supposed leisure time acting as hostess, mostly in the so-called Abbey in Aston Abbotts. Though a much grander house than 26 Gwendolen Avenue, in Putney, it was not Hradčany, the Prague castle where presidents officially resided. WWII is widely seen as a 'social leveller', which accurately reflects what the majority of Czechoslovak refugees initially experienced in Britain: however, the Beneš's life-style in government, diplomatic and military circles, was far removed from that of 'an average' refugee (owing to their political status rather than social class; though well educated, the Beneš's had working-class backgrounds). Entertainment was therefore on a level and scale that other Czechoslovak women in Britain could not emulate at that time. Dinners were held for large numbers of guests, and on one occasion the meat (covered in what villagers took for maggots but were actually caraway seeds), was too big for the house oven so had to be roasted in the village bakery,[98] while in grounds comprising gardens, a small lake with

---

95   Czechoslovak Military HQ used a Porchester Gate flat, Bayswater Road, W2 (see plaque outside), and 123 Porchester Terrace.
96   Despite wartime rationing and food coupons, restaurants accepted cash payments.
97   See also Jana Barbora Buresova, 'Hana Benešová: The Forgotten First Lady', in Charmian Brinson, Jana Barbora Buresova, and Andrea Hammel, eds, *Exile and Gender II. Politics, Education and the Arts: Yearbook of the Research Centre for German and Austrian Exile Studies*, vol. 18 (2017).
98   Victor Scott, AI.

rowing boats, stables and croquet lawn, Benešová hosted tea and coffee parties for the ladies of Czechoslovak and British ministers and officials. Guests included Winston Churchill and staff of nearby British military intelligence bases, while Sunday was 'open house', interviewee Anna Sonnek recalled.[99] Benešová was greatly assisted by her husband's two nieces, Jiřína Benešová and Božena Klučka/Klučková, who lived with them and acted as secretary and housekeeper for her.[100] But Benešová's most relaxed moments were when walking the dog; less reserved and speaking better English than her husband, she would exchange a few words with villagers, and enjoy the countryside, villager Victor Scott recalled (see Figure 20).[101] First and foremost, however, she was a supportive wife, homemaker, hostess, and when necessary, her husband's nurse during bouts of illness.

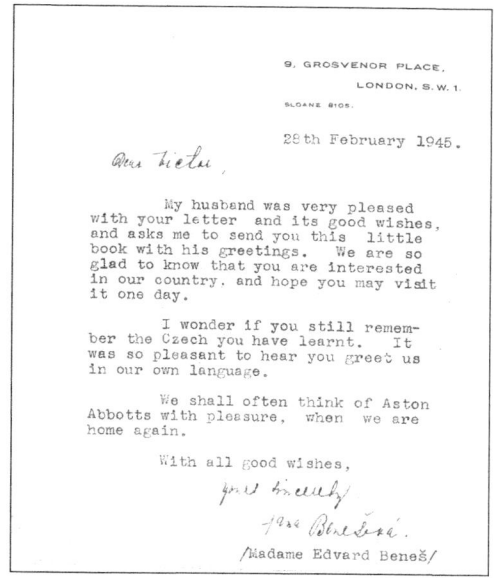

Figure 20. Letter, 28 February 1945, Hana Beneš to Aston Abbotts villager, Victor Scott. Courtesy of interviewee.

99　Anna Sonnek (Stránská), AI.

100　Neil Rees, *The Czech Connection* (Chesham: Crocksons, 2005), entry 78.

101　Scott, AI.

Reading matter

Reading matter throughout 1939 to 1950 was highly significant: émigré publications, like the social and cultural clubs, were distinguished by their languages, reflecting partisan sources, their respective objectives and potential influence over targeted social, political and/or linguistic segments of the Czechoslovak and host community. Despite wartime paper rationing, numerous Czechoslovak publications existed. Those most relevant to this study are divided into women's journals, other periodicals and books or booklets, mainly covering the war period. As Devana Pavlik observed in her overview of the WWII Czechoslovak press in exile:

> The further one is from home the more need there is to read about it, and patriotic feelings escalate when people are engaged in the fight for the liberation of their homeland. Reading in their own language reconnects them with their home and also provides a temporary refuge from the stress of the present.[102]

Newspapers and journals were read not only for their news value, but also to learn of events and programmes advertised in them, jobs, books or restaurants. Wartime censorship and propaganda ensured that news films and press reports were as positive as possible to avoid demoralizing the populace, and émigré publications were censored too.

102   Devana Pavlik, 'Czechoslovak Publications Issued in Britain During World War II', in Charmian Brinson and Marian Malet, eds, *Exile In and From Czechoslovakia During the 1930s and 1940*, *Yearbook of the Research Centre for German and Austrian Exile Studies*, 11 (2009), 183–95.

Women's journals

For the purposes of this section, two women's journals – produced by women for women – are the prime topic, *Frau in Arbeit/Pracujíci žena* [*sic*, stated in English as *Women at Work*],[103] and *Československá žena*, [given as *Czechoslovak Women's Review*].[104] Charmian Brinson's 'Frau in Arbeit: A Newspaper by Women for Women in British Exile', traces the journal's trajectory,[105] which for reasons not readily explicable but possibly rooted in ethno-politics, veered from German to joint German and Czech and back to German, with additional title and address changes until it closed in October 1945. Commencing in January 1940 as *Die Frau* [*The Woman*], under the auspices of the Communist Freunde der deutschen Volksfront [Friends of the German Popular Front], at 139c Finchley Road, NW3, it ceased briefly after April 1940 before being re-launched later that year as *Frau in Arbeit/Pracujíci žena* (*Frau/P*), noted as 'Periodical of the Working Refugee Women', averaging twelve to fourteen pages, and published by the Gemeinschaft berufstätiger Frauen [Community of Working Women], based at 132 Westbourne Terrace, London W2. Affordably priced at 2d and rising only to 4d throughout its precarious existence, what the monthly journal lacked in its cyclostyled format was compensated by its editorial style – consistently positive, practical, and generally humorous, thus uplifting as well as informative. From the outset, it was characterized by drawings and cartoons, and the informality of its editorial board, using first names.[106] This approach fostered a lively exchange of readers' views and experiences. Read and financially supported predominantly by fellow

---

103 'žena' is 'woman', not 'women' as per English sub-titles.
104 Sub-title 'Review' replaced 'Monthly' from 2nd edn.
105 Charmian Brinson, 'Frau in Arbeit: A Newspaper by Women for Women in British Exile', in Charmian Brinson and Andrea Hammel, eds, *Exile and Gender I, Literature and the Press, Yearbook of the Research Centre for German and Austrian Exile Studies*, 17 (2016), 237–48.
106 As at December 1942, the editorial board comprised Czechoslovaks, an Austrian and Germans including Rita Hausdorff, ed.

208 CHAPTER 5

Communist women workers, the journal covered a raft of topical and cultural issues, but did not ignore the conventional aspects that some women wished to retain in times of enforced 'make do' and utilitarianism. Topics therefore ranged from the (self-evident) 'Kosmetik kein Luxus!' advising on simple hair and skin preparations in February 1940, to cooking 'Für den Gasring'.[107] 'Unser Hostelklub', in the April 1941 edition, became a regular 'chat' feature, while 'Unser Klubprogramm' listed numerous social and cultural programmes at six venues, including a Professional Women's Club meeting at 132 Westbourne Terrace (CRTF premises). A gymnastics course for working refugee women held at 24 Clifton Gardens, W2, on Tuesdays 7–8 p.m. and Sundays 11.30–12.30 cost 1/6d per month. Work-related sections on pay and conditions in various types of work, were followed by information on British government training centres. Entries in Czech, centred on compatriots in America and Karel Čapek's entertaining observations of London's East End during his 1924 visit to Britain.[108]

Current affairs and social issues always featured strongly, with extensive Communist-influenced coverage of developments in Czechoslovakia and the USSR. In August 1941 Frau/P produced a *Special English Edition*, telling readers 'a little about the life and struggle of the German, Austrian and Czech peoples, and the life in England of the émigrés who have never lost their love for their own country', and hoping that the periodical would help to strengthen bonds with women's organizations in Britain – complemented by 'Spotlight on British Women'.[109] The September *Special English Edition* reported the hugely successful International Friendship Garden Party in London, organized by a committee of Frau/P and attended by some 1,500 people in August.[110] 'Tschechoslovakische [*sic*] Frauen sprechen im Radio' [Czechoslovak Women Speak on the Radio] noted in October that Hodinová, Jurnečková and Karla Pfeifferová had spoken publicly as émigrées on 30 August, regarding the situation in Czechoslovakia and the USSR, particularly concerning women and their common struggle against

107 *Die Frau*, 2 (February 1940), 10–11.
108 *Frau/P*, 10 (April 1941), 5–8, 11–12.
109 Ibid., *Special English Edition*, 14 (August 1941), 1, 5.
110 Ibid., 15 (September 1941).

Nazism. Another item centred on Jurnečková's talk on 29 September 1941 at a conference at Canterbury Hall (University of London), when she addressed 200 women about women from occupied countries.[111]

Inexplicably, in November 1941 the Czech part of the title was dropped then reverted to *Frau in Arbeit/Pracující žena* in January 1942 published under the slightly different German name Gemeinschaft werktaetiger Frauen [Community of Working Women]. An English edition focused on the formation and unifying objectives of the Council of Czechoslovak Women, and the 'newly constituted State Council of the Czechoslovak Government' in exile, which from November 1941 included two women former Deputies, Hodinová, and Jurnečková.[112] Another gap ensued between the January and May 1944 edition – re-named *Die Frau*, with an 'open letter' to readers explaining the change and shift of focus and content away from the war and war effort, towards repatriation and the homeland.[113] It would therefore incorporate Czechoslovak and Sudeten German women's activities through culture, and appears to have been written by Käthe Beckmann as editor. This was an important change. Whereas Rita Hausdorff was a Reich German Communist journalist in the CRTF Schmidt group, Käthe Beckmann, the last editor, was a Sudeten German Communist activist. Beckmann perceptively drew material from her circle of friends, such as Hedwig Huenigen and Marga Tomášková (also Tomaschek), a regular contributor. Familiar names thus recurred and unexpectedly linked some of this author's diverse interviews. The March 1945 issue declared the end of German occupation 'in unserer tchechoslowakischen Heimat' [in our Czechoslovak homeland]. Repatriation features included 'My unknown homeland' by Margaret Hünigen [*sic*], Hedwig Huenigen's English Communist sister-in-law who described what she would or would not miss, and what British people (despite the outreach endeavours described earlier) thought she would be wearing, that is, national dress, and doing the washing in the

111   *Frau/P* (October 1941), 7–11.
112   *Ibid., Special English Edition*, 19 (January 1942).
113   *Die Frau*, 42 (May 1944).

nearest river.[114] *Die Frau*'s subtitle by May 1945 incorporated the publisher's name, 'Women of the Committee of Democratic Germans from Czechoslovakia', as at 189 Westbourne Grove, W11. While the liberation of Paris, women in Palestine and letters from imprisoned women were all presented, above all readers were urged to unite, prepare for their future in Czechoslovakia and their role in the 'new' democracy – and to learn Czech. By September/October 1945, however, the Potsdam Conference and *Volksdeutsche* expulsions were noted in the periodical. German-speaking Czechoslovaks faced an especially uncertain future; they would need their wartime stoicism. One of the strongest impressions of the journal was the ability of women to laugh at themselves, to draw upon what interviewee Jana Tanner called the 'Švejk in all Czechs', when times were trying.[115]

Unlike *Die Frau/P*, *Československá žena* [*Czechoslovak Woman*, CZ] was published solely in Czech. The first edition, towards which Benešová donated £5.00, appeared in June 1943, priced 6d (1/6d per quarter, 3/- half year, 6/- year).[116] Though similar regarding topics, it was altogether more formal than *Frau/P* in style and presentation, comprising four to eight pages of small print (depending on the availability of paper and funds from readers), with black and white photographs instead of sketches. An overtly patriotic journal, its front page was dedicated to the first anniversary of the destruction of Lidice and the fate of its women and children. Jurnečková's introduction headed 'Nový spolubojovník' ['New comrade in arms' or 'fellow combatant'], directly addressed working women, stressing their importance during the war years, as well as their role in upholding Czechoslovak culture and traditions, a concept followed through in a piece subtitled, 'vzpomínky na domov' [remembering home], about the Czech school at Hinton Hall, accompanied by a photograph of a woman teacher with some pupils. Whilst acknowledging that everyone worked long hours daily, women were encouraged to go out one evening a week and join in activities, talks and practical projects such as help for

114   *Die Frau*, 52 (March 1945), 13–14.
115   A reference to Jaroslav Hašek's novel, *The Good Soldier Švejk*.
116   CZ, 1 (June 1943), 1–8.

Czechoslovak soldiers at 'Náš Klub' [Our Club], 19 Pembridge Villas. Highlighting a much more leisurely activity, a photograph showed women at easels enjoying art courses held in Czech and English on Mondays, Thursdays and Fridays 6–8 p.m. or 7–9 p.m., at the Czechoslovak School of Art at London's Chelsea Polytechnic, in Manresa Road, SW3. Fees were 3/- (per term?). Events in the regions were also listed, such as a film show about the USSR, organized by the CCWGB together with the Czechoslovak-British Friendship Club, and chaired by the Mayoress in Stoke-on-Trent. As with *Frau/P*, political issues, especially concerning the USSR and its women and children, were all-pervasive, yet 'Passed by censor'. The topic was balanced by Slovak literature, and subsequent issues had a stronger cultural focus.

While the July 1943 issue's front page bore a personal reminder and photograph of Prague's last major Sokol event in 1938, the 'Kulturní hlídka' culture column's approach was cross-cultural, recommending 'what to see in London', the National Gallery, Wren churches, etc., and compared Britain's private theatre with the Czechoslovak state theatre system.[117] 'Náš Klub', without deviating from its support for the USSR, arranged a talk by Dr Glasnerová on work in Kew Gardens, but reminders of the war and the war effort remained constant and inescapable. 'How American women work for the war' featured efforts of Czechoslovak Americans via the Red Cross, and with attention shifting towards the eventual return home, Lída Drtinová gave a detailed account of an Allied Women's Social Welfare Course, organized in conjunction with the Liaison Committee of International Women's Organizations and the British Council; eighteen Czechoslovaks were then participating in it. By August 1943, the culture column was discussing women in English literature, citing authors Fanny Burney and Jane Austen.[118] In contrast, the ever-practical Council of Czechoslovak Women provided recipes and advice on a healthy diet, and notices about short Czechoslovak cookery courses plus elementary Czech courses it had arranged for BBWs. Nor did Czechoslovakia lapse in terms of remembrance; Munich dominated the

117 CZ, 2 (July 1943), 1–6.
118 CZ, 3 (August 1943), 5–8.

journal's September issue's front page.[119] 'Light relief' came via an insert inviting readers to celebrate St Václav on 26 September, with food, dancing, and a tombola, organized by women at the Czechoslovak Institute, but in October, Czechoslovak Independence Day and politics regained the front page.[120] While Senator Plamínková's death in Czechoslovakia was further cause for remembrance, the problems of the living were encapsulated by a Scottish BBW who described her experiences seeking accommodation with her Czechoslovak pilot husband. 'We don't like foreigners – or children!' would have resonated with some readers, though not for much longer. As the October 1944 edition optimistically but accurately declared, with a photograph of central Prague on its front page, '28 říjen 1944 – poslední v cizině, příští doma!' [28 October 1944 – last [Independence Day] abroad, next [one] at home!].[121]

Other newspapers

With Ota Šling's help, the YC's own organ, *Young Czechoslovakia*, was founded on 5 May 1940, and produced in Czech with some German and English editions until 4 August 1945;[122] Hana Vodičková's journalist-soldier husband Adolf (Ada), was the last Chief Editor from May 1945.[123] It was the only newspaper G's husband allowed into their home; though not a Communist herself, caring for their young child alone in London while he served as a soldier prevented her from going to Czechoslovak clubs, and she had limited opportunity to read other newspapers in

---

119   CZ, 4 (September 1943), 1–3.
120   CZ, 5 (October 1943), 1–5.
121   CZ, 16 (October 1944), 1 (known editions to no. 21, March/April 1945).
122   *Young Czechoslovakia*, May 1940–September 1941); continued as *Mladé Československo*, September 1941–December 1942); continued as *Nové Československo*, January 1943–August 1945; discontinued [BL].
123   Vodičková, AI.

Czech to balance the Communist stance. Duly 'Examined by Censor', *Einheit* [*Unity*] described itself as a 'Sudeten German Anti-fascist Fortnightly'. Produced from 23 May 1942 until 17 November 1945 by the Publishing Board of *Young Czechoslovakia* and Management, based at 90 Sutherland Avenue, London W9, it was professionally printed and cost 6d. In contrast to the specifically women's journals, it had a broader male/female readership and corresponding range of contributions, albeit overlapping with other journals. Nonetheless, its announcements were informative and not London-centric, noting cultural events in Manchester, and that details of Christian and Jewish 'Divine Services' were obtainable from the Czechoslovak Centre, advertising its existence.[124] As Jennifer Taylor comments, reinforcing earlier observations here: *'Einheit's* contribution to the identity of the German-speaking population of Czechoslovakia was not confined to the political sphere. Value was also attached to cultural identity'.[125] Yet despite its idealistic name, *Einheit*'s readers were not entirely united, since some readers rejected President Beneš as their leader in exile. *Einheit* nevertheless publicly supported the British war effort, and organized political conferences that aimed to create a united anti-Fascist front of both Czech and German-speaking citizens. From December 1944, the independent weekly *Čechoslovak* carried English supplements for BBWs, proffering advice on preparations for their departure to Czechoslovakia post-war. Cultural events were additionally reviewed in Czechoslovak émigré journals printed in English in the latter war years, thereby attracting both British and Czechoslovak readers; J. P. Hodin's article, 'Czechoslovak Art in Exile' in *Review-45* for example, praised the work of Mary Durasová and Bedřich Feigl, who had exhibited at the Czechoslovak Institute and elsewhere.[126]

124   *Einheit*, 3, 21 (24 October 1942), 24.
125   Jennifer Taylor, 'Einheit', in William Abbey, *et al.*, eds, *Between Two Languages. German-speaking Exiles in Great Britain 1933–4* (Stuttgart: Heinz, 1995), 169–88.
126   J. P. Hodin, 'Czechoslovak Art in Exile', *Review-45* (Summer 1945). II, 2, 80–3 [Czechoslovak quarterly in English covering arts and sciences].

Books

It suffices here to note that most Czechoslovak governmental and some civilian publications targeted Czechoslovak servicemen/women, or aimed to inform and influence British readers about Czechoslovakia's situation. Some titles were available through the Czechoslovak bookshop at 71 Edgware Road, W2, others via The Right Book Club, of which Christina Foyle (later director of Foyle Bookshop in Charing Cross Road, Soho) was Secretary, and associations like the Czechoslovak Institute and the National House had their own libraries. Among the few publications for or about Czechoslovak women other than commemorative works or those published by the Czechoslovak Red Cross, was Jurnečková's nostalgic *Women of Czechoslovakia*[127] (reviewed in *Die Frau*, November 1944),[128] while in BBWs' homes *Czechs in the Kitchen. 100 Quick and Easy Wartime Dishes* that 'still retain their native character', might well have vied with Mrs Beeton's classic British cookery guide.[129] The metric weights and measures conveniently converted to the British Imperial system helped immensely, but in meeting a need, the book also highlighted the domestic pressures some BBWs and Czechoslovak women were under to cook Czech meals in wartime Britain without all the necessary ingredients – in addition to their daily work and war effort contribution.

127 M. Jurnečková and M. C. Matheson, *Women of Czechoslovakia* (London: New Europe Publishing, 1944).
128 *Die Frau*, 48 (November 1944), 12.
129 Maria/e Mikulíčková, *Czechs in the Kitchen. 100 Quick and Easy Wartime Dishes* (London: New Europe Publishing, 1944).

Cinema

The cinema was a major wartime leisure activity that was solely in English, yet especially enjoyed by women at Fortis Green hostel in north London, and by Marie Řehulková, who lived near the Kensington High Street Odeon which she fortunately had left just before a bomb damaged it. This did not deter her from cinema-going however, for ticket prices were low, and women could take their babies with them. Pathé News reels helped keep refugees informed about developments in Britain and abroad, while feature films provided an escape from them. In addition, refugees could hear music by Czechoslovak composers broadcast by the BBC Home Service for both adults and school-children, or read reviews in *The Listener*, from 1944 to 1945.

Assimilation and alienation

Despite considerable endeavours to promote Czechoslovak culture and involve British people, not only did the Czech/German dichotomy persist, but con-tradictory attitudes arose regarding Czechoslovak culture and identity; the lure of assimilation on the part of some Czechoslovaks led to alienation from family members. A Fulneck School pupil was ashamed of her mother's foreign accent and poor English. To avoid being regarded as 'different', she rejected her mother's, and thus her own culture, identifying instead with British friends and customs. Another refugee observed, however, that 'there was wealth but no culture' in the home of her British Jewish guardians, while Morton felt that 'intellectuals were not appreciated in Britain', and compared enthusias-tic inter-war Sunday morning visits to Prague museums with British 'laxity' about the arts. Culture was thus not merely an occasional afterthought for the majority of Czechoslovak refugee women, but a way of life preserved, and perhaps considered all the more precious when at risk of being engulfed by an alien British culture. It was a matter that was also to concern the next cohort of refugees, from post-war Communist Czechoslovakia.

Repatriation, Retribution and (Re)migration to Britain

For all the determined efforts to foster and preserve a Czechoslovak national identity and culture in exile in wartime Britain, when the longed-for opportunity to return home finally became a reality, refugees were generally slow to take it up, and it appears that less than half of the refugee men and women returned to Czechoslovakia. Various reasons accounted for this. Whilst the end of WWII on 8 May 1945 was indisputably cause for jubilation, in the war's wake new traumas and challenges arose: some were unforeseen or on a greater scale than anticipated, and as the records show, large numbers of refugees 'watched and waited' in Britain, uncertain about their prospects, or awaited visas for onward migration overseas. Repatriated Czechoslovak refugees seemed largely unprepared for what they encountered. Retribution, population transfers, escape and (re)migration were not what they had envisaged as the 'new post-war world', yet these developments were to drastically impact on the lives of women and those dear to them. The three faces of new 'pull-push' factors regarding which women might have had little or no agency – repatriation, retribution and (re)migration – form the basis of this chapter.

Repatriation 1945–1947: Preparations and aspirations

Just as Homer's Odysseus wished to return home to Ithaca after the siege of Troy and his subsequent adventures, to be reunited with family members and friends, regain property or possessions and ultimately to resume lives in an egalitarian, democratic Czechoslovakia, where neither ethnicity nor religion diminished citizens, was a natural desire of refugees. Thus, without disrupting their war effort work for Britain, idealistic women trained and prepared to realize that goal by contributing to Czechoslovakia's post-war social reconstruction on their return. From October to December 1944, Hedwig Huenigen participated in the British Council's Fifth Social Welfare Course for Allied Nationals in London, followed by a British Red Cross First Aid course in January 1945, and via the Council of Czechoslovak Women in Great Britain (CCWGB) urged more women to do likewise.[1] As an employee of the Czechoslovak government in exile, Elisabeth Tauber was 'very patriotic and pleased' to be sent on a similar social work course especially for women at the London School of Economics and Political Science, organized by the British Council,[2] and her school-friend Eve Road took one in Cambridge.[3] The trajectories of these women, and the application of their training, however, were to diverge considerably.

'Newly Czech' women, too, prepared for life in a Czechoslovakia they had yet to see. To help them in this difficult cultural situation, two-sided English-language monthly supplements addressed 'To the British-born Wives of Czechoslovaks' (BBWs), acting as a substitute Czechoslovak mother-in-law proffering guidance and information, were inserted in *Čechoslovák*, a newspaper read by Czechoslovak soldiers and airmen.[4] The well-intended advice seems somewhat daunting, though. The March 1945 issue detailed ten 'Do's and Dont's' emphasizing differences in English and Czechoslovak customs and etiquette, the need to learn 'Czechoslovak methods of cooking' and the Czech or Slovak language – all without losing one's 'English' identity. The author had attempted to be jovial, but the piece was underpinned by serious items: the Czechoslovak Institute's conference and talks on life in Czechoslovakia, 'Registration for Repatriation' and how to obtain a Czechoslovak passport. Marian

1   Hedy Fromings (Huenigen), AI, PP.
2   Elisabeth Tauber, AI.
3   Eve Road, AI.
4   *Čechoslovák*, independent weekly edited by President Beneš's nephew, Bohumil Beneš; known BBW supplements commenced September 1944, ended no. 9, September 1945(?).

Jeary remained in Britain with her husband Jaroslav Knap, who headed the Institute until its closure in 1948, but BBWs who did go to Czechoslovakia included Winifred Plocka (previously New, later Horáková)[5] and New Zealand-born Marian Šlingová,[6] whose lives became embroiled in the shifting political situation.

Paradoxically, as practical preparations for repatriation escalated from February 1945, the excitement and hope for the future felt by some refugees was marred by distress on the part of others. This was due to known or feared losses, particularly in the case of Jewish refugees like Renee Morton, for whom the end of the war was 'very upsetting as everyone was celebrating, whereas I waited anxiously for the post for three months – but there was no news'. Although Morton's parents had been sent to Terezín, their names had yet to be found, and at the end of 1945 an uncle in New York advised that she should 'assume the worst'.[7] In her last year at the University of St Andrews, Morton had married a former boyfriend from Prague who had joined the Czechoslovak air force; both stayed on in Britain. Throughout the war WAAF Corporal Theresie Lowit thought she would return to Czechoslovakia, but on hearing that Sudeten Germans were being expelled in 1945 she, her Social Democrat parents and soldier future husband decided against repatriation. Her parents 'were shattered'; that 'they felt German but were good Czechoslovaks'[8] is a paradigm of the complex dichotomy between identity and nationality referred to in preceding chapters. Eighteen-year-old Hedy Fromings was loathe to leave her boyfriend in Britain, but despite Hedy's tears and entreaties, Hedwig Huenigen insisted that her daughter 'did her patriotic duty' in returning to help re-build Czechoslovakia.[9] Furthermore, things and places that had become familiar, and perhaps rendered a measure of comforting security during the war years, were suddenly to be supplanted by a homeland that younger children no longer fully remembered, or had never known because they were born in the diaspora. As

5   Winifred Plocka (New, later Horáková), AI.
6   Marian Šlingová (Wilbraham, later Fagan), AI.
7   Renee Morton, AI.
8   Theresie Lowit, AI.
9   Hedy Fromings (Huenigen), AI.

at April 1945, the following people (approximately) were registered with the Czech Refugee Trust Fund (CRTF) and eligible for repatriation:[10]

Individuals	Families
4,500 Czechoslovaks	2,500
3,000 Sudeten Germans	1,600
1,100 Germans	600
800 Austrians	450
600 Miscellaneous	350
10,000	5,500

Despite their relative wartime independence, most married women would have placed their husband's preference to remain or be repatriated above their own, as did ophthalmic surgeon Jindřiška Koděková, who had joined her Jewish scientist husband studying in Britain in 1939, but unlike him wished to return to Prague.[11] It was a testing time for women of all ages and backgrounds, with major issues to be addressed, and far-reaching decisions to be made. 'Pull-push' issues arose again. How were women and their families going to uproot themselves and cope with the fresh upheaval and adjustments? Some older refugees felt that they could not do so, raising concerns from 1944 about the CRTF's responsibility for 600–700 elderly and infirm people 'who would not compete in the labour market or become charges on public assistance', and whom the Trust 'might therefore expect to go on supporting for the rest of their lives'. With the Trust's continued existence in doubt, the question of when a refugee ceased to be one so far as the Trustees were involved was highly relevant, since it was thought unlikely that the Czechoslovak government in exile, once repatriated, would

10   The National Archives, London [TNA], HO 294/31, Repatriation: CRTF, Resettlement – General Questions, Rough Outline for Discussion at Trustees' Meeting, 12 April 1945.
11   Jindřiška Koděková, questionnaire respondent.

be willing to support refugees remaining in post-war Britain, particularly German-speaking families from the Sudetenland.[12]

Repatriation process: Statements of intention

In order to ascertain for planning purposes who wished or did not wish to be repatriated, individuals or heads of family (or women then in Britain without their spouse), were required to complete a form printed in Czech and English, and submit it to the Czechoslovak Ministry of Social Welfare's specially created Repatriation Department, at 53 Cadogan Gardens, London SW3. The Ministry first sent out an 'Appeal' in January 1945 to all civilian Czechoslovak citizens who wished to be repatriated to get in touch. A questionnaire would then be sent to the applicant, to be completed and returned by 15 February 1945.[13] The CRTF had a one-page form comprising five questions which simply concerned the number of individuals, spouses and families involved in each case, their plans for 'final settlement' and possible occupation outside Britain. Notably, 'Your nationality?' in English/Czech/German ranked last of the main questions. The Czechoslovak government's three-page *Dotazník* [Questionnaire] listing twenty-nine key questions, was far more searching, however, than the Trust's.[14] Added to the basic data required were questions about military service and rank, education, languages spoken, place of birth, the respondent's passport number and registration details at the Czechoslovak Embassy in London (or other relevant documents), the British identity card number, and date and place of arrival in Britain. Question 21, was 'Reason for leaving Czechoslovakia?' while Question 22, pointedly asked what the person had done since September 1938 (the date of the Munich Agreement). Not until Question 23 were refugees asked if they wished to be

---

12   TNA, HO 294/31, CRTF, Note of Discussion at the Home Office, 17 February 1944.
13   National Archives, Prague [NAP], Ministerstvo Sociální Péče [Ministry of Social Welfare], Czechoslovak Repatriation Mission, ref: MV–L 259, 2–68-3, sub-file 8.
14   NAP, *op. cit.*, ref: 1639, inv. č 918, karton 1, file 2–1-1 to 2–1-11, Ab-Ad, sub-file 6, list 2.

repatriated, with Question 24, 'Where to?' Questions regarding luggage led to disclosure of one's personal financial position 'abroad' (presumably outside Czechoslovakia), deposits, shares and valuable possessions, 'particularly immovables', that is, property, and whether one had ever been a 'member' (registered refugee) of the CRTF, fined or convicted abroad. The implications of certain sensitive questions posed are considerable, and indicate that applicants were being vetted regarding their 'suitability' for repatriation.

Prague's National Archives contain innumerable completed questionnaires filed alphabetically: sample batches viewed were all signed by the respondent and 'witnessed' (presumably checked and passed), by Colonel F. Langer,[15] at 134 Piccadilly, London,[16] in March 1945. Ironically, the information supplied in order to start life afresh disclosed more about the individuals' histories than their plans for the future. Recurring 'Reasons for leaving Czechoslovakia' for example, were 'political'. Ida Antuschová, an ethnic German from Liberec and former resident of Fortis Green CRTF hostel, stated in Czech that the Gestapo had arrested her husband in Prague.[17] Interestingly, one woman gave her *národnost* [nationality] as *židovska* [Jewish], while Leona Andrášková, a British-born wife (BBW) from Crewe, was listed as 'Czechoslovak (former[ly]) British'. Her husband, a mechanic in 311 Czechoslovak Squadron of the RAF, apparently completed the form on her behalf; to Question 15 he answered, 'English perfect, Czech 20%', then wrote 'boxis' ('boxes') regarding luggage.[18] Agneša Adorjánová's surname had also been changed to a more 'Czech' one; her army doctor husband was 'Adorjan, Paul alias Rosenbaum'. Adorjánová had worked as a secretary at the International Rotary Club, where her knowledge of German, Hungarian, French and English would have been advantageous. Nevertheless, she wished to return to Slovakia, which became part of Czechoslovakia again post-war.[19]

15   Playwright František Langer then headed Czechoslovak army medical services.
16   Czechoslovak Ministry of Social Welfare, and Ministry of Defence offices were in Latymer House, Piccadilly.
17   NAP, *op. cit.*, file 2–1-33 to 2–1-40, Ant-Ast, sub-file 2–1/33/3, list 2.
18   NAP, *op. cit.*, file 2–1-22 to 2–1-32, Am-Ant, sub-file 2–1/28/8, list 2.
19   NAP, *op. cit.*, file 2–1-1 to 2–1-11, Ab-Ad, list 11.

Refugee statistics are never absolute, thus the CRTF's table of Recorded Intentions of Certain Registered Refugees in the U. K. Regarding Their Future (Answers Recorded June and July 1945), could merely reflect the mood of the moment. Like other CRTF statistics, those reproduced here do not always tally exactly and cannot be adequately explained; however, they do usefully highlight the three options open to refugees (whether CRTF-assisted or not). Furthermore, they illustrate the dilemma in choosing between them, and affirm some civilian refugees' reluctance to commit themselves to a course of action. As the following figures show, only approximately half of the refugees registered in each group participated in the survey, but for the Trust's own assessment purposes it surmised that the other half was like-minded.

Czechs and Slovaks

Of some 4,500 Czechs and Slovaks still registered with the Trust, only 1,700 (38 per cent) answered the Trust's letter and form of March 1945; of those who did so, 334 had 'Not decided'. Only 811 respondents expressly intended to return to Czechoslovakia, 378 preferred to remain in Britain if permitted, and 177 to emigrate elsewhere.

Sudetens

Of 2,978 registered Sudetens 1,625 (55 per cent) replied: although 285 remained undecided, 1,007 chose to return (possibly unaware of the situation in their home region, or planning to live elsewhere in Czechoslovakia), 226 to remain in Britain, and 107 to emigrate elsewhere.

Others

'Others' (unspecified, probably ethnic Hungarians, Russians, Ruthenians and other minorities, but like the Sudetens listed by the Trust under the overall heading 'Czechoslovaks'), surprisingly numbered 7,748 registered refugees, of whom 3,399 (44 per cent) responded. They, too, hesitated; 623 refugees wrote 'Not decided'. Nonetheless, it was proportionally the largest group opting to return, perhaps because the 1,875 refugees in question had nowhere else to go following border shifts, or preferred to stay on the familiar Czechoslovak side of a new border. 611 wished to remain in Britain, and 290 to emigrate elsewhere.[20]

Some Reich Germans and Austrians who had previously sheltered in Czechoslovakia, however, were not keen to return to their respective countries – barely 479 refugees of 1,860 then registered with the Trust. (This may seem questionable given the high percentage of political refugees who, it might be assumed, would wish to help reconstruct their homeland and resume their political activities there. It must be remembered, however, that a high proportion of these refugees were also Jewish, unwilling to return to societies that were and could still be hostile to them, and where reminders of family and friends who had died in the Holocaust would be too acute to endure).[21] Whilst CRTF group leaders helped refugees seeking Czechoslovak nationality in order to return to Czechoslovakia, Germans and Austrians were left to resolve their post-war repatriation problems through other channels, discussed in the House of Commons on 16 July 1946.[22]

20   TNA, HO 294/31, CRTF, Table of some refugees' repatriation intentions recorded in June–July 1945.
21   CRTF statistics re: German and Austrian refugees.
22   Hansard, House of Commons Official Report 425 H. C. DEB. 5 s., 'Austrian and German Refugees (Repatriation)', cols 1043–4, 16 July 1946, noted that application forms were available from the Control Office for Germany and Austria, Norfolk House, St James's Square, London.

These statistics unfortunately made no distinction between men and women, but were supplemented by another Trust table which did so: Approximate Tabulation of Registered Refugees from the Sudetenland As at 1st April 1945, Allocation of Breadwinners According to Family Units and Normal Types of Occupation. The Sudetens had been the core focus of the British Committee for Refugees from Czechoslovakia in 1938; in 1945 they were again deemed in need of special attention, albeit in different circumstances. Thus, though limited by geographic and time-scale factors, the data has provided a rare breakdown of a number of men and women from the region. Extrapolated statistics concerning women follow (probably excluding women no longer registered with the Trust due to marriage and permanent settlement in Britain):

Total number of women: 2,374
Age range: 21 to over 55
Marital status: Single: 202 (versus 560 men)
Married couples: 608
Couples with children or other dependents: 1,564
Breadwinners: the majority of women worked in diverse occupations,
      including industry and commerce.[23]

The largest group in all these sections was that of women aged 31 to 45, and would have included a number of this author's interviewees, rendering the table of particular interest and relevance to the study.

Logistical problems and policies

Repatriating citizens across war-ravaged Europe with its millions of refugees and people forcibly displaced for whatever reason was a massive and costly logistical task. While the over-arching policy centred

23   TNA, HO 294/31, with CRTF note, 12 April 1945.

on prisoners of war and concentration or forced labour camp survivors, the repatriation of exiles in Britain called for co-operation between the Home Office, CRTF and other charitable refugee entities and the Czechoslovak Government's Repatriation Department. The rate of repatriation, though, was determined by two interfacing factors: the limited availability of transport, which necessitated a 'priority schedule' of repatriates as set out in the Trust's summary dated 11 May 1945 of discussions with Czechoslovak embassy officials. Point 3, on priorities, categorically stated that 'selection will be made by the Repatriation Mission in London from the register of people who have applied to be repatriated'. It was carefully expanded in Point 4; the Mission would be responsible for 'organising the departure from the United Kingdom of people selected for return, and also the provision of transport to Czechoslovakia and for the custody of such baggage as does not accompany the traveller. The Government in Czechoslovakia will make all necessary arrangements for [the] reception and dispersal of people'.[24]

Primarily, military personnel and 'key people', mostly government and diplomatic staff-members and those 'to be directed to specific tasks by the Czechoslovak Government', were repatriated by the Czechoslovak government throughout spring and summer 1945.[25] Elisabeth Tauber was among the government employees flown home in a dakota in May 1945 approximately two weeks after the end of the war, while her husband, serving with the Czechoslovak Brigade High Command, was repatriated by the army.[26] They were all people who 'would be assured of paid employment immediately on arrival', therefore did not require CRTF resettlement grants. Dependents of 'key personnel' were the second priority. Thirdly, Czech/Slovak-speaking refugees with useful skills or experience (doctors, nurses and social workers were badly needed); a few business people were also repatriated early

---

24   TNA, HO 294/31, CRTF, summary of repatriation discussion with Czechoslovak embassy officials, 11 May 1945.
25   *Ibid.*
26   Tauber, AI.

and allowed to 'rebuild their businesses',[27] possibly including Anna
Abelesová, a Czech businesswoman who had never depended on the
CRTF, and wished to return to Prague.[28] Repatriation was not, however, automatically guaranteed. Point 7 left no doubt about the vetting
process: 'The general policy of the Czechoslovak Government is that
they will accept the application only of those who are considered to
have been loyal citizens; each case will be considered individually [...].
Applications from Czechoslovak nationals of German race [Sudetens]
will be subject to special scrutiny'.[29]

   There were, though, special cases for the CRTF to consider, too. Whilst
CRTF group leaders were not entitled to preferential repatriation, requests
in March 1945 for clothing and financial assistance for eight returning
helpers who had earlier lost earnings due to poor health, were channelled
via MP Anežka Hodinová of the Czech Group.[30] MP Karla Pfeiferová,
for instance, had chronic anaemia and could not work as a weaver, so had
helped the Czechoslovak Red Cross. Anna Mondok, an ethnic Hungarian
in the Beuer group, had been a volunteer worker in the Trust's clothing
department, receiving a maintenance allowance before working as a dressmaker at the Austrian Centre's Astu Studios Ltd earning £3 per week,
but suffered 'nervous shock' on the death of her fiancé. Some 172 unaccompanied minors constituted another special group under the Trust's
care as at 1 August 1945, of whom 140 were Czechoslovak nationals to be
repatriated.[31] As the Czechoslovak state boarding school in Britain would
not re-open after the summer vacation, thirty-four pupils aged under 18
needed to be repatriated in time to resume their education in the autumn
term. Though it was claimed that they all wished to be repatriated, the
Trust's problem was who, if anyone, would receive them. Consequently, it
was suggested that no child should return 'until there is a suitable private

27 TNA, HO 294/31, CRTF, repatriation discussion, *op. cit.*, 11 May 1945; see 'Discussion on Repatriation', 2, English supplement for BBWs, no. 7, *Čechoslovák* (June 1945).
28 NAP, *op. cit.*, file 2–1-1 to 2–1-11, Ab-Ad.
29 TNA, HO 294/31, CRTF, repatriation discussion, *op. cit.*, 11 May 1945.
30 *Ibid.*, CRTF, Repatriation. Individual cases, 28 March 1945.
31 *Ibid.*, CRTF, Repatriation of Unaccompanied Minors, 1 August 1945.

home ready to receive him/her'. Furthermore, 'in view of the unsettled and severe position in Czechoslovakia both politically and economically, children should not be allowed to return unless their parents wish it. This applies especially to Czech youngsters of German race or extraction'. By August 1945, news that the maltreatment and expulsion of ethnic Germans from eastern Czechoslovakia was becoming widespread, and not solely the random acts of ultra-nationalists as originally thought, helped to crystallize attitudes concerning deferred repatriation.[32] One Czechoslovak CRTF respondent observed that support from Jewish friends or family in Czechoslovakia could not be counted on, 'they will be either dead or unable to help us'; another was conscious that she spoke 'the Czech language only insufficiently', while a Sudeten man with a British wife and small child would seek British citizenship.[33] Although respondents to the Czechoslovak government's questionnaire included Germans and Austrians, Austrians were referred to an Association of Austrians Office, complicating matters for married women. Viennese Gisela Altschulová was a Czechoslovak army doctor's wife therefore a Czechoslovak citizen, and supported in Britain by the CRTF, but she could 'not make any decisions about repatriation', and sought to remain in Britain until her husband in France was demobbed 'because I should have nowhere to go in Czechoslovakia'.[34]

Departure from Britain

Co-ordinating the departure of those who did return to Czechoslovakia was likewise fraught with dilemmas, involving vaccinations against smallpox, typhoid and typhus, for example, at the Czechoslovak section of Hammersmith Hospital in London, resettlement allowances, subsidies for

---

32   *Ibid.*, CRTF, Intentions of Refugees Regarding Their Future, 7 August 1945.
33   *Ibid.*
34   NAP, *op. cit.*, inv. 918, file 2–1-12 to 2–1-21, k1, Ae-Al, sub-file 2–11/14–3, list 3.

suitable clothing especially in autumn and winter, transport, and luggage. Refugees had accumulated clothing and possessions in Britain, or transferred them from Czechoslovakia before WWII, thus, a Sudeten widow had 'a complete household'. Wartime nurse Marie Řehulková, returned to Prague in November 1945 with her British-born daughter but only 'regular' luggage, and re-joined her soldier husband.[35] Significantly, her Czechoslovak Repatriation Office Registration Certificate was printed in Czech, Russian and English – not a word in German. It was an ominous indication of things to come. Hedwig Huenigen also returned home permanently, after 'winding things down' at the Czechoslovak-British Friendship Club where she worked. She was 'included in the 4th Repatriation transport by boat and rail', leaving at the end of November via Belgium. Without special permission from the Bank of England repatriates, regardless of age, could take only £5 in £1 notes plus £10 in another currency. Personal luggage, she was instructed, was limited to '200 lbs of weight per person. 15 lbs of food not more than 2 lbs of each commodity and 2 lbs of soap are included in the 200 lbs', and she was advised to take food (still rationed) for seventy-two hours for the journey. While bomber aircraft were cold and uncomfortable but fast, journeys in overcrowded trains typically took several days, with bombed bridges and damaged rails causing major delays. Travellers in 1945 did indeed need an adequate supply of food, BBW Winifred Plocka recalled, and Hedy Froming's English aunt, Margaret Huenigen, found travel with a baby particularly trying; but just how difficult circumstances would be at their journey's end they had yet to discover.

35　　Marie Řehulková, AI.

Rejection and retribution

'Odsun' vs *'Vertreibung'*

Many repatriates were plunged into the vortex of a tense domestic political situation that was not of their making, and beyond their control, arriving while others were departing during the population counter-movements of 1945–6. Two works epitomize the opposing Czechoslovak and German perspectives of *'Odsun'* vs *'Vertreibung'* ['transfer' vs 'expulsion']: Radomír Luža's *The Transfer of the Sudeten Germans*,[36] and Theodor Schieder's *The Expulsion of the German Population From Czechoslovakia*.[37] These population 'transfers' have been a taboo subject in Czechoslovakia, where each party perceived itself as a victim of the other's aggression, but the internal turmoil and external influences of the period are increasingly documented in the country's historiography and examined in the ongoing discourse, facilitated by access to archive material in the freedom of the post-Communist era. The objective here is not to add to that controversial debate, but to contextualize it with an overview of developments before discussing the homecoming of individual female refugees.

The Potsdam Conference of 16 July to 2 August 1945 on post-war borders in Europe, and the transfer of Germans from territories east of Germany to Germany as agreed by Stalin, Roosevelt, Churchill and British Prime Minister Clement Attlee, had effectively legitimized the displacement of Reich and ethnic Germans, strategically 'corralled' and controlled to minimize a resurgence of German power in Europe (see map on p. vii; the shaded areas denote ethnic German settlements in the Sudetenland). It seemed the ultimate cleavage between ethnic Germans and Czechs or Slovaks in an era when the notion of the nation state, comprising one racially homogeneous nation sharing a common language and

36   Radomír Luža, *The Transfer of the Sudeten Germans, A Study of Czech German Relations, 1933–1962* (New York: New York University Press, 1964).
37   Theodor Schieder, ed., *The Expulsion of the German Population From Czechoslovakia* (Bonn: Federal Ministry for Expellees, Refugees and War Victims, 1960).

culture, was vigorously upheld – impracticable and complicated as it was in reality by mixed ethnic backgrounds and marriages. Czechoslovakia was thus not unique in its '*odsun*' of about 2.5 million of its *Volksdeutsche* minority,[38] nor in the manner in which it sometimes took place, contrary to Article XIII of the Agreement stipulating that transfers be carried out 'in an orderly and humane manner'.[39] Understandably though regrettably, resurgent ultra-nationalism was articulated verbally or expressed physically in extreme acts of revenge across post-WWII Europe, particularly in the immediate post-war months. Poland expelled some ethnic Czechoslovak Polish citizens, while minority groups were also expelled from other countries. The official measures taken in Czechoslovakia, but partly activated pre-Potsdam, were formulated and codified in a series of Decrees of the President of the Republic, collectively known as the Beneš Decrees. Prompted by wartime bitterness and fear of renewed irredentism post-war, these were wide-ranging and far-reaching; they targeted alleged ethnic German and Hungarian 'fifth columnists', Nazi collaborators and 'traitors' such as Jozef Tiso, President of wartime devolved Slovakia,[40] and established the jurisdiction of Special People's Courts and District National Committees to try them and pronounce the punishment deemed due. Lawyers like Frederick Gellner (interviewee Elisabeth Tauber's father) endeavoured to be just when sitting on the tribunals of ethnic Germans accused of disloyalty to the Czechoslovak state during WWII,[41] but the system was open to abuse through unfair accusations or personal vendettas, and like the British internment tribunals of 1940, the decisions reached could be very arbitrary.

38 Figures vary: 3 million according to some sources.
39 Art. XIII, Orderly Transfer of German Populations, that is, from Poland, Czechoslovakia and Hungary, approved 2 August 1945 by Stalin, Truman and Attlee, <http://potsdamer-konferenz.de/dokumente/protokoll_en.php#XIII>, accessed 31 May 2018.
40 Slovak National Council announced a separate retribution law, 15 May 1945, though retaining links with Prague, Benjamin Frommer, *National Cleansing* (Cambridge: Cambridge University Press, 2005), 64, 76–7.
41 Tauber, AI.

At Beneš's instigation, the Decrees emanated from plans drawn up much earlier in Britain by Jaroslav Stránský, then Minister of Justice in the Czechoslovak Government in exile. When Stránský's horrified daughter, Anna Sonnek, heard about them, she declared that 'they were inhuman'; he replied, 'inhuman but necessary'.[42] Ministers, however, did not unanimously support the harsh terms later favoured by Russia and reflected in President Beneš's Statute Issued in Košice, Slovakia: Programme of the New Czechoslovak Government [...] April 5 1945. Sections VIII and IX dealt explicitly with the German and Hungarian 'question', and it was these same precepts that had informed the Czechoslovak government's repatriation policy, discussed here earlier.[43] Rebutting criticism from 'abroad', the Czechoslovak government sought to justify its racial policies in a formal statement headed, 'The Germans and Hungarians in Czechoslovakia', published in *Čechoslovák's* July 1945 English supplement. Citing 'its desire to rid the country of these dangerous and hostile aliens', it added that Germans who had been loyal to the Republic and 'fought for her freedom' would be exempted from property confiscations.[44] The principle, however, was not always evident in practice.

The 'homecoming'

The 'homecoming' in numerous instances consequently failed to be a happy or even welcoming one, as portrayed by interviewees' experiences recounted here, and which accounted for their ultimate departure, together with a host of other reasons. Czechoslovakia had not been a 'Golden Age' for everyone inter-war, and was definitely not so post-war, whether people had remained in the country or not. An entrenched 'we stayed, suffered and fought while you left' attitude,

---

42   Anna Sonnek (Stránská), AI.
43   Wilhelm K. Turnwald, *Documents on the Expulsion of the Sudeten Germans* (Munich: University Press, 1953), Appendix VIII, *Collection of Documents, issued by the Ministry of Information, Publication No. 2/45*, 264–5.
44   'The Germans and Hungarians', no. 8, *Čechoslovák* (July 1945).

engendered resentment against the repatriates, creating a 'them and us' situation fuelled by Moscow-tutored Communists whose power steadily increased. That people had fled the Nazis was comprehended, but why to the 'Imperialist west rather than east to the Soviet Union?' was a burgeoning issue.[45] Despite minimal structural war damage compared with Britain or Germany, Czechoslovakia's economy was at base-level, sapped by Reich Germany for its own war effort, and Fascists had taken over the principal institutions during the Nazi occupation. Witnesses of both sexes described the 'dire' and 'wild west' situation, with strict food rationing including in restaurants (unlike even wartime Britain), a rampant 'black market' and shortage of work and accommodation, particularly in overcrowded Prague unable to cope with the influx of repatriates. Hedy Fromings and her Czechoslovak state boarding school friend, Susan Groag Bell, were flown to Prague in late August 1945 to attend a 'crash course' for their Czechoslovak *Maturita* [matriculation examination]. They spent the first night in a Young Men's Christian Association hostel, sleeping on mattresses on the floor alongside men and women with shaved heads, still in their striped concentration camp clothing. Soon afterwards, the girls were followed after a concert, and 'though conversing in English [or perhaps because of this], were threatened in the same way that Germans were', Fromings recalled.[46] 'It was all', Groag wrote later, 'a rude awakening'.[47]

Elisabeth Tauber also found her return to Czechoslovakia challenging. 'Some Czechoslovaks preferred those who fled east rather than west', thus she 'was not persecuted, but not welcomed, and for a short time was rebuffed'. Furthermore, 'there was hardly anyone left'; her husband's family had mostly perished in the Holocaust, and 'it was a great shock'. Nonetheless, she persevered, using her British Council training course in Czechoslovakia's 'devastating' Terezín to help rehabilitate

---

45   This did not consider the difficulties of reaching the USSR, or the risk of being apprehended en route and returned to Czechoslovakia.

46   Fromings, AI.

47   Susan Groag Bell, *Between Worlds* (New York, USA: Dutton, 1991), 139.

survivors,[48] supplying women (possibly including Heda Franks and her mother) with civilian clothes and dealing diplomatically with women's wishes to have the best ones, before establishing their identity and any family contacts so that they could prove who they were, where they had been during WWII, and crucially, obtain identity cards to draw rations for their continued survival (see Figures 21 and 22).[49]

Figure 21. Czechoslovak Repatriation Card issued to Heda Wernerová (later Franks) on release from Terezín, 1945. Courtesy of interviewee.

48   Tauber, AI.
49   Heda Franks, AI, PP.

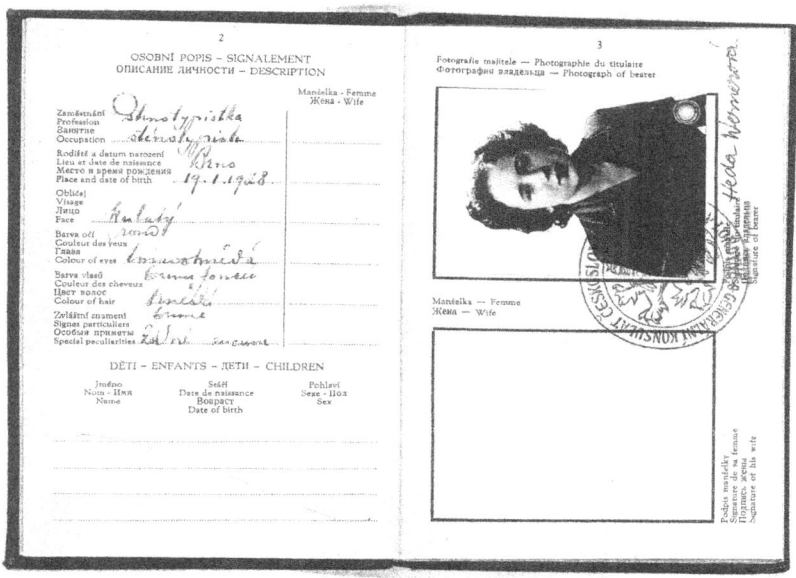

Figure 22. Extract from Heda Wernerová's (later Franks) passport, showing her photograph. Courtesy of interviewee.

Post-traumatic stress disorder had yet to be fully recognized and treated, and though there were some disturbing moments, Tauber was undeterred, only ending this work in December 1945 to give birth to her daughter. The Taubers 'did not starve, but there was very little food, despite the many fruit trees', so they were grateful for the food parcels from Britain. These, however, aroused the suspicion of the porter in the apartment block where the Taubers lived, and Elisabeth always 'felt that he was spying and report-ing on them' – which was most probably the case. She continued doing social work, yet felt increasingly 'uncomfortable, and homesick for Britain' where she still had a few friends. After six years in the Czechoslovak army, her husband worked as a scientist; he too felt 'an atmosphere'.

In 1945, Josef (Pepí) Horák, a pilot in the Czechoslovak air force in exile, returned to his home village, Lidice, after the Nazis had razed it to the ground on 10 June 1942, in retribution for the assassination of Deputy Reichsprotektor, Reinhard Heydrich. Despite having been informed in

Britain by his friend Václav Student of the execution of some 173 men and
boys aged over 15 against a wall of the Horák family's farm, he was deeply
shocked by what he saw. Horák's English wife Winifred joined him in
nearby Kladno, and tried hard to console him, as previously, but 'people in
Lidice called him a murderer', erroneously blaming him for their suffering
at a time when he had been serving in Britain, unconnected with either the
assassination plot or the Czechoslovak resistance movement as alleged by
the Nazis. Plocka herself (then Horáková) was 'blamed for Chamberlain's
misbehaviour' over the 1938 Munich Agreement. Moreover, she had two
sons, the first babies in Lidice since the reprisals.[50] Whilst this was ostensibly a reason to rejoice, it was outweighed by the wartime removal of 105
Lidice children, most of whom had been gassed in Chelmno concentration camp; nine were selected for 'Germanization' because of their Aryan
appearance, and only seventeen were traced and returned to Lidice through
the efforts of two Lidice mothers, the President's wife, Hana Benešová
and two policemen. The jealousy and resentment directed against Plocka
by certain Lidice mothers who had survived Ravensbruck concentration
camp (143 of some 200) was therefore intense.[51] These circumstances
were particularly painful as Plocka's own sister-in-law, Anička, had had
her baby taken away after her birth in Ravensbruck, never to be returned
or traced.[52] Plocka attended the trial, though not the public execution by
hanging on 22 May 1946, of Sudeten German Nazi Karl Hermann Frank,
Deputy Minister of the Protectorate of Bohemia and Moravia, for his role
in organizing the executions in Lidice and Ležáky.

Plocka found it 'an extremely lonely life' in Kladno. 'Very drunken
Russian soldiers' were still in the area in 1945, so gates were locked against
them for safety, and people lived off the land as much as possible. Some
people were friendly, and neighbours helped her do her shopping as 'everything was on coupons' and she could not speak Czech. The only other
English woman there was half-Jewish, married to a Jewish man, and they

50 Plocka, AI.
51 'History of Lidice Village', <http://www.lidice-memorial.cz/en/memorial/
    memorial-and.../history-of-the-village-lidice/>, accessed 31 May 2018.
52 Plocka, AI.

could occasionally meet and shop together. There was little else to enable her to socialize; a small English club which included two local shopkeepers, the miners' balls and a group of women who sang, which she joined. Josef met his friends and discussed shifts in Czechoslovak politics that Plocka was unaware of: 'I was sorry I hadn't opened that book from Josef to learn Czech' when still in Britain, she stated ruefully, 'I was too busy caring for the children'. She did, though, gradually learn to cook the Czech way, helped by the aunt of Josef Stříbrný, the other Lidice man who had served in the RAF during WWII but was, like Horák, nonetheless accused of causing the atrocities, as well as the deaths of most members of their respective families as an extra punishment meted out by the Nazis. Although extended family members helped Plocka with the children, unused to Czech food as she was, and under considerable strain, she fell ill. 'What's wrong with this English woman – can't cook, skate, ski people asked Pepí, but he treated me as if he was my father and suggested that I go home to visit my mother', she recalled. When he applied for a visa on her behalf, however, her Czechoslovak passport was confiscated.[53] Retribution took many forms, at many levels.

Treatment of ethnic German, Communist and Jewish repatriates

The prevailing Czechoslovak attitude was that 'the only good German was a dead one', Hedy Fromings (formerly Huenigen) remembered clearly,[54] but that ethnic German citizens could simultaneously be Jewish (by birth if not conviction), Communist or Social Democrat and loyal to Czechoslovakia, did not seem to register strongly with the general populace. 'Miraculously', her non-Jewish family was reunited in 1945 in Ruprechtice, near Liberec in the Sudetenland; however, life would never be as it was inter-war. The local

---

53   Plocka, AI.
54   Fromings, AI.

Hitler Jugend [youth group] had used the family home as a hostel, turning part of the garden into a parade ground complete with flagpole. Hedwig Huenigen, the staunch Communist and active supporter of women's groups, ever keen to use the social care training and experience gained in Britain for the benefit of her compatriots, was told by them that her help was not needed. Her husband, former MP Edmund Huenigen, was repatriated from Germany's Flossenburg forced labour camp, thus also had 'strong credentials' regarding his loyalty to Czechoslovakia. He and his brother, Gerhard, spent much time during 1945–7 in the Liberec Antifa (stemming from *Antifaschismus*) office dealing with appeals against expulsion, or the confiscation of property. Edmund took up cases of known ethnic German Communists, Social Democrats and anti-Nazis he believed were wrongly assessed as Fascists, and travelled to the Communist Party HQ in Prague to 'demand the right' of these appellants to stay in Czechoslovakia and retain their property – support that was viewed unfavourably by extreme nationalists or 'Czech opportunists'. The government's official apology to 'those who suffered wrongs' due to 'inappropriately applied measures' during this dangerous period was not offered until 2005.

Fromings rationalized and adopted a philosophical outlook. Nevertheless, at college in Liberec in 1946 people appeared to her 'parochial and hostile, jealous of my clothes obtained with coupons in Britain, and a very stylish handbag from the USA which I was accused of flaunting', she recalled. 'There was an atmosphere', and she did not feel part of things: 'why did you return after being pampered in Britain? Don't tell us what to do!'[55] Most educational establishments had been closed after Heydrich's assassination, and the universities were full in autumn 1946, so she worked for the British Council which had opened in Prague, then commenced studies in autumn 1947 at the prestigious Academy of Arts, Architecture and Design in Prague, winning one of only eleven available places due to limited resources. Having seen so much destruction during WWII in Britain, and been influenced by the work of Elizabeth Denby, one of the few women architects of the time, Fromings had decided to

55   Fromings, AI.

become an architect. 'Told that I was German I still felt an outsider but [...] informed everyone that my parents considered themselves Czechoslovak citizens, and later it was better, the students became more friendly'. 'One must step back and view the situation at two levels: "grass roots" and the official level, versus propaganda', Fromings declared.

'Everyone in Fortis Green [CRTF] hostel wanted to return to Czechoslovakia', stated Věra Vohlídalová, daughter of former resident Markéta/Marga Tomášková, an ethnic German Communist from the Jablonec region in northern Bohemia, but after the war 'we could not speak Czech, so we felt very alone. All mother's relatives were away.' Vohlídalová's uncle was an expert glassmaker 'and could stay', whereas 'an aunt was sent to a camp in Mladá Boleslav for expelled Germans. My mother and friends watched'. After leaving the hostel in 1944, Marga's husband, Alois, became a United Nations Relief and Rehabilitation Administration (UNRRA) officer in a Displaced Persons (DP) camp in Mannheim, Germany, and did not return to Czechoslovakia until November 1946. Vohlídalová's parents none- theless 'lost work and friends', who were increasingly 'afraid to speak to them and avoided them in the street' as Germans and émigrés who had spent WWII "in the west"' (similarly from August 1968 to the 1989 'Velvet Revolution' because they opposed the invasion and occupation of Czechoslovakia by Warsaw Pact forces). Vohlídalová was therefore 'very pleased that her parents wanted their children to be cosmopolitan and tolerant'; it was her parents' 'philosophical way of moving forward, not through hatred'.[56]

Anti-German sentiments nevertheless permeated all strata of Czechoslovak society, with a widespread lack of sympathy for Jews, many of whom had identified themselves as German in the pre-war official census, and were solely German-speaking, hence endeared themselves to neither Czechoslovaks nor Soviet Russians. The 'Germanization' of the Austro- Hungarian Empire's subjects had included Jews, broadening their education and resulting in the Jewish attachment to German culture with an inherent belief in its racial and class superiority over Slavs, but this 'boomeranged' on them negatively. Groag Bell, among others, was refused employment on

---

56   Věra Vohlídalová (Tomášková), AI.

giving her nationality as German, instead of Czech. In some instances, Jewish repatriates from concentration camps were, like non-Jewish ethnic Germans, obliged to wear white armbands with the letter 'N' for '*Němec*' [German] to mark them out,[57] and 2,000 Jews were not reinstated as Czechoslovak citizens until 1947.[58] In addition, 'as more and more women returned from the concentration camps, with shaved heads, emaciated and in rags, how could one understand or relate to them?' Fromings commented, though not unsympathetic.[59] Catholic fellow Czechoslovak school pupil Franci Dražil, repatriated in 1946 as a 15-year-old, remembered having 'guilt feelings' on seeing the returnees.[60] The difference between German and Czech-speaking Jewish refugees repatriated from Britain, like Groag Bell, and those repatriated from concentration camps, appears to have been blurred: their loyalty to Czechoslovakia was disputed, their return doubly unwelcome according to numerous accounts, where Jews requested the restitution of their or their family's possessions and/or property. According to US Records, of some 120,000 Jews from Bohemia and Moravia, only 10,000 survived WWII, and 10,000–15,000 of approximately 90,000 Slovak Jews survived.[61]

Ethnic Czechoslovaks and revised borders

Ethnic Czechoslovaks, like Russian Orthodox Christian, Nina Dobosharevich, who had been living in Poland before WWII and were distinguished by their Czech dialect, could also encounter problems when repatriated to

---

57   The policy was not uniformly implemented, and only for a short period, hence some denials of it.
58   Bernard Wasserstein, *Vanishing Diaspora* (London: Hamish Hamilton, 1996), 38–40.
59   Fromings, AI.
60   Franci Dražil (Šmolká/Schmolka), AI.
61   'US National Archives and Records Administration, Records of the Foreign Service Posts of the Department of State (RG 84) Czechoslovakia', <http://www.archives.gov/research/holocaust/finding-aid/civilian/rg-84-czech.html>, accessed 31 May 2018.

Czechoslovakia. Despite the fact that her grandmother and other family members had not left Czechoslovakia, that her Polish-born brother was a serving officer in the Czechoslovak Army in Czechoslovakia, and despite her own loyal wartime service with the Czechoslovak section of British Auxiliary Territorial Service (ATS) in the Middle East, Dobosharevich 'had difficulties with the Czechoslovak authorities' who initially did not recognize her as a Czech. These were finally resolved by General Andrej Gak, responsible for Czechoslovak recruitment in the Middle East, who vouched for her.[62] Czechoslovaks of all backgrounds, however, returned to a diminishing territory, contrary to Article 6 of the 8 May 1944 agreement with the USSR that Soviet-liberated territory would revert to Czechoslovak control. President Beneš's plans to reinstate Czechoslovakia's pre-Munich borders were unravelling,[63] causing yet more DPs.

(Re)migration: Last migration periods, 1945–1946 and 1948–1950

The potent combination of radical internal policies buttressed by the Beneš Decrees and external pressures from the fiercely anti-German USSR with its embedded Communist agenda, acted as a watershed for the last periods of forced migration from Czechoslovakia within the time span of this study. These occurred during two specific periods, 1945–6 and 1948–50, and were distinct in nature, hence are discussed separately below, but both were rooted in the war, both remain 'scars' in modern Czechoslovak history and collective memory. Unlike 1938–9, however, there was no British Committee for Refugees from Czechoslovakia or other charitable entities to rescue women directly from Czechoslovakia. The reasons and means by which women (re)entered Britain

---

62   Nina Dobosharevich, AI.
63   TNA, FO 371/46811, Interview, President Beneš to Reuter's Correspondent in Prague,
      11 July 1945, with covering note from British Delegation in Prague, 23 July 1945.

from 1945 to 1950 therefore differed considerably, and for ease of reference are divided into expellees, escapees, re-émigrées and those entering for other reasons.

1945– 1946: Expellees, Britain via Germany

Post-war repatriation and the parallel expulsions from Czechoslovakia were largely completed by the end of 1946.[64] Neither process was clear cut though; the quagmire of disputed data based on differing criteria or periods and from conflicting sources, is compounded by unregistered outward population movements. It is even more difficult to ascertain figures specifically about women, but Schechtman's survey provides two insights:

(a) a transport of 4,200 women, children and aged people left Troppau (Opava) in Silesia for Berlin in late August 1945 and
(b) Jan Masaryk's summary of 24 October 1945, noted that the circa 2,500,000 ethnic Germans scheduled to be transferred included 1,010,000 women aged thirteen to sixty, and 172,000 women over sixty years-old.[65]

In principle, German-speaking wives of Czechoslovak men and their children were not subject to expulsion, and Czechoslovak Ministry of the Interior statistics as at 8 October 1946, presented a total of 2,165,135 ethnic Germans officially expelled: 1,415,135 to Germany's American zone, and 750,000 to the Soviet zone, both bordering Czechoslovakia. An estimated 300,000 'Germans' remained in Czechoslovakia, but by 1948 most of them, Prauser and Rees posited, had left Czechoslovakia for Germany, 'fearing further persecution following the rise to power of the Communists'.[66]

64   Jaroslav Vaculik, 'Post-War Repatriation of Czechoslovak Persons', *Historica* vol, 11 (Institute of History, Prague, 2004), 139–40.
65   Joseph B. Schechtman, *Postwar Population Transfers in Europe 1945–1955* (London: University of Pennsylvania Press, 1962), 73, 76.
66   Steffen Prauser and Arfon Rees, eds, *The Expulsion of the 'German' Communities From Eastern Europe at the End of the Second World War*, EUI Working Paper HEC

That *Volksdeutsche* women who identified closely with German society and culture should then move to victorious post-war Britain seems an anomaly, yet strong 'push factors' can be deduced from Julius Isaac's study of assimilation problems in bankrupt West Germany. Discrimination was prevalent against destitute Czechoslovak *Volksdeutsche* refugees, 'treated by the native population as unwelcome intruders and as a group with inferior social status'[67] (as were some refugees in Britain 1938–9). The *Volksdeutsche* women who left Czechoslovakia during the mayhem of 1945–6 and finally settled in Britain had not all envisaged leaving Czechoslovakia permanently, but they constitute an inseparable strand of this work on forced female migration from Czechoslovakia by physical or psychological means, and cannot be 'airbrushed' away. It is fitting that their 'voices' be heard within a Czechoslovak context, thereby adding another dimension to the discourse. Thus, three very contrasting *Volksdeutsche* interviewees confronted by their own sense of identity versus that perceived by others, recounted their difficulties, attitudes and reception in Britain.

Dorothea Koehler, a devout ethnic German Catholic from Silesia's Těšín (Teschen) region described herself as 'pro Czech'. Her father had 'kept faith with the Czechoslovak state and was on the side of the hard-fighting Czechs', so he was allowed to remain in Czechoslovakia after WWII, but dual Czech/German usage was no longer acceptable. Not speaking Czech nor feeling able to learn it adequately for employment purposes, he and the family reluctantly 'went voluntarily' to Thüringen in Germany's Soviet zone in April 1946. Reflecting the age- gap, 'the situation went very deep' for Koehler's parents; for Dorothea it was 'an adventure'. Exceptionally, the 'Marshall Zhukov Aktion Agreement' allowed anti-Fascist German émigrés to transport half a railway wagon

No. 2004/1 (European University Institute, Florence), 18–20, <http://cadmus.eui.eu/bitstream/handle/1814/2599/HEC04-01.pdf?sequence= 1>, accessed 31 May 2018.

67   Julius Isaac, 'Problems of Cultural Assimilation Arising From Population Transfers in Western Germany', *Population Studies*, vol. 3: *Cultural Assimilation of Immigrants: Supplement* (March 1950), 23–37.

of furniture and personal belongings;[68] in Germany, however, 'people were hungry' and could offer new arrivals little help. The Anglophile Dorothea had been a trainee stenographer for the daily *Deutsche Post* in Czechoslovakia and found work in Germany, but in 1948, aged 24, she joined an uncle married to an English woman and living in Trinity Church Square in Borough, London. 'I had come to a free country and liked everything!' Koehler quickly 'found her feet', settling with a Christian couple in Golders Green, where she was taught English and read many English books; although without English friends, she 'was not accused of being a German'. At the bomb-damaged Catholic Church in Whitechapel, a small weekly club provided a service held by a German priest and tea for about ten girls, all in domestic employment, nursing or factory work. Some of Koehler's acquaintances 'were quite nationalistic and critical of Britain, very, very German in outlook though not dangerously so'. The depth of her own feelings was expressed in 'an act of atonement', when she apologized to a Slovak priest 'for all the wrong that has been done [by Germany] to provoke Czechoslovakia' from 1938, about which she 'felt guilty as an ethnic German. Sudetenland was part of Czechoslovakia – you can't get away from it' she asserted. In time, she went on her 'pilgrimage to the Abbey at Aston Abbotts out of admiration for Beneš' to see where he lived and to symbolically reaffirm her loyalty to Czechoslovakia. Although Koehler did not wish to return permanently to Czechoslovakia as 'there is nothing there now' for her, she retained 'tender memories – not painful but joyful memories of times past', and has never regretted coming to Britain. Appreciated by her long-term employers who provided for her in their will, and in turn valuing 'the feeling of tolerance', she duly obtained British citizenship and felt 'very British, with my budgies and milk tea!'[69]

In a counter-narrative to Koehler's, Maria Stanzl, also a staunch Catholic from the Těšín region, held to her German origin.[70] Nonetheless, she 'never thought that she would leave Czechoslovakia'. 'There was no

68   Confirmed in Schechtman, *op. cit.*, 85.
69   Dorothea Koehler, AI.
70   Maria Stanzl, AI.

time to think over why or wherefore!' Her sister had overheard Czech farm workers in September 1945 saying that all Germans would be 'thrown out or placed in concentration camps – and we were [ethnic] German, educated in German'. She 'could not speak Czech and did not consider it culturally worthy', but whilst her parents had been expelled in August 1945, Stanzl 'could not imagine such a thing happening' to her. Pretending to go on a pilgrimage, the sisters obtained permission to leave the village, still wearing their 'N' armbands. 'I expected to go home to Vienna to *our* Reich. I had always hoped to see *the real homeland*. We were *very Österreichisch!*' ['Austrian'; Stanzl's emphasis]. Crossing into the Russian then the American zone, however, they were 'disappointed by the Americans' attitude'. 'Why didn't the Allies do something about the expulsions?' the dislocated Stanzl asked, 'people could have lived together if the Beneš Decrees hadn't been introduced'. Though this was plainly speculative, Stanzl's views 'were based on Christian morality, not politics. How can people treat others with such inhumanity?' She finally helped on a farm in impoverished, unwelcoming Austria, before arriving in London in January 1947 recruited, like some 20,000 German women by December 1951, via commercial agencies or private individuals to meet demands by British households, despite the recent hostilities.[71] Aged 22, Stanzl became a governess in Kensington, London, praying and singing to the children in German, but was unexpectedly given notice, and as a parlour maid in the Richmond home of a British Brigadier and his wife, was very lonely. Not until Stanzl lived and worked with the Dentzers, cleaning and sewing, was there 'plenty of love and laughter. The misery was soon forgotten' through walks in Kensington Gardens and visits with her employers to the German Club in Kilburn, with its organized outings to other cities and 'educational evenings' about Britain. These events reflected efforts made during 1948–50 via clubs, hostels, churches and charities, to inform émigrés about the 'British way of life' and draw them into it (just as the British Council had done in wartime). Ministry of Labour booklets in joint German/English, *To Help You Settle*

---

71   Inge Weber-Newth and Johannes-Dieter Steinert, *German Migrants in Post-war Britain. An Enemy Embrace* (London: Routledge, 2006).

in Britain, were distributed through the same channels.[72] Stanzl attended English classes, but did not make many English friends. On the other hand, she 'did not experience animosity being German-speaking', and became a British citizen in the 1970s.

Of these three *Volksdeutsche* interviewees, Maria Gokorsch from Mähren (Moravia Silesia/Polish border) was the only one to be expelled – by the Red Army in 1946.[73] From April and May 1945 the town hall issued 'N' armbands, and 'having seen Jews wearing armbands we found that shocking' Gokorsch recalled; then in May 1946 there were 'verbal announcements concerning the Beneš Decrees'. Her civil servant father was sent to a forced labour camp in the USSR, while other ethnic Germans were expelled by soldiers at very little notice, street-by-street, district-by-district, using lists from the town hall. Allowed only 25 kilograms of luggage per person, 'or more realistically what one could physically carry', Gokorsch's mother took the lead in the forced absence of her husband, packing practical items – duvet, cutlery and cooking pots. Maria and her sister packed their most useful clothes and small mementos. But how does one select which portable mementos to take in a great hurry? And does one mourn for articles perforce left behind? David Parkin discusses their significance in *Mementoes as Transitional Objects in Human Displacement* [*sic*].[74] In the face of such emotional and physical disruption to their lives, families 'clung together'; thus grandmother, mother and daughters, overseen by Russian soldiers, were sent on a three-day journey to Germany in packed open cattle-wagons, but 'were grateful to be alive [...] many, many people had committed suicide' fearing Soviet brutality. Nevertheless, life in Hessen in the American zone held little promise for the future, so when in 1947

---

72   *Ibid.*, 49.

73   Maria Gokorsch, AI; military historian Eduard Stehlík advised although most Soviet soldiers had officially left Czechoslovakia in 1945, 'it was very possible as an exception' that Gokorsch and others were expelled by Soviet soldiers in 1946; they regularly crossed the Czechoslovak border, were closely involved in Poland's claim regarding Těšín, and had a forced labour camp near the Soviet/Polish border.

74   David Parkin, 'Mementoes as Transitional Objects in Human Displacement', in *Journal of Material Culture*, 4:3 (1999), 303–20.

'well-off' relatives in Austria wrote that the situation was better there and offered to obtain permission for Gokorsch to stay with them, she readily agreed, but was 'treated as a servant, like Cinderella'.

European Voluntary Workers scheme

Gokorsch subsequently joined the European Voluntary Workers (EVW) scheme.[75] As in 1938–9, Britain boosted its labour force in selected services and industries, while providing refugee women with a means of escape from hunger and unemployment. The prospect of legal entry into Britain and the right to work, albeit in restricted posts, particularly drew women marooned in the 'no-man's land' of DP camps across Germany and Austria. From 1948 on, 1,304 German female refugees from the Sudetenland were recruited under the 'Westward Ho!' project for the cotton industry in Lancashire,[76] and 192 Czechoslovak displaced women volunteers arrived in Britain between October 1946 and December 1949.[77] Numerous Czechoslovaks with predominantly Slav names, however, were erroneously recorded as 'Jugo-Slavs', causing yet more confusion regarding Czechoslovak refugees.[78] Healthy volunteers (EVWs) aged 21 to 40 had free transport to their respective places of employment, 95 per cent of which were in the textile industry or domestic positions, the snags being that EVWs could not bring family members, and had to remain in post for three years or repay the fare:[79] like

75 Gokorsch, AI.

76 Johannes-Dieter Steinert, 'British Post-War Migration Policy and Displaced Persons in Europe', in Jessica Reinisch and Elizabeth White, eds, *The Disentanglement of Populations* (Basingstoke/New York: Palgrave Macmillan, 2011), 229–47 (here 235).

77 Diana Kay and Robert Miles, 'Refugees or Migrant Workers? The Case of the European Volunteer Workers in Britain (1946–1951)', *Journal of Refugee Studies*, vol. 1, nos 3, 4 (1988), 214–36.

78 TNA, HO 213/943, EVW scheme, Czechoslovaks.

79 Kay and Miles, *op. cit.*

Gokorsch though, many volunteers settled in Britain permanently. Aged 20, she reached Bradford, Yorkshire, in 1949, and later spoke very positively of her time there – 'it was an adventure'. 'Everything was so organized, and the Women's Voluntary Service tea-trolleys at railway stations provided an introduction to English biscuits and tea with milk'.[80]

EVWs at Gokorsch's placement were accommodated two to a room and cared for by a matron in the mill's comfortable hostel. After three weeks' training, Gokorsch was fully employed from 7 a.m. to 5 p.m. on piecework, weaving, as she wrote to her parents, 'the finest worsted cloth in England', and earning over £4 per week (rising to £6 after six to nine months for 'urgent export order work' involving better quality material), from which she paid around £1 at the hostel for lodging and 'good food'. She was made 'very very welcome' by colleagues. 'Everyone was treated equally by the overlooker of looms even when looms broke down' and awaited repair, 'but when English workers stopped for tea and a cigarette, émigré(e) workers continued, to earn extra money'. Gokorsch was fortunate, it seems, for according to Weber-Newth and Steinert, Sudeten German EVWs 'experienced more discrimination than any other groups of EVWs', facing 'resentment and animosity [...] from both the British population and other foreign workers', causing some women to 'fall back' on their Czechoslovak identity, or leave the mills as soon as possible. One EVW wrote of her short stay in the Hyde Park hostel, London, in January 1949, 'The welcome was awful, because Polish and Czech women work at this hostel, and these did not like us at all'.[81] Such tensions are partly attributable to WWII, but Sudeten German women were also a physical reminder of Chamberlain's disastrous 1938 appeasement policy over the Sudetenland issue, of which both Czechoslovaks and the British public would have been conscious, to the extent that 'where possible, the [British] government avoided publicly announcing the nationality of the women'.

Following a Ministry of Labour conference on 5 November 1948 to discuss the moderation of inter-racial friction between European migrants, regional newspapers encouraged British families to befriend

30   Gokorsch, AI.
31   Weber-Newth and Steinert, *op. cit.*, 86, 107–8, 186.

EVWs portrayed as lonely DPs, notably in Lancashire and Yorkshire,[82] possibly prompting Gokorsch's invitation to Sunday afternoon 'high tea' in an English colleague's terrace house.[83] It was a new experience. 'We were apprehensive as we came from Germany; we never spoke German in town, we didn't provoke anyone'. Puzzled, she observed that her hosts had a 'front room' with upholstered furniture, but an outside toilet – the reverse of at home!' Noting 'the doilies and nicely laid table', Gokorsch was amazed by the array of food offered despite rationing – ham, cold roast beef left from lunch, cakes, jelly, fruit salad and biscuits. When thanking her hosts but declining any more food, she mistakenly stated that she was 'fed up' instead of 'full': 'nobody corrected me, not a murmur, unlike Germans'. Despite various kindnesses, Gokorsch 'suddenly felt an outsider. English people did not understand refugee life'. She tried hard to learn English in evening classes using the standard booklet *English for Foreigners*, but always spoke German in the hostel, so responded to a Bradford relief teacher's advertisement for a companion, with light housework in return for 'a nice room', and dispelled the teacher's initial reluctance to accept a foreigner. Gokorsch later moved to London, embarking on a new career. Meanwhile, developments in Czechoslovakia were creating many more women refugees.

1948–1950 escapees: Britain via Austria and Germany

Astute observers in Czechoslovakia and Britain noted shifts in political ideology which aroused concern for the future, and proceeded with caution, or decided against repatriation after the free parliamentary election on 26 May 1946. President Beneš was re-elected, but Klement Gottwald became the first Communist Prime Minister, strengthening Communist power. The Communist coup occurred on 25 February 1948.

82   *Ibid.*, 45–7.
83   Gokorsch, AI.

On 10 March 1948 Jan Masaryk, Minister for Foreign Affairs, died in suspicious circumstances, and on 7 June 1948 President Beneš was obliged to resign for the second time, succeeded on this occasion by Gottwald (see Chronology). When Beneš's government courted Soviet support during WWII, it had done so in the expectation of duly governing Czechoslovakia with its own liberal form of socialism, not that of a hard-line Moscow diktat, but the USSR's apparent magnanimity was underpinned by expansionist objectives resulting in the 'Communist Bloc' of satellite countries, including Czechoslovakia, which became a security buffer between Soviet Russia and West Germany. With Czechoslovakia in the USSR's thrall, repatriates and BBWs had barely settled in when they were unnerved by these developments, and as Dražil recounted, 'people started being afraid in 1948';[84] some feared being trapped in Czechoslovakia, some feared for their lives, others were arrested, yet others ominously 'disappeared'. Prospects of an enlightened 'new postwar world' became a mirage under the new authoritarian regime.

In contrast to the 1945–6 forced migration period based on German and Hungarian ethnicity, 1948–50 escapees were principally, though not exclusively, Slav 'politicals' (accompanied if possible by their families). At the cohort's core were political activists, Beneš supporters, Social Democrats, 'Western Communists' plus servicemen/women who had served in Britain not the USSR during WWII, hence were targeted as 'imperialist traitors'. They were joined by intellectuals and scientists such as Gerta Vrbová,[85] artists and writers who found restrictions to freedom of expression intolerable and feared persecution for 'not toeing the party line'. Anyone removed from post as 'politically unreliable' understood that her or his career was blighted. Zdeňka Pokorná, the outspoken headmistress of a school in Břeclav, Moravia, was demoted to teacher, then sent to a village school in Hrušky. After helping others to escape, she herself had to flee to Austria in July 1948.[86] There was also a cross-section of nationals who did not openly resist the new regime, yet were disillusioned and

84   Dražil(ová), AI.
85   Gerta Vrbová, *Betrayed Generation* (Kings Lynn, UK: Zuza Books, 2010).
86   Zdeňka Pokorná, AI.

feared what they might have to endure under it. The wrench of uprooting so soon after WWII reflects the degree of desperation. In addition to 'first timers', numerous Czechoslovak nationals fled for the third time, having escaped from the Sudetenland to rump Czechoslovakia, then to Britain, and subsequently back again. If caught, even apolitical escapees were punished on the ground of imputed political opinion. Unauthorized departures were illegal and deemed a rejection of the status quo, potentially leading to active opposition to the Communist regime by those in exile: the 'Cold War' had begun. Subsequent re-settlement in a free country was far from immediate however, and what linked post-war escapees and expellees at this juncture was the grim interim refugee and DP camp experience, described by Sylva Šimsová.[87]

Like Šimsová and her Social Democrat parents, the majority of escapees relied on clandestine contacts to escape on foot at night in small groups, carrying minimum luggage without incriminating photographs of family or friends. With the Soviets entrenched in East Germany by 1948, any Czechoslovak escapees discovered there were forcibly repatriated: 1,100 Czechoslovaks therefore escaped to Austria, but most fled to West Germany. Conditions in refugee camps there were notorious, especially in German-administered camps in the American zone, where refugees were reported to be starving.[88] This caused Ernest Bevin, Secretary of State for Foreign Affairs, to comment in May 1948 that an estimated 2,000–3,000 refugees were sheltering in the British zone, with 7,000–10,000 in the American zone, while some 200 more refugees arrived each day, many of whom applied to enter or return to Britain. 'A first impulse', Bevin stated, is to 'let the I. R. O. [International Refugee Organization] solve the problem', but added, 'I feel nevertheless, that something will have to be done to help this enterprising, and, on the whole, most deserving class of refugees'.

87   Sylva Šimsová, 'Taking up life as a refugee 1949–1950: The decision to go into exile', *British Czech and Slovak Review* (October/November 2011), 6–8.

88   TNA, HO 294/5: History of the CRTF, Report on Czechoslovak Refugees, undated, around 1948/9.

Resettlement in Britain

Czech Refugee Trust Fund, post-war role

How to rescue Czechoslovaks stranded in refugee camps – not uncommonly for years rather than months while competing for entry into a third country and subject to increasingly stringent quotas and visa requirements often conditional upon employment – was a major problem, though the reason for their predicament in part provided the remedy. Political developments in 1948 Czechoslovakia obliged the British government to retain the new £1 million balance[89] of its 1939 Grant to Beneš's (now dissolved) government, as 'there could be no question of releasing money from a refugee fund to a government whose policy was creating refugees in large numbers'.[90] Arguments over the Fund's future use rested on the CRTF's remit: legal definitions of 'refugee' and time frames were examined and interpreted. 'There is no express reference to refugees from Nazi oppression', concluded the Treasury's Principal Assistant Solicitor, R. W. A. Speed, which allowed Trustees and the Secretary of State to include refugees from the Communist regime if they so wished.[91] Parliamentary pressure helped override Treasury opposition, and in November 1948, the Secretary of State directed that the Trust's remit be widened to include the 'new' post-war refugees. The government was also willing to admit from Germany and Austria all Czechoslovak citizens who had a former association of any substance with Britain; those who had lived and worked here during the war, had British-born wives or close relatives here, and those who had served with the Allied armed forces. Furthermore, 'Students, businessmen,

---

89   TNA, HO 213/983: Secretary of State document, 30 April 1948, three-quarters of a million pounds sterling were set aside from the balance for future expenditure by the Trust, for example, refugees remaining in Britain after the war, leaving £1 million.
90   TNA, HO 294/5: History of the CRTF, Introduction to the Fund, undated.
91   TNA, HO 213/982: letter, R. W. A. Speed, Principal Assistant Solicitor, Office of H. M. Procurator General and Treasury Solicitor, to a Mrs M. D. Montgomery, 22 April 1948.

diplomats and Olympic Games competitors – who were unwilling to return' would be granted asylum in Britain. They too were assisted by the CRTF, without neglecting the 'old' (Nazi era) refugees.[92] Between December 1948 and December 1949, 1,281 'new' refugees registered with the Trust with a further 1,020 in 1950.[93] The number of maintained refugees then rose from 290 as at 31 March 1948, to 540 by March 1949 and 433 in 1950.

The broadened British immigration policy and CRTF remit greatly facilitated entry into Britain and support thereafter, but subsequent reports rarely distinguish between Czechoslovak post-war 'first timers' and re-émigrés to Britain, nor explain how they came except in individual case files, which mostly (to date) remain closed under the Data Protection Act. Interviewees' accounts therefore helped reconstruct the means, roughly categorized as follows:

   a. direct from Czechoslovakia, helped by friends, family or associates at home or abroad (especially BBWs, or refugees still holding a valid visa for Britain).
   b. via the EVW scheme.
   c. assisted by other organizations and charities dealing with refugees in Europe or family reunion.
   d. through marriage to a British citizen.
   e. authorized visits to Britain on business or other pretexts.
   f. temporary entry into Britain when migrating to another country (or supposedly doing so).

Like their predecessors, most 'new' and re-émigrés preferred to be in London, but heavy bombing had left severe housing shortages. The CRTF's additional role from 1949 as a 'non-rapacious landlord' was therefore as vital to them as it was to the dependent 'old' Nazi era refugees who had remained in Britain. Instead of organizing hostels as in WWII, up to March 1955 the Trust purchased some forty-five buildings in the Greater London area, converting them into over 150 furnished flats rented out at only 80 per cent of the commercial rate, less in cases of acute hardship.[94] Close

---

92   TNA, HO 294/5: History of the CRTF, Introduction, *op. cit.*
93   *Ibid.*, History of the CRTF, General Report 1952.
94   *Ibid.*, History of the CRTF, Annual Report to 31 March 1955.

proximity to compatriots in CRTF accommodation could renew wartime ambivalence between refugees of diverse political affiliation or ethnicity, but frequently facilitated 'sharing and caring'. Not everyone needed CRTF help to rebuild his or her life, however, or only initially, as some interviewees emphasized.

Re-émigrés

High profile government members, officials and prominent political activists found escaping as a family extremely difficult, even with contacts at home and abroad and 'hard decisions had to be made. Right through the war, I never thought in any other terms, going home was wonderful', Anna Sonnek recalled; then she was forced to leave again.[95] From 1946 until the 1948 Communist putsch, her father, Jaroslav Stránský, had been Minister of Justice then Education, but purges were imminent: the provisional National Front coalition government formed in April 1945 of several anti-Fascist political parties, including President Beneš's, was dominated by Communists. Sonnek eventually crossed the border at Cheb, but could only subsequently arrange her small son's escape and her parents followed later. She is remembered as a very committed helper to her Czech general practitioner husband in Canvey Island. When Elisabeth Tauber's husband was nominated as a delegate for a science conference in 1949, they seized the opportunity to return to Britain permanently with their baby, leaving everything behind in Prague except basic essentials for a few days.[96] 'Free but a refugee again', Tauber was not to see Czechoslovakia for forty-three years. She already spoke English so, like Sonnek, could reintegrate easily with little or no recourse to the CRTF, and rejoin her nucleus of friends, especially Eve Road who had stayed on, duly becoming a social worker. Tauber's earlier social work course in Britain complemented by experience

95   Sonnek, AI; Karel A. Machacek, *Escape to England* (Sussex: Book Guild, 1988), 253, 287.
95   Tauber, AI.

with Terezín survivors, likewise led to satisfying social work in London, notably at Queen Mary's Hospital, Roehampton.

The Horáks, however, abandoned their attempts to escape together. 'Josef was too well known therefore not taken immediately [...] but we were spied on, a Czech man at the English Club in Kladno was arrested, and people disappeared', BBW Winifred Plocka (previously Horáková) stated. As the British Nationality Act, 1948, allowed dual citizenship, BBWs who had lost their British citizenship on marriage to an alien (and become, e.g., Czechoslovaks) effectively regained it, so in principle could leave legally, especially if they had British-born children. However, the Horáks' bank account had been 'frozen', causing financial difficulties.[97] Furtively, Plocka reached the British embassy in Prague, but her anxious question about 'how we stood' if she and her ex-RAF husband reached Britain separately met with silence, owing to 'the 'bugs'. Supposedly visiting her mother in Britain, Plocka was strip searched before leaving Prague with the children in April 1948; the £7 the embassy had given her plus her beloved gold bracelet from Josef were confiscated. 'Astonishingly, British European Airways literally carried me "cash on delivery!"' Once safely in Britain, she approached MP Barnett Stross,[98] whom she and Josef had met in Lidice, for help, 'and the next day he had Josef flown out of Austria!' It was not, though, the end of their problems. Plocka took various jobs while her sister cared for the children (who then spoke little English), but like other women of her generation, felt that she was 'not equipped for anything, and did not have self-confidence'. Since the Horáks' return to Britain preceded the Trust's revised remit, they did not qualify for CRTF assistance, nor did they receive any from the Czech community.

---

97   *The General Acts and the Church Assembly Measures of 1948*, British Nationality Act, 1948, S. 14–19 (London: HMSO).

98   Labour MP of Polish-Jewish origin, founded *Lidice Shall Live* campaign in Stoke-on-Trent, 1942.

Figure 23. Wall of Horák family farm, Lidice – with commemorative rose placed by
Josef Horák's widow, Winifred (interviewee), 2011. Author's image.

After some difficulty finding work, Horák joined Coastal Command, but
was killed when his plane crashed in poor weather conditions in January
1949 (see Figure 23). Overcoming memories and tensions, Plocka has
returned to Lidice annually for the commemorations post-Communism.[99]
Marian Šlingová, however, did not return to Britain until after 1968, having
endured imprisonment, her husband's execution following the 1952 Slánský
trials and internal exile with her sons. Despite everything, she remained
loyal to the Communist Party.[100]

99   Plocka, AI.
100 Šlingová, AI.

Unexpectedly, Hedy Fromings returned to Britain too. Her future husband led a group of architectural students from London; she was the designated interpreter for English-speaking visitors at the July 1947 first World Festival of Democratic Youth and Students in Prague. With much in common, they married in Liberec in 1948, but 'political obstacles' delayed Fromings' departure until 1949. 'I was interviewed at the Czechoslovak Foreign Office [in Prague] by a lady representative who pointed out the perceived disadvantages of losing my citizenship. I explained that it was unlikely that my husband would learn enough Czech to be able to work in Czechoslovakia'. Determined, and finally permitted to leave Czechoslovakia, Fromings completed her studies at the Regent Street School of Architecture, qualifying in 1952 as an architect recognized by the Royal Institute of British Architects.[101]

'First timers'

'First timers' generally could not speak English and lacked the re-émigré(e)s' experience of making a fresh start in a foreign country. In common with their contemporaries throughout Europe, young Czechoslovaks usually had few or incomplete qualifications due to WWII, or had belatedly started careers which could not be pursued in Britain, while older women were often unaccustomed to working outside the home, or even in it. Older men, however, could not always find employment to support their families (and retired men without resources who might become a financial liability were refused entry into Britain, impacting on family reunion as in the case of Zora Karas's father).[102] Consequently, regardless of their age and background, most 'new' refugee women faced downward mobility, just as their 1938–9 predecessors had done, but likewise determined to reverse the trend for their own fulfilment and their children's future. Refugee women (sometimes pressured by their husband as some interviewees disclosed), tended to have no children or only one child due to financial constraints,

---

101 Fromings, AI.
102 Vera Sturgess (Karas), re: Zora Karas, AI, PP.

inadequate accommodation, work and the absence of extended family support. Regaining self-esteem, social and/or professional status was a slow process in which sustained effort and education were significant elements, as illustrated by the following interviewees' accounts.

Zdena Kolařová, for instance, a Moravian Brethren adherent and Social Democrat from České Velenice, south Bohemia, together with her former businessman husband had evaded arrest by paying 50,000 Czech crowns each to cross into Austria in June 1949, using false passports to travel safely from Vienna in the (then) Soviet zone to Linz in the American zone.[103] However, her husband was passed over when manual workers were sought, and they were 'not wanted until 1951, when they could work as a couple' for a family in Northwood, Middlesex, only to 'feel like bonded slaves' after requesting a change of post. The Home Office 'mentioned the small print' binding them to a four-year, not one-year contract; release 'for study was not possible'. Plans for a family life had to be postponed. Kolařová's husband later worked at Queen Mary's Hospital, Roehampton, Zdena at the BBC from 1958 to 1998 as a secretary, then reading and translating. She appreciated the Smutný family's help, and the CRTF accommodation at 29 Gwendolen Avenue, SW15. Ironically, it is close to the Beneš's temporary residence at No. 26; life had gone full circle from 1938.

Aged seventeen, Olga Smutný fled to Vienna in 1948 with her mother and father (Secretary General of the Czechoslovak Parliament, pre-coup).[104] Both parents had been arrested then amnestied, 'so we were extremely happy to arrive in London in March 1949', Smutný explained. With the help of influential friends and associates, they were 'VIP refugees' granted political asylum with 'free entry and "indefinite" residency', and photographed for *The Lady*,[105] but received no financial support, so relied on the CRTF for 'a modest allowance'. The 'good days in Prague' were over. Smutný's father found no work, and died in August 1949, 'but we did *not* give up hope'. 'Mother was a very brave lady who had never worked in her life, daddy provided everything', yet 'in her fifties she learned to become a milliner

103   Zdena Kolařová, AI.
104   Olga Smutný (Madarová), AI.
105   'Dr. Josef Madar', vol. CXXIX, no. 3345 *The Lady* (31 March 1949), 286.

at a friend's firm'. Though alone in a foreign country and grieving, both women proved their ability and will to 'get on with their lives' and to fend for themselves. Since the Trust only paid university fees for science courses or viable 'continuation studies' commenced in Czechoslovakia, Smutný valued the Pitman's College secretarial course in Russell Square, paid for by the CRTF. Living in CRTF property in Brook Green, Hammersmith from 1951 to 1956, she worked for the Czechoslovak Intelligence Office at the War Office in London,[106] and afterwards at the National Coal Board and All England Lawn Tennis Club. During her first two years in Britain, Smutný 'missed Czech food, there were ration coupons, but the type of food available was limited', and she maintained links with the Czechoslovak community in exile, stressing however that 'it was never a ghetto'. Whilst it took a long time to acquire friends, she did not feel ostracized or resented. On the contrary, 'by not believing that I would return to Czechoslovakia I became more rapidly assimilated' – an outlook not adopted by all refugees.

Rose/Růžena Bernard from Teplice, was an official of the Presidium of the Czechoslovak Trades Union Congress in her own right, and married to a Social Democrat MP.[107] Likewise evading arrest, they fled to Vienna in March 1948, and 'were full of anxiety, with not a penny' on reaching Britain. Helped by the Labour Party and friends for the first few months, they turned to the 'quite bureaucratic' CRTF which, only after the birth of their son, provided two 'not very suitable rooms' in Pembridge Crescent, Notting Hill Gate. Later they moved to Chelsea, then to Reading in 1958, when the Trust 'was a great help', lending £500 for the deposit on a house. While Bernard's politically active husband ultimately held a BBC monitoring post in Caversham, wrote articles for journals and occasionally spoke publicly, she had worked to augment their income and provide a 'solid' home-life, so crucial to refugees. Her 'first job was to learn English', registering with the local council for classes, she stated. Thereafter, she worked in a Lyons Teashop kitchen on Saturdays and Sundays from 1 p.m. to 11 p.m., 'meeting English people and making friends'. As the BBC in London did not then allow women

---

106 The CIO existed in Britain 1948–57, Eduard Stehlík confirmed.
107 Rose Bernard, AI.

to be announcers, Bernard typed Czech translations and 'liked it, since it meant a step up' after a range of jobs. In further 'steps up' she became a part-time then full-time German teacher at Wokingham Grammar School, with the added security of a pension, and was 'very pleased' that her son graduated from the University of Oxford and had a successful career as a history professor.

Another mother, Dana Čadská, had been an agricultural student in 1948, but was 'forced out of university as her father was a rich landowner' whose farm plus her own was confiscated.[108] Her law student husband Otakar, was forced out too, and accused of 'contact with the enemy' by the Communist authorities. The purge was substantiated in the *News Chronicle* of 18 March 1949, noting that one out of every eight students was 'eliminated'.[109] The couple therefore escaped to Germany in February 1949, but decided against emigration to Australia as 'it was too far away, and we wanted to go home eventually'. 'Coming to England was traumatic' in 1950, feeling like slaves bound by a two-year contract in Woking as cook/housekeeper and chauffeur/gardener respectively. 'I never cleaned my own shoes until I left Czechoslovakia', Čadská remarked, but setting her background aside demonstrated how resourceful women could be – of necessity. In London she variously cooked for six German men, baked for Decmar patisserie in South Kensington, and set then closed the 'legs' over stones in 'hand-made' jewellery for a Czech jeweller in Greek Street (women also went to one in Ladbroke Grove). Often working late at night, women's eyes burned from the prolonged glare, but the smaller the stone the better the pay; Čadská earned £10–15 per week, mainly before Christmas. 'In typical Czech style', her husband expected her 'to be there for him whenever he was at home'; nevertheless, she took a diploma course and became a comptometer operator, earning ten guineas (£10.10s) per week with a pension at AXA and other large companies. Understanding decimal points in pre-decimalized Britain was a distinct advantage. Feeling empowered, Čadská proudly bought a motor scooter with her own earnings. Her husband was

108   Dana Čadská, AI.
109   'Czech Purge of the Varsities', *News Chronicle* (18 March 1949).

employed by the CRTF from 1952 until 1972,[110] initially to help refugees obtain jobs: unable to complete his law studies, he gained a degree in sociology through evening classes at Birkbeck College, University of London. Together, the Čadský's ensured that their future doctor son had a good education, and as an only child did not 'miss out on things'.

Exceptionally, the 15-year-old Aryan-looking Jana Tanner[111] arrived from Slovakia with her Buchenwald survivor brother and the first of *The Boys* group[112] (which included a few girls), flown from Prague in a British bomber in August 1945. Under the (Jewish) Central British Fund scheme, 732 child or juvenile orphans and concentration camp survivors were resettled and reunited, where possible, with family members in Britain, Canada and the USA. First though, they were taken to a hostel near Lake Windermere for rehabilitation, where Tanner spent some two weeks. Most boys were Polish, and the helpers spoke Yiddish and English, not understood by the few Czechoslovaks who 'stuck together' with Kitty Rosen and the future Rabbi, Hugo Gryn.[113] To Tanner the hostel 'was paradise after a year hiding with partisans' children in an orphanage' in Modra, run by Lutheran nuns in constant fear of Nazis and then Russians. Having had very little food there, mostly beans and potatoes, the usually eschewed British 'bread as white as snow, *and you could put margarine and jam on it* was sheer luxury!' Discovering her Jewish origins, however, had been a culture shock, 'we were Czech and did not consider ourselves Jewish'. Now, Tanner had to adjust to life in Britain. While her brother joined an uncle in America, Tanner 'had a home' in Notting Hill Gate with her married sister who had been in Britain since 1939 (working for the Czechoslovak government in exile, then later the Czechoslovak Embassy and BBC), and her opera singer husband, Otakar Kraus. Both Tanner and her sister studied

---

110 Imperial War Museum [IWM], Papers of R. J. Stopford, RJS 3/13–3/17, file 3/14: Czech Refugee Trust Fund, Note from Home Office, 1971, on winding-down the Trust, liquidated 1974–5.

111 Jana Tanner, AI.

112 Martin Gilbert, *The Boys* (London: Weidenfeld and Nicolson, 1996), 1–2.

113 *Ibid.*, 333, 390–1, 399.

English at Regent Street Polytechnic,[114] and Tanner quickly made Czech
and English friends, completing her matriculation and a secretarial course.
'Accepted' in the friendly National Buildings Record Library and photo-
graphic archive, she duly became secretary to the director, and enjoyed
meeting poet John Betjeman and eminent professors.

Entering Britain for other reasons

Not foreseeing the 1948 Communist coup and clampdown in
Czechoslovakia, women also came to Britain early post-war for normal
peacetime reasons such as a better life, to learn English, or just for a holiday.
As in 1939, though, they soon became refugees '*sur place*', fearing or unable
to return home due to the new political situation. Their predicament is
representative of the period, and two different instances are recorded here.
    Aged twenty-two, Eva Halata left her Slovak village, Staškov, and came
to Britain in 1946 seeking 'a new life'.[115] Owing to 'a [minimum] six-month
wait for emigration to Canada or America' from the DP camp in Umstadt,
Germany, Halata opted for Britain instead (probably the EVW scheme).
Segregated men and women travelled by train via Holland escorted by
policemen, Halata recounted. She first tasted baked beans en route to
a mill in Shipley, Yorkshire, where for one year she earned £3 per week,
paying 30/- for hostel accommodation and food and retaining 30/- 'Plenty
of money!' Restricted to factory or hospital work, Halata chose cleaning
and washing-up in Ilkley maternity hospital, but later earned £6 for similar
work in a London restaurant. It was hardly the new life she had envisaged
(though she later married and opened a grocery shop), nor was it without
reminders of her provisional status in Britain. Both Halata and Gokorsch
mentioned having to register as aliens at the local police station on arrival

114   University of Westminster from 1992.
115   Eva Halata, AI.

at their first job, reporting periodically thereafter, then re-registering in London and informing the local Labour Exchange of work and residential changes.[116] The British authorities were ever-cautious regarding guest workers and refugees, whether in wartime or peacetime.

To improve her English and obtain the Cambridge English Certificate, 22-year-old Zora Flajsner from Jindřichův Hradec, spent a 'miserable' year from September 1947 as an au pair at Queen Anne's public girls' school, in Caversham.[117] Compounding this, her application to extend her stay in Britain after the Communist coup was refused by the Czechoslovak authorities, so she remained illegally in their view, though 'acceptable to Britain'. Unlike Smutný, Flajsner resisted the CRTF's proposed secretarial course to improve her employment prospects, but since it would not pay for her chosen course as a cutter, she borrowed the necessary £120, repaying her brother £1 weekly. Through a compatriot, she obtained a job as a cutter earning £8 per week from 1949 to 1951, with the Jewish firm Toplett, which produced jerseys for Harrods store in Knightsbridge. To earn extra money she took wrinkled knitting material home to Earls Court at night, pressing it under a damp cloth for use the next day: paid by the yard, workers measured carefully. Flajsner did not regret her decision: skilled and self-supporting, she 'could do many practical things' for herself, including upholstery and decorating.

Adjustment to new situations was also necessary on the part of those who had remained in Britain. Vera Sturgess wrote of her parents in a family biography, 'After the war, the darkness of their earlier years remained with them and took a heavy toll as they struggled to forge a new life in the UK'. Far from being defeated though, 'they built a sound and meaningful life [...] for themselves and their family'.[118]

116   Registration was compulsory until 1961.
117   Zora Flajsner, AI.
118   Sturgess, AI.

Conclusion

Contrary to expectation, exile in Britain exceeded the life-span of many older refugee women, stretching into that of their Czechoslovak or British-born children and beyond. Thus, women's life-changing experiences since the 1938 Munich Agreement, together with the disjunctive effects of WWII, impacted across generations and should be viewed holistically rather than as discrete incidents. Were, then, the women helpless victims of circumstances? Moreover, were they ultimately losers or contributors, and did they gain anything from their experiences? There is no single answer. Whilst there were undoubtedly times of profound misery or depression, and some older women could not adjust, life was not all negative. Hence, Edward Said's argument quoted in the Introduction to this study that the exile 'exists in a median state, neither completely at one with the new setting, nor fully disencumbered of the old [...] nostalgic and sentimental',[1] is countered or modified, since refugee women settled, integrated and were gradually assimilated over the years, absorbing 'British' culture without necessarily abandoning their own. An analysis of the women's lives by a nuanced combination of reference sources and interviews allowing the refugees 'to have a voice', reveals considerable fortitude, adaptability and even humour. They might well have been nostalgic and sentimental at times – who would not be in such circumstances? Yet these women not only persevered but largely overcame their difficulties. As preceding chapters attest, the disruption of family life, isolation, identity clashes and conflicting cultures or ideologies, all lay in freedom's wake. Innumerable situations and emotions consequently had to be confronted then surmounted if the women were to 'move on', and not just in wartime. Post-war expulsions from Czechoslovakia 1945–6, and the lengthy 'Cold War' Communist era

---

1   Edward Said, 'Intellectual exile: expatriates and marginals', *The Independent* (8 July 1993).

created additional cohorts of refugees and returnees in 1948 and 1968. Most British-born wives [BBWs] of Czechoslovak men trapped in Communist Czechoslovakia were ultimately repatriated, albeit not without difficulty; some, like Marian Šling,[2] only escaped thanks to the 1968 'Prague spring', and even then with only one of her two sons. The stresses and strains of life continued.

Reviewing exile life in Britain

Adjusting to peacetime

Whereas the wartime 'fighting spirit' shared by British and Czechoslovak women had helped to carry them through their hardships, adjusting to peacetime was equally essential. It was a whole new phase, but no easy task, as Vera Sturgess witnessed. With thousands of British servicemen demobbed and competing for work, women like her mother Zora Karas, who had replaced men and contributed to the war effort, were no longer in great demand. Suddenly they were expected to revert to dutiful mother/wife figures, devoid of personal aspirations beyond the home. Yet Karas's bomber pilot husband, Tibor, was without transferable kills for peacetime, and as Sturgess observed, 'civilian life was very different; ex-servicemen had to make their own decisions, go to the authorities – who did not like foreigners – and find out what their rights were'. After a stint at the Forest Trading Estate in south Wales, he started an electroplating business in Manchester, and Sturgess recalled 'sitting around the kitchen table doing the jigging for him to plate the following day and Zora did all the invoicing. She wasn't trained for that, but that's what she did in the evenings'. During the day she had no time for formal education, and bought bones to cook broth. Whilst 'Father was strong and a very hard worker', the previously

---

2   Marian Šlingová, AI.

cosseted Zora 'was the leader, the thinker and planner of the family [...] without her he wouldn't have known where to turn as a refugee in a strange country, I don't think he could have coped, and yet *she* planned the life and made sure it went ahead'. 'My parents were so poor, but they still occasionally took me and my brother to a restaurant so that we would know how to behave'; it 'was always uppermost in their minds, something that they kept from their homeland and weren't prepared to give up'. Typically, they dedicated 'all their efforts to the upbringing of their children'.[3]

Identity and culture revisited

Unable to indulge in expensive pursuits, refugees essentially replicated wartime leisure activities, congregating in their own clubs, speaking in their own language and joining student movements and political meetings. Social Democrats gathered in South Kensington's Daquise Restaurant, but the range of activities linked to Czechoslovakia early post-war depended on both location and individual interests. Several societies ceased to function, as there were fewer Czechoslovaks in Britain to organize or attend events. Anglo-Czechoslovak entities had achieved their wartime objectives, and the Czechoslovak PEN Club was temporarily re-established in Czechoslovakia. Leaders of the Czechoslovak women's groups and editors of journals had also returned home: a new Association of Czechoslovak Women in Exile was not formed until 1959 (and ceased in 1983), its first secretary Zdena Kolářová stated.[4] With the Czechoslovak armed forces and government in exile speedily repatriated, the regional spread of clubs and societies narrowed to concentrations of Czechoslovaks, notably in Manchester and London. President Beneš's parting gift of some £3,000 enabled London's Czechoslovak National House to purchase premises in 1946 at 74 West End Lane.[5] Known simply as 'the Czech club', it contin-

3   Vera Sturgess, AI.
4   Zdena Kolářová, AI.
5   Renamed Czech and Slovak National House, January 1993, reflecting Czechoslovakia's separation into Czech and Slovak republics; rejuvenated by au pairs meeting there.

ued to host Czechoslovak Legionnaires' meetings and the Czechoslovak
Colony Club, but became the main social centre, with a library, bar and
popular restaurant serving Czechoslovak dishes. St Mikuláš [Nicholas] Day
with treats and (always black) Baťa shoes for each 'good child', Christmas
and *Silvestr* [New Year] were all celebrated there: life continued. Women
met with friends, looked for familiar faces among new arrivals and some
Czechoslovak partners at the regular dances became husbands. Only nine
of the refugee women interviewees had married British men (see Table of
Interviewees), and as Lady Grenfell-Baines (formerly Milena Fleischmann)
pointed out, 'since women were expected to follow their husband, marriage,
whether to a Czechoslovak or British-born man, usually directed their
cultural activities along nationalistic lines not just social ones'.[6] Indeed,
Eva Halata's engineer husband had served in Czechoslovak units of the
RAF and loved dancing; he was happy that she could 'dance the Czech
way, especially the waltz and polka, as British women "walked!"'[7] Zora
Flajsner, too, met her businessman and former Czechoslovak army officer
husband at a Czech club dance.[8] She also joined the Sokol group; needing suitable space and equipment, sessions were held one evening a week
in Kensington schools 'the venue changing each year like the rent'. While
the men played volleyball [still played in 2018 by a mixed male/female
group of 1968 refugees every Saturday], Flajsner and some fifteen women
exercised under the leadership of Sister Uhlířová. Flajsner did not think
anyone paid a membership fee, 'as no-one had any money'.

Supplementing the social and cultural organizations, *Otec* [Father]
Jan Lang's arrival in London in 1949 heralded a stronger religious and
cohesive phase in London's Czechoslovak community.[9] His pastoral care
embraced everyone, but as a teacher his special concern was Czechoslovak
youth and he furthered plans for a Saturday Czechoslovak school in the

6   Milena Grenfell-Baines (Fleischmann), AI.
7   Eva Halata, AI.
8   Zora Flajsner, AI.
9   Milan Kocourek, *Krajanská Farnost v Londýně. Pamětník: Otec Jan Lang S. J.*
     [*Compatriots in the London Parish. Father Jan Lang S. J.*] (London: unnamed pub-
     lisher/printer, 1994), 11–17, 85.

Notting Hill Gate area, which women such as Dana Čadská duly helped to run. Slovak Eva Halata was among the refugees who attended services held in Czech in the convent chapel of the Holy Child Jesus in Cavendish Square,[10] before the congregation transferred to the larger Church of the Immaculate Conception in Farm Street, Mayfair,[11] and she read the monthly church news, *CM Věstník* [*Cyril and Methodius Newsletter*] launched in 1949.[12] *Věstník* provided a tangible link between the church and the exile community, especially for refugees living outside London, and Čadská remembered notices about activities Father Lang had organized: dances for adults and young people, Czechoslovak national dance sessions for young people, seminars and concerts. Post-war exile was initially expected to be short-term like WWII, so the preservation of Czechoslovak culture and identity, particularly by 'new' 1948–50 refugees, was primarily a continuum of the wartime approach. Church and club became central to national commemorative occasions, observed for the same reasons as those prompting them during WWII, and they bound together those in exile, overriding different political and religious views. The Czechoslovak national flag was placed near the altar, children and young people wore national costume, and patriotic hymns and prayers for the homeland and loved ones were offered. Participation in Czechoslovak community activities did not, though, signify total immersion in them, or the rejection of British society.

Reflections on inter-personal Anglo-Czechoslovak relations

It was very clear early on in this study that escape to the relative safety of Britain was only half the battle; adapting to life in a foreign country when totally unprepared, was the other. Nevertheless, hardship in Britain was

---

10 Later, site of Heythrop College, Halata, AI.
11 Czechoslovaks had use of the English church at certain times.
12 Kocourek, *op. cit.*, 14–15, 85.

not confined to refugees either during or after WWII, and no 'hierarchy of suffering' is intended here. Both British and Czechoslovak women ranging from teenagers to the middle-aged, actively participated in the war effort and suffered personal loss, while refugees remaining in or reaching Britain in the early post-war years shared the country's years of austerity. What distinguished between and sometimes distanced hosts and refugees, were their respective socio-political backgrounds, trajectories and aspirations. The dynamics of inter-related hardships described by this author's interviewees or respondents and endorsed by independent sources cited in this work, may be summarized as psychological, physical and financial, widely compounded by little or no knowledge of English. The psychological element stemmed primarily from forced flight and displacement, but partly also from socio-historical factors. Unlike Continental Europe, Britain's occupation by foreign invaders was beyond living memory and, in the main, unimaginable: whilst British society was not entirely xenophobic, its sense of superiority over other peoples was legendary. Class differences and social prejudice prevailed throughout the turbulent times covered here therefore, although refugee women were grateful to be in Britain and usually willing to work, those restricted to domestic service during 1938–9 and 1945–50 (discussed in Chapters 1 and 6) generally felt trapped and exploited. Moreover, they resented being treated as lowly servants, particularly by social equals or someone deemed to be of a lower social or cultural standing than themselves. Lonely refugees reportedly found this aspect harder than the work itself, which was often physically demanding, carried out in uncomfortable conditions and low-paid.

Despite the received wisdom that WWII was a 'social leveller', this author suggests that it was not a blanket leveller and that the statement requires qualification. Rather than be 'helpless downtrodden victims', refugees were keen to improve their circumstances and regain something of their former living standards, particularly if they had children. Zora Karas and her mother, for example, were never accepted by co-workers in factories where they helped produce military uniforms and folded parachutes as their war effort contribution.[13] The gulf between working-class British women arriving with their hair in curlers under head-scarves knotted above their forehead, and the smart, intellectual Karas's was never bridged. Class-based tensions also prevailed between Czechoslovak, Reich German and Austrian women internees billeted in overcrowded boarding houses or hotels on the Isle of Man, and between the proprietors and refugees in 1940–1. Reports and personal accounts at Manx National Library and Archive, however, show that women internees devised spirited schemes to meet their material and intellectual needs, which helped prevent the majority of women from becoming entirely demoralized and suicidal. Women from Czechoslovakia participated in the projects, including the chronically sick Anna Tschapek,[14] thereby demonstrating their fortitude and adaptability in particularly adverse conditions.

Lives transformed

Research carried out for this study established that Czechoslovak refugee women's lives were forcibly transformed by political events beyond their control, which both shaped their experiences and informed their responses to them: these could be positive, negative or, paradoxically, both. For many adolescent and young women WWII meant tragedy and a disrupted youth but, as was widely stated by interviewees, it also brought adventure and independence. Marie Řehulková spoke of her 'definite feeling of freedom during the war', and liberating financial independence as a married woman working as an auxiliary nurse in London, while her soldier husband was based elsewhere. 'Life was more modern and desirable, a break with the past'.[15] Refugee women who joined the

---

13 Sturgess, AI.
14 Walter Tschapek, AI.
15 Marie Řehulková, AI.

armed forces, like WAAF Corporal Theresie Lowit, also became more independent than if they had remained within a family environment – whether in Britain or the homeland – and enjoyed the camaraderie of a close-knit team.[16] Alexandra Kučerová even described her stay in Britain as 'the happiest years of my life'. She went dancing, met her Czechoslovak pilot husband, and their daughter was born.[17] Conversely, for older women not accustomed to working, the situation thrust upon them could be stressful and burdensome rather than liberating; whilst generally not impoverished in the homeland, they usually were on arrival in Britain. Obliged to work, especially if alone, they often lacked work skills and age could limit training possibilities, thereby reducing their employment opportunities in both wartime and peacetime. These women, together with aged and infirm refugees, were mainly or partly supported by the Czech Refugee Trust Fund.

Established in 1939 specifically to aid refugees from Czechoslovakia, the CRTF was one of the most important support organizations for them in Britain, thus has been repeatedly referred to in this study. Although the Quakers, YWCA, Moravian Church and many other organizations rallied to aid refugees from Czechoslovakia and those who had sheltered there until 1939, innumerable refugees would have been in dire straits in Britain without the Trust. It played a pivotal role, rendering greater support than that generally afforded to Reich Germans or Austrians in Britain, and for a much longer period. Whilst the CRTF did not organize escape from Czechoslovakia (unlike its predecessor the British Committee for Refugees from Czechoslovakia), it provided financial help and extensive welfare services, albeit unevenly perhaps, and perforce only to a very limited extent by its closure in 1975/6, when its resources were virtually depleted. Still, there were criticisms. Accusations levelled at allegedly Communist CRTF employees concerning their perceived favouring of Communist refugees caused considerable disputes and mistrust. Furthermore, refugees like Edith Sterne's husband were (unduly)

16   Theresie Lowit, AI.
17   Alexandra Kučerová, AI.

too ashamed to request even temporary assistance,[18] while some applicants found that they fell outside the Trust's remit so could not be helped, and not understanding why, believed that it had failed them. Such was the case regarding needy pre-Munich arrivals not classed as refugees, destitute resident domestics initially in Britain under the aegis of the YWCA's 1938–9 domestic service project, and post-war returnees to Britain prior to the Trust's extended remit in 1948, such as Josef Horák and his BBW wife Winifred. Nevertheless, thousands of refugees were aided in some way. The CRTF continued to assist refugees post-war, providing vital financial support, accommodation and, as far as possible, (re)training courses. Much as CRTF tenants disliked being means-tested and reporting periodically to the Trust's offices, they nonetheless benefited from subsidized furnished CRTF accommodation they could not otherwise have afforded in bomb-damaged London. 'Living in each other's pocket' might also be disagreeable, but flats were infinitely preferable to CRTF wartime hostels, where residents shared rooms in addition to 'house duties'. For all its imperfections, the Trust was an invaluable institution and 'stepping stone'.

Olga Smutný gained professional skills through a secretarial course paid for by the Trust, for example; her widowed mother was also initially assisted by the Trust in 1949 but, like other women, she showed her mettle by training in a friend's private business and working as a milliner when in her fifties, despite never having worked prior to Czechoslovakia's 1948 Communist coup and subsequent purges.[19] Britain's post-war reversion to stay-at-home wives and mothers may have suited some women, but could be problematic. The situation was especially difficult in a refugee community with a high proportion of male doctors, lawyers, administrators and businessmen, unable for various reasons to follow their career paths and provide for their families as they would normally have done. WWII had drained Britain's economy, retraining was costly and time-consuming, and British citizens had priority over aliens who might in any case not stay in the country. Consequently, contrary to Czechoslovak tradition, instances

18   Edith Sterne, AI.
19   Olga Smutný, AI.

of gender role swap not infrequently occurred in exile; women like teacher
(later headmistress) Edith Sterne, became the breadwinner or mainstay of
her family for a time.[20] Moreover, some women had to cope with their
husband's sense of humiliation and inadequacy (sometimes angrily vented),
in addition to their own suppressed disappointments, anxieties, work and
childcare. 'Women *had* to be strong for the sake of the family', Sturgess
asserted.[21]

Contribution to Britain

Determined to 'do their bit' against Hitler, young Czechoslovak women
served in units of the British armed forces, but were 'unsung heroines'
of WWII compared with Czechoslovak servicemen, about whom there
are published works and even a feature film about the airmen, *The Dark
Blue World*. Yet whilst women did not fight like their Czechoslovak
counterparts in Russia, they were still key contributors – an aspect of
their legacy that this study has helped to reveal. Some native German-
speakers in the armed forces like Ruth Tosek, were assigned to the then
secret 'Y service', making radio contact with German pilots to deliberately misdirect them,[22] while civilian native German speakers like Valery
Fuhrmann, worked secretly as translators in 'X service' at Bletchley
Park,[23] or passed coded messages in BBC broadcasts from London. Only
after the fall of Communism in 1989 were some women commended by
the Czechoslovak government, but many remain unacknowledged. The
war effort took numerous forms depending on the women's ages, skills
and available time, and included nursing, knitting items for servicemen
and/or helping the Czechoslovak Red Cross in Britain, headed by Hana

20   Sterne, AI.
21   Sturgess, AI.
22   Ruth Tosek, AI.
23   Dorrit Epstein, AI.

Benešová, wife of the President in exile. Less obviously, contributions were also made through medical research and culture. Uplifting recitals by pianist Líza Fuchsová and violinist Maria Lonová, gave pleasure to unknown numbers of listeners while simultaneously promoting Czechoslovak music (which Fuchsová resolutely continued doing after WWII via the stage and radio). Thus, whilst individual Czechoslovak women's efforts may have been qualitative rather than quantitative, collectively they constituted a not insignificant contribution to Britain and the war effort.

Czechoslovak women's involvement with the host society increased exponentially with time and confidence, particularly once they could communicate adequately in English. A longer-term view is necessary, however, to consider their broader achievements and contribution to Britain or society in general. It is conceded that this entails going beyond the stated end date of 1950, but crucially within the context of this study, their achievements underpin the argument that in common with, for example, German and Austrian refugees, Czechoslovak women on the whole were not hapless victims depending indefinitely on charity, but willing contributors wanting to move forward. Naturally they were not all ambitious or career-minded, and never attained prominence like US Secretary of State, Madeleine Albright, former wartime Czechoslovak refugee in Britain.[24] Nor is it suggested that this author's interviewees represent all Czechoslovak women. They nevertheless represent a range of women of different ages, who came to Britain in different refugee cohorts and circumstances at different stages in their life. Without undermining the achievements and contributions previously mentioned, the following examples are presented within the context of wartime and post-war limitations that Czechoslovak and other women experienced, and highlight the transition from refugee life to permanent settlement in Britain.

That women's experiences as refugees could heighten their compassion for others and similarly influence their children, is notably conveyed through medical and other caring professions such as teaching (see Table

24 Madeleine Albright, *Madam Secretary. A Memoir* (Basingstoke/Oxford: Pan Books/ Macmillan, 2004).

of Interviewees, Occupation). Eve Road[25] and Elisabeth Tauber[26] were both social workers, Tauber's last post being at Queen Mary's Hospital, Roehampton. As a clinical psychologist at Great Ormond Street Hospital for Sick Children Marianne Lowe, together with psychologist Anthony Costello wrote *Trends in the Development of Representational Play in Infants From One to Three Years – An Observational Study*. They devised the *Symbolic Play Test*, allowing young children unable or unwilling to speak about disturbing experiences to express them through play.[27] All royalties from sales of the published test (amounting to over £50,000) were donated to the hospital. The test is still cited in scholarly works and conferences, and various versions are displayed in London's Science Museum. Renee Morton researched in the Dunn Nutritional Laboratory in Cambridge with Egon Kodíček, developing a freeze-drying method for food originally intended for soldiers but ultimately benefiting millions of people.[28] Josefina Bruegel was the first woman to be awarded the special Czechoslovak Medical Degree, Medicinae Universae Doctor (MUDr) at the University of Oxford, in February 1943.[29] One year after qualifying as a doctor, Slovak Charlotte Bushell became the youngest woman member of the Royal College of Physicians in 1948 and around 1975 was elected to a Fellowship of the College. Regarded as a dedicated consultant in rheumatology, with a lectureship at Hammersmith Hospital, Bushell acknowledged that she had accomplished a great deal, but remarked, 'success was at a price concerning my children and social life'.[30] Kate Thompson's career culminated at the National Institute for Medical Research, researching the ageing of human cells, while her contribution to society continued as a British Library volunteer participating from

25   Eve Road, AI.
26   Elisabeth Tauber, AI.
27   Marianne Lowe, AI; Marianne Lowe, and Anthony J. Costello (Windsor: NFER-
      Nelson Publishing Co., 1976, 2nd edn, 1988).
28   Renee Morton, AI.
29   Bodleian Library, University of Oxford, ref: VR 6/OUC/3.
30   Charlotte Bushell, AI.

1988 to 2005 in its oral history project interviewing, among others, three Nobel Peace Prize winners.[31]

Whilst 'catching up' on missed studies and opportunities due to WWII might have been delayed due to financial constraints and family obligations, it was not impossible, as Maria Ratzer proved. She missed her homeland but had stayed on in Britain post-war caring for her sons, then with her husband's support she belatedly embarked on another major transition in her life, resuming medical studies for five years at Glasgow University. Graduating in 1953, she became a consultant in 1967, specializing in dermatology. 'As a woman and a foreigner', her son Peter wrote, 'it was not always easy for her', yet 'she was the first woman consultant in a clinical speciality in Glasgow's Western Infirmary'; Professor Rona Mackie said of her: 'she stood out for me as a superb role model'.[32] Nina Dobosharevich reached Britain in 1950 after escaping from Czechoslovakia in 1949 and ultimately working for the International Refugee Organization in Germany. Overcoming language barriers and racism, she qualified in general nursing, midwifery and psychiatric training, rising to Theatre Sister at St Stephen's Hospital, Fulham (now Chelsea and Westminster Hospital). Indomitable, she additionally coped with a suicidal husband who greatly needed her.[33] Achievements did not always coincide with women's aspirations; however, Edith Sterne, who never completed her legal studies, seemed reconciled to her alternative roles as a loved and respected teacher, headmistress and sometime breadwinner.[34] Food and newly discovered business acumen combined, as demands for Continental specialities increasingly came from British people who had sampled them abroad, as well as from refugees. Winter & MG Imports, of which Maria Gokorsch was a partner in the early 1950s, supplied delicatessen shops in London and the Midlands, Harrods and Coopers' 'flagship shops', Waitrose and British Airways.[35] While Gokorsch pioneered *Glühwein*

31   Kate Thompson, AI.
32   Ratzer papers.
33   Nina Dobosharevich, AI.
34   Sterne, AI.
35   Maria Gokorsch, AI.

a German mulled wine] in Britain, supported charities and served on committees, Susan Groag Bell's mother Edith, also succeeded in business. She became a trust tax accountant, joined women's clubs, and rose to be President of the Business and Professional Women's Club, Thames Branch, as inscribed on her medal;[36] Susan became an academic and a writer in America, with special interest in gender studies.

Former Kindertransport child Milena Grenfell-Baines, left nursing to concentrate on leading cookery courses, Czechoslovak cuisine and broadcasting.[37] In due course she promoted and became the sole UK agent for the *remoska*, an electric slow cooker relied upon in Czechoslovak homes. In recognition of her extensive charitable work, including support of the Liverpool Philharmonic Orchestra and help to Czech or Slovak music students temporarily in Britain, she became a Burgess of the City of Preston in 2012, and an Honorary Fellow of the University of Central Lancashire for her contribution to the arts and international understanding.[38] Adding to her numerous activities, and work in connection with Sir Nicholas Winton and the Kindertransports, she has latterly initiated the project and fund-raised for a memorial 'to the brave mothers' left behind at Prague's Wilson Station, platform 1; placed near the Kindertransport monument there it, too, marks the beginning of a long and emotional journey. Architect and fellow Czechoslovak school pupil Hedy Fromings specialized in designing hospitals. In her free time Fromings established and led the Beskydy Dancers, an Anglo-Czechoslovak amateur group of singers, dancers and musicians who performed at various events and entertained residents of old people's homes and patients in hospitals, well beyond the year 2000 (see Figure 24).

36   Groag Bell, AI.
37   Grenfell-Baines, AI; 'Prestigious awards recognise Lady Milena's work for arts and international friendship', *British Czech and Slovak Review* (October/November 2012), 2.
38   Grenfell-Baines, AI.

Figure 24. Beskydy Dancers – Czechoslovak folk group founded in London early 1950s
by Hedy Fromings (previously Huenigen). Courtesy of interviewee.

Dorrit Epstein's artistic talents were applied to illustrations for book covers,
magazines and posters.[39] Her work at the Central Office of Information
1946–8 included posters such as 'Coughs and sneezes spread diseases'
(revised and reissued in around 2009), and her large representation of atoms
and neutrons using brightly coloured balls was included in the 1951 Festival
of Britain. The ball theme was adapted for popular coat-hangers and coat-
stands in the 1960s, re-appearing in around 2010 in Oliver Bonas shops.
Epstein also formed her own company, Dekk, and successfully exhibited
her work. With dwindling hopes of returning to Czechoslovakia, women
had had to rise to fresh economic and psychological challenges. Forced

39   Epstein, AI.

into extended exile by the immediate post-war era's deepening ethnic and political schisms in the homeland, the majority of (re)émigrées who came to Britain between 1946 and 1950 remained for the rest of their lives. Their struggles, failures and successes have become an integral, if not fully recognized, facet of Anglo-Czechoslovak social history.

Gains and losses

Women's endeavours certainly did not end with the war. While refugee women generally worked of necessity, it was found during interviews that a number of them, like Charlotte Bushell, also felt the need to fulfil themselves and 'give something back' to Britain or contribute in some way, hence were often drawn to caring or vocational positions. The desire to break free from the stereotyped wife/mother figure and complete higher education or pursue vocational training, gradually enabled women, where possible, to obtain more fulfilling employment than domestic service or factory work. Whereas juggling careers and motherhood is now seen as mainstream in western Europe, in 1950s Britain the home was still paramount, and the shift of focus, time, energy and commitment to a career seemed quite radical. Nonetheless, moving beyond the traditional parameters could empower women. They gained by having more choices in life and some, like Maria Gokorsch, succeeded even in business careers they had never envisaged, nor thought themselves capable of pursuing, often holding responsible positions that they would rarely have reached in inter-war Czechoslovakia.

Personal achievement evaded some women, however. Typically they gained safety and a measure of security, but never realized their aspirations in exile; like so many refugees from other countries, then as now, as well as many indigenous British women, they supressed their frustrated ambition for the rest of their lives. Yet that is not to undermine women's achievements. Although Zora Karas never completed her medical studies and felt that she had 'missed out' due to WWII, family and financial constraints, 'she made the very best of her hardships' in Britain. She contributed to

British society through her valued work with the Citizens' Advice Bureau, and as a qualified counsellor involved in the rehabilitation of mental health patients in the community. 'Maybe the war years made her strong, made her a strong person to build the rest of her life', her daughter Vera reflected when interviewed.[40] Dana Čadská never completed her university studies either. Instead, she had a range of jobs while her husband worked and studied part-time in the evening at Birkbeck College for a degree in sociology, to improve his employment prospects. Čadská joined the ranks of the refugee women who sacrificed their own needs and wishes for the betterment of their children's lives, who in turn contributed to Britain.[41] Overall, Czechoslovakia's 'brain-drain' loss was Britain's gain.

Family reunion and retrospection

Time does not always bring closure to past suffering. Sadly, regardless of women's best intentions, a further finding was that some of the wartime tensions and difficulties in mother and child(ren) and family relationships discussed in Chapter 4, continued to impact on women's lives post-war, sometimes detrimentally. Moreover, various long-term ramifications were only manifested well after WWII had ended, either through new tensions, or the regrets that maturity and retrospection can give rise to, particularly in the case of Jewish Czechoslovaks. Whilst few extended families of Jewish origin remained intact after the Holocaust, some individual family members were reunited, Mrs Karlik among them. As in numerous instances, though, the reunion proved not to be a happy one; the parties concerned had grown apart without the bonding of shared experiences that might otherwise have developed. Vera Karlik had missed her parents, but was already sixteen when she heard that her mother was still alive, and 'they

40   Sturgess, AI.
41   Čadská, AI.

did not get on. Vera wanted to be a nurse, but her mother thought it highly unsuitable for a young lady, so Vera became a dental nurse instead', her Fulneck School friend Libby Dewhirst Mitchell recounted.[42] The situation is doubly revealing regarding certain generational social attitudes usually retained by the more affluent strata of Czechoslovak society, who viewed the inter-war period as the 'golden era' (still referred to as such in some literature); they held to them in the expectation that life would 'return to normality', rather than change irrevocably, as was the case. Yet despite her wartime sacrifice and good intentions regarding her children's future as described earlier, 'Mrs Karlik was the ultimate survivor – she outlived her daughter. Life can be very cruel sometimes', Mitchell observed.

Not all core families had been separated though; former Fulneck School pupils Eva Rayner and her brother Tom reached Britain in October 1938, together with their parents, cousins and an aunt and uncle. In principle, family members supported each other, but as an adult, and with the benefit of hindsight, Eva wrote of the difficulties experienced when her grandmother was reunited with the family in Britain:

> After the war, Granny came to live with us. She used to follow my mother everywhere like a shadow hardly wanting to let her out of sight, which was understandable but very hard on my parents. I wish I had asked them much more about how they felt leaving all their friends and family behind but they never talked about it and I did not ask. My Granny never talked about her time in Terezín. When she came to England I could still speak Czech and we got on very well. I cannot imagine how it must have felt not knowing what is happening to your family for so many years.[43]

Like a number of other children of refugees, especially daughters it seems, Rayner became her family's 'memory and memento keeper'. Perhaps compensating for the 'missing years' and tangible extended family links, she has kept the post-war telegrams her mother received informing her that her mother was alive; she has also kept the Stars of David that dead family

---

42 Libby Dewhirst Mitchell, AI.
43 Eva Rayner, autobiographical note to Libby Dewhurst Mitchell, May 2001, for *Moravian Messenger* on Holocaust's fiftieth anniversary, and subsequent correspondence with this author.

members had worn, some currency and soap from Terezín, and the treasured gold bracelet given to her mother 'by Granny at the railway station, just as they [the family] were leaving Czechoslovakia' and concluded, 'Tommy and I were the lucky ones, we had our parents with us'.[44]

Such wartime parents are now elderly or dead, but it is evident from this author's interviews that even where parent(s) and child(ren) were reunited after WWII, time has not eradicated memories of events that separated them. 'In the absence of parents, pupils supported each other. I think most of us tried to be "brave and independent" as a matter of necessity', Kindertransport and Czechoslovak state boarding school pupil Marion Feigl reflected.[45] Feigl joined her parents in America in 1944; other pupils were devastated to find at the end of the war that they had none. Whilst mothers and children had perforce dealt with situations when confronted by them, the full impact of forced separation as a dynamic of exile was sometimes manifested only in the longer term. Feigl for instance, developed a fear of travelling, hence rarely returned to Czechoslovakia or joined in school reunions, and Eva Fleischmann (also reunited with her parents), who had 'stoically never cried when with her foster family', could only in her later years express her hidden pain in poetry.[46] The question of silence about damaging wartime experiences remains a recurring element in the narratives of refugee women and their children.

'Rusalka effect'

In spite of every effort to minimize the negative effects of WWII, the legacy of 'difference' in an era that pre-dated the high level of multiculturalism in twenty-first-century Britain, was sometimes transmitted to refugee women's children, especially those who were born or brought up

---

44   *Ibid.*
45   Feigl, correspondence with author.
46   Grenfell-Baines, AI.

in Britain. As in Dvořák's opera *Rusalka*, about a water-nymph who falls in love with a mortal prince and is transformed into a human being to be with him, yet never totally succeeds in being accepted as one, children of refugees might similarly be regarded as neither totally English nor Czechoslovak. A daughter's identity in a central European family would normally have been closely tied to her mother's, but in Britain there were exceptions. Interviewees observed that some boys and girls even if directly involved in the Czechoslovak community in exile, inclined towards an English identity, spoke neither Czech nor German, and displayed a distinct lack of interest in their parents' homeland and culture in order to avoid being perceived as 'different' by their peers. This attitude could be hurtful to parents. Zora Karas's daughter Vera recalled her parents' distress when her brother 'rejected Judaism and any connection with Czechoslovakia, and refused to join in Czech folk songs the family sang in the car on long journeys'. For refugees then still cherishing the hope that 'one day' they might yet return to Czechoslovakia, it was a worrying matter. Furthermore, some interviewees were sad that whatever they might have (re)gained from Czechoslovakia to pass on to their children, typically old (if not always valuable except in sentimental terms) books, paintings, china or cut glass were not always appreciated and would not be preserved within the family. A treasured porcelain coffee set with a design of violets that Edith Groag somehow brought to Britain was left to her daughter, who noted that it was not liked, not 'dish-washer safe' and unused by the next generation. Most women irrevocably lost what they had expected to retrieve or inherit. They may not have dwelled on such losses, but it did not prevent Edith Sterne from wishing that she could have given her daughter what she had had, the life that she had enjoyed at home, a sentiment echoed by other interviewees. Times and life-styles had changed enormously, however, in post-war Britain as well as in Czechoslovakia, and the dynamics of generational differences were strong in both countries.

From integration to assimilation

In this study, assimilation is acknowledged as an important component of ultimate settlement in Britain, driven by the eventual realization that the Communist regime would endure for the (then) foreseeable future, and the associated need for security. Nonetheless, the transition from integration to assimilation was not a smooth linear process, and to some Czechoslovak interviewees relinquishing one's national identity in favour of naturalization had meant surrendering or losing something of oneself. Interviewees from the various periods of migration grew accustomed, though, to speaking to their children and grandchildren in English, and even Prague school friends Eve Road and Elisabeth Tauber lapsed into English when meeting. Eva Halata still spoke to her dog in Slovak,[47] but some interviewees admitted to having forgotten (through irregular usage rather than forgetfulness) every-day Czech or German words and terms when speaking or corresponding in either language, and their 1940s idiomatic language marked them out as émigrées when visiting the homeland. In some instances, first names were gradually anglicized, for example, Eva to Eve and Jana to Jane, either by the interviewees themselves or their English partners and associates; surnames were changed, too, sometimes by omitting the feminine 'ová' ending. Apart from simplifying names, for the women concerned it was a way of moving forward and distancing themselves from their former insecure refugee status as 'the other': but older women especially, rarely lost their foreign accents – to their chagrin and their children's irritation. Interviewees had resented being asked where they were from by English people, regarding the question as an unsettling reminder that they were 'not quite one of us' in the early post-war years, whatever documentation they held. By the time that the former refugees were interviewed by this author, they had lived longer in Britain than in the homeland, and almost all were long-standing British citizens, generally feeling 'very British' and drinking 'gallons of tea' with milk not lemon. Their perception of themselves

---

47   Halata, AI.

may not entirely conform to that of the indigenous British population, but the psychological human need 'to belong' somewhere and enjoy full citizenship rights had mostly overcome any lingering feelings of disloyalty to Czechoslovakia that naturalization had caused. Practical issues inevitably arose, such as passports. Some stateless refugees had previously only held a (1921 format) Nansen Passport, superseded by the 1951 UN Convention Travel Document 'valid for all countries' – with the ominous hand-written proviso, 'except Czechoslovakia'. A British passport was therefore valued, signifying security and acceptance to both the holder and officialdom. When Lord Alf Dubs' mother sought naturalization soon after WWII, applicants were asked what they had done during the war. Her war effort contribution with the (then) Women's Voluntary Service was cited as a recommendation to approve her application.[48] Conversely, ultra-patriotic to the end, former headmistress Zdeňka Pokorná loyally never became British, so never received the customary hundredth birthday congratulations from HM the Queen.[49]

Supposedly 'the weaker sex', pragmatic refugee women from Czechoslovakia nevertheless proved markedly capable and resourceful in adverse circumstances. Like refugees from other countries, to a considerable extent they not only came to terms with their experiences, but transformed them into positive action, as is evidenced throughout this work. They could all have sunk into permanent embittered apathy, which leads one to question whether they were inherently strong, resilient and adaptable? Again, there is no one answer. Women may well not have known their own strengths until tested in exile, when sheer necessity drove them on; women, after all, especially as mothers or carers in some capacity, were highly motivated. Their experiences may have heightened pre-existing personality traits, but youth, hope and a sense of adventure played a part too, as did variables such as opportunity, confidence and self-esteem. Both Gokorsch and Sturgess considered women more adaptable than men, observing that women 'just got on with things' (echoed by other women), while Tanner believed that humour helped, noting the intrinsic 'Švejk in

48 Alf Dubs, AI.
49 Pokorná, AI.

all Czechs' that pushed them to 'work around' difficulties and problems as in Hašek's *Good Soldier Švejk*. Nina Dobosharevich agreed. Her strong sense of humour helped her throughout her life and in her nursing career; her personal maxim was 'Never give up!'[50]

Perhaps above all, the key determining factor was the resolve to 'live life to the full' and not to be perpetually treated either as a victim or a survivor, as Heda Franks insisted.[51] Naturally, there were regrets and unhappy memories. Franks' own mother was very unhappy in Britain and unable to adjust to her new life after their release from Terezín. Other women needed extra care in Brett House, the CRTF 'rest home', where Zdeňka Porkorná worked for a time as a psychiatric nurse.[52] Even when women readily adjusted to life in exile, the war and its aftermath left some interviewees re-living experiences or suffering from nightmares: 'I still hear the high boots of the Gestapo running up the house, I feel it in my bones' Zdena Kolářová acknowledged. Yet despite their experiences and the freedom to say what they felt when interviewed, hardly anyone mentioned an aversion to Germany and all things German. Does time heal, or is there a generational differential governing 'forgiving' and 'forgetting'? In exceptional cases interviewees were anti-Semitic, and occasionally interviewees resented the influx of more recent refugees with whom they did not identify on the grounds that they were 'not European', or 'too many for a small country', views currently voiced by segments of the indigenous population too, and partly resulting in 'Brexit'. Does human nature change with locations? Nevertheless, while most interviewees were happy that they had at last been able to visit their homeland post-Communism, all except one woman chose not to return permanently; they had 'outgrown their home' or 'put down roots' in Britain, and some had no wish to return to a painful past. But they all valued British democracy, the years of freedom of speech and life without the dreaded knocking on the door by Fascist or Communist soldiers and police. Edward Said's assertion that exile was 'one of the saddest

---

50   Dobosharevich, AI.
51   Heda Franks, AI.
52   Pokorná, AI. Lord Layton granted use of his house at the junction of Putney Heath Lane and West Hill, London SW15, replaced by flats and houses.

fates', therefore – in their own opinion – resonated only minimally with people interviewed or contacted by this author. Whilst women were indisputably hindered at times by their respective situations, their fate was not immutable, and as has been shown, they themselves helped to re-shape it positively as far as possible. Moreover, interviewees were proud of their ability to 'make a fresh start in life', their achievements and contributions to the wider British community.

In conclusion, this study has aimed to unify diverse facets of the experiences of forcibly displaced Czechoslovak women in exile in Britain from 1938 to 1950. By the fusion of disciplines, namely social history, politics and oral history, the women have been placed within the context of Anglo-Czechoslovak history. Conceived as a pioneering study, it has endeavoured to be comprehensive, but is not finite: word limitations prohibit the inclusion of more material, and interviews merit fuller reports than is possible here. Czechoslovak refugee women's vision of the 'new post-war world' was initially predominantly of the homeland, not Britain, but the expulsion of ethnic Germans and the dominance of Communism permanently altered the course of their lives. The 'Iron Curtain' to which Winston Churchill first referred in his speech on 5 March 1946 in Fulton, USA, denoting the separation of east from west Europe, had 'descended'. Britain continued to provide a safe haven for the refugees beyond 1950, mainly escapees already in Austrian and German camps awaiting resettlement, but the reinforcement of Czechoslovakia's borders effectively prevented escape thereafter. The next major period of migration to Britain was not until 1968, a new era, and minus the Czech Refugee Trust Fund. Tragically, wars and harsh authoritarian regimes continue to exist around the world; millions of refugees flee, seek shelter, are accepted or rejected. Asylum is but reluctantly granted. Despite the time element, some of the interviewees' difficulties cited in this study remain remarkably similar to what a woman or girl refugee might experience in Britain today; they are universal and transferable to other contexts, to other countries. Indeed, certain issues seem perennial: a 1944 PEP Pamphlet posed the question – as pertinent then as now – *Are Refugees an Asset*? Yes, it argues.[53] Former MP David Miliband likewise argues in their favour in his 2017 publication, *Rescue: Refugees and the Political Crisis of Our Time*,[54] and Lord Alf Dubs, a former Director of the Refugee Council, works ceaselessly on behalf of refugees, especially unaccompanied children. Such approaches will doubtless continue to be challenged, as indeed they were in Parliament in 2018. Kapp and Mynatt, however, notably declared during WWII that 'in championing the cause of the refugees, we take a stand for our own democratic rights; in fighting for these we vindicate the refugees'.[55] Since then, membership of the European Union from 2004 has allowed the free movement of Czech and Slovak citizens, many of whom work in key services and industries in Britain; will 'Brexit' preserve or destroy Britain's goodwill towards them in the future?

53 *Are Refugees an Asset?* Political & Economic Planning Pamphlets (London: Europa Publications, 1944).
54 David Milliband, *Rescue: Refugees and the Political Crisis of Our Time* (London: Simon & Schuster/TED Books, 2017).
55 Yvonne Kapp and Maragaret Mynatt, *British Policy and the Refugees 1933–1941* (London: Frank Cass, 1997, largely written in 1940).

Chronology

28 October 1918	Czechoslovak Republic established (National Day/Independence Day).
12 March 1938	*Anschluss*, Germany annexed Austria; some Austrian and German refugees sheltered in Czechoslovakia.
29 September 1938	Munich Agreement ceded Czechoslovakia's Sudetenland region to Germany; Sudeten anti-Fascists fled to rump Czechoslovakia.
October 1938	British Committee for Refugees from Czechoslovakia (BCRC) formed.
5 October 1938	President Beneš obliged to resign.
22 October 1938	President Beneš and wife Hana left Czechoslovakia for Britain.
Dec. 1938-Jan. 1939	Nicholas Winton helped BCRC representatives in Prague.
January 1939	British Grant of £4 million to Czechoslovak government to assist refugees from the Sudetenland.
14 March 1939	Slovakia declared independence; Nazi 'puppet state'. Re-joined Czech regions 1945; first Winton Kindertransport left Prague for Britain.
14/15 March 1939	Germany seized Bohemia, and Moravia.
1 April 1939	New regulation: refugees without a visa refused entry into Britain.
July 1939	BCRC helped last group of women to escape to Britain; succeeded by Czech Refugee Trust Fund (CRTF).

2 August 1939	Penultimate Winton Kindertransport.
1 September 1939	Germany attacked Poland, Czech borders closed; Winton's last Kindertransport never left Prague; the children were never seen again.
3 September 1939	Britain declared war on Germany.
17 November 1939	Order in Council briefly permitted refugees to work in Britain.
May 1940	Small number of Czechoslovaks interned in Britain.
June–July 1940	Czechoslovak soldiers and airmen evacuated from France to Britain.
July 1940	Czechoslovak National Committee in France re-established in London as Provisional Czechoslovak Government in exile, headed by Beneš.
August 1940	Blitz and Battle of Britain began; Czechoslovaks fought in the RAF.
13 November 1940	Beneš's moved to Aston Abbotts, Buckinghamshire, for security reasons; government officials and Presidential Guard lived nearby.
May 1941	Most Czechoslovak refugees released from internment in Britain.
21 June 1941	Some Nuremburg Laws against Jews enacted in Czech Lands.
22 June 1941	Germany attacked the Soviet Union.
9 September 1941	Slovak legislation passed based on Nuremberg Laws.
27 September 1941	Reinhard Heydrich named Deputy Reich Protector of Bohemia and Moravia; is associated with 'Final Solution' of the 'Jewish problem'.
27 May 1942	Heydrich assassinated by Czechoslovak parachutists from Britain.

9–10 June 1942	Lidice destroyed in retribution for Heydrich's death.
11 June 1942	Anglo-Soviet Treaty of Alliance signed.
18 June 1942	Czechoslovak parachutists killed in Prague church.
18 July 1942	Czechoslovak Government in exile recognized by British government.
29 September 1942	Britain and France revoked 1938 Munich Agreement; Beneš government in exile in London deemed 'de jure'.
12 December 1943	Czechoslovak-USSR Treaty of Friendship and Mutual Collaboration.
8 May 1944	Agreement with USSR that Soviet-liberated territory would revert to Czechoslovak civilian control (not strictly adhered to).
29 August 1944	Slovak Uprising against Germany commenced.
8 September 1944	Battle of Dukla Pass on Polish/Slovak border began; Soviet 'liberators' and Czechoslovak soldiers won through.
4–11 February 1945	Yalta Conference: post-war Europe and spheres of influence.
11 March 1945	Beneš and government officials left Britain for talks in Moscow; proceeded to liberated Slovak regions.
4 April 1945	New Czechoslovak government temporarily based in Slovakia; National Front coalition government comprised, for example, Czechoslovak National Socialist Party, Social Democrats, and Communists.
5 May 1945	Prague Uprising against German occupation.
8 and 9 May 1945	VE Day, end of WWII; Soviet troops entered Prague; Czechoslovak refugees in Britain prepared for gradual repatriation.

16 May 1945	Czechoslovak government re-established in Prague.
July 1945	Wives and children of government officials repatriated, others follow.
16 July–2 Aug.1945	Potsdam Conference: Europe's post-war borders, transfer of Germans from territories east of Germany; 'Beneš Decrees' and expulsions.
26 May 1946	Czechoslovak national elections: President Beneš re-elected.
2 July 1946	Communist Klement Gottwald became Prime Minister.
25 February 1948	Communist putsch; regime caused post-war cohort of refugees.
10 March 1948	Jan Masaryk, Minister for Foreign Affairs, died in suspicious circumstances in Černín Palace, Prague.
7 June 1948	President Beneš obliged to resign for second time.
14 June 1948	Gottwald became Czechoslovakia's first Communist President.
19 June 1948	Czechoslovakia announced an Amnesty allowing 'illegal' émigrés to return within three months without penalty – hardly taken up.
3 September 1948	Edvard Beneš died in Czechoslovakia after a long illness.
January 1949	Czechoslovakia forced to join USSR's Council for Mutual Economic Assistance (Comecon) in preference to US Marshall Plan.
1950	Communist government closed Czechoslovak borders; 'Iron Curtain' remained until 1989 'Velvet Revolution', except for brief liberalization in 1968 'Prague Spring'.
1952	Rudolf Slánský and Stalinist 'show trials' of prominent Czechoslovak Communists, mostly Jewish.

20 August 1968	USSR instigated invasion of Czechoslovakia by Warsaw Pact forces; subsequent Communist crackdown ended 'Prague Spring'.
2 December 1974	Hana Benešová died in Czechoslovakia.
November 1989	Fall of Berlin Wall, start of Communist fall in Czechoslovakia.
1 January 1993	Slovakia seceded from Czechoslovakia, became Slovak Republic; Czech Republic comprises Bohemia and Moravia.

Population of Czechoslovakia Showing Ethnic Groups According to the 1930 Census

Total population: 14,729,536		
Ethnic Group	Total	Per cent of Total Population
Czechoslovaks	9,756,604	66.24
Russian and Ruthenian	568,941	3.86
Sudeten Germans	3,318,445	22.53
Hungarians	719,569	4.89
Jews*	204,779	1.39
Poles	100,322	0.68
Gypsies	32,857	0.22
Rumanians	14,170	0.10
J[Y]ugoslavs	6,026	0.04
Others (unspecified)	7,823	0.05

*The actual figure would have been higher, as many Jewish people did not register as such in the census; an unknown number registered as Germans.

Source:
Czechoslovak Ministry of Foreign Affairs, Department of Information, *Statistická Příručka Československé Republiky*, Československé Ministerstvo Zahraničních Věcí, Informační Oddělení, *Statistical Handbook of the Czechoslovak Republic* [dual Czech/English] (London: 1942), 10–11.

Interview Questionnaire

Date .... Place...

NAME: PLACE/DOB:

1. Which part of the former Czechoslovakia are you from?
2. When did you leave Czechoslovakia?
3. Why?
4. When, where and how did you arrive in Britain?
5. How old were you then?
6. Were you alone, or with family or friends?
7. What were your first impressions?
8. What help did you receive when you first arrived and/or later?
9. Where did you settle in Britain initially AND later?
10. What work (paid or voluntary) did you do, if any:
    (a) in the homeland?
    (b) in Britain?
11. How did you obtain it? AND how did you feel about it and your UK colleagues?
12. How did your UK colleagues behave towards you?
13. Where did you live e.g. independently, with own/other family, with friends, in Czech Refugee Trust Fund property …?
14. How did you spend your free time?
15. How soon did you make any British friends or feel accepted or 'integrated'?
16. What problems did you experience adjusting to life in Britain?
17. Did you ever plan or try to return to Czechoslovakia? If so, what was the outcome, and why did you ultimately stay in Britain?
18. What do you think you have gained from living in Britain?
19. What do you feel you have contributed to society in Britain?

Any other comments or observations

Key Interviewees, Respondents and Testimonies*

Name	DOB	Place (as currently known)	Lang. (plus Eng.)	Occupation (peacetime)	Religion	Polit. Party	Arr. UK	Repat. CzS	Ret. UK
A. CzS Refugees & Children									
Bell, Susan Groag	1926	Opava, Silesia	Ger/Cz	Writer, lecturer	Luther'n/J	–	1939	1945	1946
Bernard, Rose (Volinová)	1912	Teplice, Bohemia	Cz/Ger	TUC rep., teacher	–	SD	1948	–	–
Bradbrook, Bohuslava (Nečasová)	1922	Zlín region	Czech	Educationalist	Christian	–	1953	2007	–
Burton, Alena (Knap)	1931	Birkenhead, UK	Czech	Publishing	Christian	–	–	–	–
Bushell, Charlotte (Feldman)	1924	Bratislava, Slovakia	Ger/Slovak	Rheumatologist	Jewish	–	1938	–	–
Čadská, Dana (Straková)	1925	Statenice/ Prague	Czech	Comptometer op.	Catholic	–	1950	–	–
Dobosharevich, Nina (Vignerová)	1920	Wolin, Poland	Cz/Polish	Theatre Sister	Russian Orthodox	SD	1950	–	–

Name	DOB	Place (as currently known)	Lang. (plus Eng.)	Occupation (peacetime)	Religion	Polit. Party	Arr. UK	Repat. CzS	Ret. UK
Dražil, Franci (Šmolka/Schmolka)	1932	Prague	Czech	Teacher	J/Catholic	-	1939	1946	1966
Dubs, Lord Alf	1932	Prague	Czech	MP	Chr/J	Labour	1939	-	-
Epstein, Dorrit (Fuhrmann)	1917	Brno, Moravia	German	Artist	Jewish	-	1938	-	-
Feigl, Marion	1929	Prague	Czech	Designed school textbooks, mags.	Jewish	-	1939	-	USA
Flajsner, Zora (Novotná)	1925	Jindřichův Hradec	Czech	Cutter	Catholic	-	1947	-	-
Franks, Heda (Wernerová)	1928	Brno, Moravia	German	Secretary, transl.	Jewish	-	1946	-	-
Fraser, Glenda (Hodbod)	1939	Lancashire, UK	Cz/Russ.	Research Asst.	Christian	-	-	-	-
Freistadt, Berta, also re. Freistadt, Ludwig (father)	1942 1903	Northern UK Bratislava, Slovakia	English German	Writer, teacher Businessman	Chr/J Jewish	- Soc'list	- 1939	- -	- -
Frejková/Freund, Hana	1945	London	Czech	Actress/singer	Jewish	-	-	1945	-

Name	DOB	Place (as currently known)	Lang. (plus Eng.)	Occupation (peacetime)	Religion	Polit. Party	Arr. UK	Repat. CzS	Ret. UK
Friedl, Tommy (Tomaš) (see also Rayner, Eva, sister)	1927	Budapest (but Czech national)	Czech	Wool merchant	Jewish	–	1938	–	–
Fromings, Hedy (Huenigen)	1926	Liberec, Bohemia	Ger/Cz	Architect	–	–	1939	1945	1949
Fuhrmann, Valerie (mother of Epstein, Dorrit above)	1893	Brno, Moravia	German	Translator and various posts	Jewish	–	1938	–	–
Gissing, Vera (Diamant)	1929	Čelákovice, Boh.	Czech	Teacher, translator	Jewish	–	1939	1945	1949
Gokorsch, Maria	1929	Mähren, Silesia	German	Businesswoman	–	–	1949	–	–
Gould, Kate/Katja (Löw)	1919	Mistek, Silesia	German	Secretary, WIZO	Jewish	–	1938	–	–
Grenfell-Baines, Lady Milena (Fleischmann)	1929	Proseč, Bohemia	Czech	Nurse, cookery expert/writer	Jewish	–	1939	–	–

Name	DOB	Place (as currently known)	Lang. (plus Eng.)	Occupation (peacetime)	Religion	Polit. Party	Arr. UK	Repat. CzS	Ret. UK
Groag, Edith (Wolf) (mother of Bell, Susan Groag above)	1900	Opava, Silesia	Ger/Cz	Businesswoman	Jewish	–	1939	–	–
Halata, Eva (Grečmalová)	1923	Staškov, Slovakia	Cz/Slovak	Mill worker, ran grocery shop	Catholic	–	1945	–	–
Hodbod, Anna (mother of Fraser, Glenda, above)	1903	Prague	Czech	Various; home-maker	–	–	1935	–	–
Huenigen, Hedwig (mother of Fromings, Hedy, above)	1900	Frydlant, Bohemia	Ger/Czech	Liberec Co-op.	–	Communist	1939	1945	–
Karas, Zora (Mayer) (mother of Sturgess, Vera, below)	1922	Trenčín, Slovakia	Cz/Slovak	Counselling	Jewish	–	1938	–	–
Karlik, John/Jan, and Karlik, Vera (sister)	1930 1928	Prague Prague	Czech Czech	Bio-chemist Nurse	J/Chr J/Chr	– –	1939 1939	–	Australia 1950s

Name	DOB	Place (as currently known)	Lang. (plus Eng.)	Occupation (peacetime)	Religion	Polit. Party	Arr. UK	Repat. CzS	Ret. UK
Knap, Jaroslav (see wife in part B, daughters Burton, Alena, Vivo, Nadia de, in A)	1901	Dvůr Králové, Boh.	Czech	Cotton exporter, Director CzS Inst.	–		mid-1930s	–	–
Koděková, Jindřiška	1908	Prague	Czech	Ophthalmic surg.	–	–	1939	–	–
Koehler, Dorothea	1924	Těšín, Silesia	Ger/Cz	Stenographer	Catholic	–	1948	–	–
Kolařová/ Šrámek, Zdena (Karousová)	1923	České Velenice, south Bohemia	Czech	BBC, UK	Moravian Brethren	SD	1951	–	–
Koschland, Bernd	1931	Fürth, Bavaria	German	Rabbi	Jewish	–	1939	–	–
Kučerová, Alexandra (Olmerová)	1924	Brno, Moravia	Czech	Czech Red Cross in UK	–	–	1939	1945	–

Name	DOB	Place (as currently known)	Lang. (plus Eng.)	Occupation (peacetime)	Religion	Polit. Party	Arr. UK	Repat. CzS	Ret. UK
Lowe/Marianne (Adler)/ Dorrit Maltby, daughter	1913	Prague	German	Psychologist	Jewish	Left-wing	1940	–	–
Lowit, Theresie (Schneider); Lowit, Herbert (husband)	1923 1923	Karlovy Vary, Boh. Teplice-Šanov, Boh	German Cz/ Ger	WAAF, mother army, businessman	Jewish Jewish	SD SGSD	1938 1938	– 1945	– 1947
Morton, Renee (Stránská)	1920	Prague	Czech	Scientist	Jewish	–	1938	–	–
Pokorná, Zdeňka	1905	Brno, Moravia	Czech	Headmistress, nurse	Moravian Brethren	–	1948	–	–
Ratzer, Maria (Stegmüller)	1914	Marianské Lázně	German	Doctor/ consultant	Catholic	–	1938	–	–
Rayner, Eva (Friedl)	1929	Brno, Moravia	Czech	Director textile co.	J/Mor. Br.	–	1938	–	–
Řehulková, Marie (Semanská)	1918	Bečváry u Kolín, Bohemia	Czech	Nurse, mother	Christian	–	1938	1945	–
Road, Eve (Adler)	1916	Prague	Ger/Cz	Social worker	Chr/J	SD	1939	–	–

Name	DOB	Place (as currently known)	Lang. (plus Eng.)	Occupation (peacetime)	Religion	Polit. Party	Arr. UK	Repat. CzS	Ret. UK
Roden, George	1923	Ostrava, Moravia	Czech	RAF, tailoring	–	–	1940	1945	1946
LS (anonymized as req'd.)	1921	Teplice, Bohemia	German	ATS, Palestine	Jewish	Zionist	1946	–	–
Seifter, Pavel (son of Seifter, Anna)	1938	Ostrava, Moravia	Cz/Ger	Historian, lecturer, Ambassador	Chr/J	Diss-Ident	1939	1947	1997
Smutný, Olga/Olina (Madarová)	1931	Prague	Cz/Ger	CzS. Foreign Intelligence Service, AEL Tennis Club	–	–	1949	–	–
Sonnek, Anna (Stránský)	1917	Brno, Moravia	Czech	CzS Trade Union	Chr/J	–	1939	1945	1948
Stanzl, Maria	1925	Šumperk, Moravia	German	Governess, domestic help	Catholic	–	1947	–	–
Sterne, Edith (Bader)	1911	Karlovy Vary, Boh.	German	Headmistress	Jewish	L-wing	1939	–	–
Sturgess, Vera (Karas)	1944	Cornwall, UK	Czech	Teacher	Jewish	–	–	–	–
Tanner, Jana (Grafová)	1930	Bratislava, Slovak.	Czech	Secretary/PA	Jewish	–	1945	–	–

Name	DOB	Place (as currently known)	Lang. (plus Eng.)	Occupation (peacetime)	Religion	Polit. Party	Arr. UK	Repat. CzS	Ret. UK
Tauber, Elisabeth (Gellner)	1916	Prague	Czech	Social worker	–	–	1939	1945	1949
Teich(ová), Alice (Schwarz), Teich, Mikuláš (husband)	1920 1918	Vienna (later CzS) Košice, Slovakia	Ger/Cz Cz/ Slovak	Professor Professor	Jewish Jewish	Comm-unist	1938 1939	1949 1946	1969 1969
Thompson, Kate (Herrnheiser)	1919	Czechoslovakia	Czech	Genetic research	Jewish	–	1939	–	1945
Tomášek/ Tomášková, Markéta/Marga (Bílek) (see Vohlídalová, Vera, daughter)	1915	Albrechtice, Liberec region	German	Executive secretary	–	Comm-unist	1938– 1939	1945	–
Tosek, Ruth (Ornsteinová)	1925	Prague	Cz/Ger	WAAF, BBC	Jewish	SD	1939	1946	1966

Name	DOB	Place (as currently known)	Lang. (plus Eng.)	Occupation (peacetime)	Religion	Polit. Party	Arr. UK	Repat. CzS	Ret. UK
Tschapek, Walter (and Tschapek, Anna, mother)	1928 1902	Schöenwalt Krásy Les, Nrn. Bohemia Oberbadsdorf	Ger/Cz German	Lecturer Housewife	– –	Communist (both)	1939 1939	1945 1945	– –
Vivo, de, Nadia/ja (Knap)	1934	Liverpool, UK	Czech	Mother	Christian	–	–	–	–
Vodičková, Hana (Lewitová)	1918	Czechoslovakia	Czech	Nurse	Jewish	Communist	1939	1945	–
Vohlídalová, Věra (Tomášková)	1942	London	Cz/Ger	Politics, women's groups	–	–	–	1945	–
Warnholtz, Elizabeth/ Elsbeth (mother of Frejková, Hana)	1907	Hamburg, Germany	German	Actress	Jewish	Communist	1938–1939	1945	–
Weiss, Elizabeth	1919	Radwanice/ Karlovy Vary	German	Nurse	Catholic	–	1939	1946	1966

Name	DOB	Place (as currently known)	Link to CzS	Occupation (peacetime)	Religion	Polit. Party	Arr. UK	Repat. CzS	Ret. UK
B. British-born Men, Women/ Wives									
Bower, Esther/ Hetty (Rimel)	1905	London	CRTF hostel warden	Book-keeper Political/anti-war Activist	Jewish	Labour/ Comm.	–	–	–
Freistadt, Esther (Dunn)	1899	London	Husband, and taught refugees English	Housewife	Catholic	–	–	–	–
Knap, Marion (Jeary)	1898	Martham, Norfolk	Husband, culture	Teacher	Christian	–	–	–	–
Mitchell, Libby, Dewhirst	1929	UK	Moravian Brethren School	Theatre, mother	Christian	–	–	–	–
Plocka, Winifred, previously Horáková (New)	1923	Swindon	Husband, Lidice	Mother	Christian	–	–	1945	1948

Name	DOB	Place (as currently known)	Link to CzS	Occupation (peacetime)	Religion	Polit. Party	Arr. UK	Repat. CzS	Ret. UK
Roginson, Joan (Jeffs)	1923	Bedworth, Midlands	CzS Sokol Group	Secretary	Christian	–	–	–	–
Šling(ová)/ Schling, Marian (Wilbraham)	1913	New Zealand	Husband, politics	Writer, translator	–	Comm-Unist	–	1946	1968
Winton, Sir Nicholas	1909	London	BCRC and CzS Kind-transport	Businessman, philanthropist	Christian/J	–	–	Dec. 1938	Jan. 1939
C. Villagers of Aston Abbotts, Buckinghamshire			via		–	–	–	–	–
Higgs, Natalie (and son)	1911	Skinningrove, North Yorkshire	Pres./Mrs Beneš and	Retired nursery maid, housewife					
Higgs, Colin	1935	Grantham, Lincs.	President'l	Tile company					
Petry, Barbara (Williams)	1927	Tring, Herts.	Guard and	Sister, midwife					
Scott, Victor	1928	–	Govt. staff	Horticulturalist					

Name	DOB	Place	Link to CzS	Occupation	Religion	Polit.	Arr.	Repat.	Ret.
		(as currently known)		(peacetime)		Party	UK	CzS	UK
(Brief discussion also with Bystra, Andy, Curnow, Andy and April)			in Aston/A and nearby Wingrove						
*Key									
Boh. – Bohemia									
Comm. – Communist									
Cz/Ger – Czech/German									
J – Jewish									
SD – Social Democrat									
SGSD – Sudeten German									
Social Democrat									

Bibliography

Archival material held at institutions

(UK): Bodleian Library, Oxford; British Library; Imperial War Museum; London School of Economics and Political Science; Manx National Heritage Library; Modern Records Centre, University of Warwick; Moravian Church in Britain Archives, and archives of Fulneck Girls'/Boys' School; School of Slavonic and East European Studies; The National Archives; University of London: Institute of Advanced Legal Studies, also Institute of Germanic Studies/Senate House Libraries; Wiener Library for the Study of the Holocaust and Genocide; Women's Library at LSE. (Czech Republic): Antonín Dvořák Museum, Prague; Liberec Library; National Archives, Prague.

Refugee publications in exile, including internment [IoM]

Čechoslovak, with English supplement *To the British-born Wives of Czechoslovaks* 1944–5); *Československá žena; Central European Observer; Einheit; Frau in Arbeit/Pracující žena* (also called *Die Frau*, variously in German or joint German/Czech, special editions in English); *Hamaccabi* (joint English/Czech); *Mladé Československo* (Czech and German versions, some in English); *Naší Cestou* produced by *Naše Noviny; Refugee Teachers' Association* (joint German/Czech); *Review-45; Spirit of Czechoslovakia; Věstník; Camp Tribune; The Camp; Pioneer* (IoM).

Private papers

Denoted as PP in footnotes.

Select official publications

Czechoslovak Ministry of Foreign Affairs, Department of Information, *Statistická Příručka Československé Republiky*, Československé Ministerstvo Zahraničních Věcí, Informační Oddělení, *Statistical Handbook of the Czechoslovak Republic* (London: 1942) [joint Czech/English].

Czechoslovak Ministry of Foreign Affairs, Department of Information, *Two Years of German Oppression in Czechoslovakia* (Woking: Unwin, 1941).

Hansard, House of Commons Official Report 425 H. C. DEB. 5 s., 'Austrian and German Refugees (Repatriation)', cols 1043–4, 16 July 1946.

Hansard, Parliamentary Reports, House of Commons, 339 H. C. DEB. 5 s., Oral Answers, 'Government Policy', col. 364 and cols 427–34, 5 October 1938.

Hansard, Parliamentary Reports, House of Commons, 340 H. C. DEB. 5 s., Oral Answers, 'Czechoslovakia (Refugees)', cols 369–70, 3 November 1938.

Home Office, *Czech Refugee Trust Fund and Directions to the Trustees* (London: HMSO, July 1939).

Jacobsen, Karen, and Landau, Loren, *Researching Refugees: Some Methodological and Ethical Considerations in Social Science and Forced Migration*, New Issues in Refugee Research, Working Paper No. 90 (Geneva: United Nations High Commissioner for Refugees, Evaluation and Policy Analysis Unit, June 2003).

League of Nations International Assistance to Refugees, Report by Herbert Emerson, High Commissioner for Refugees, C.25.M.25.1942.XII (Geneva: February 1942).

Schieder, Theodor, ed., *The Expulsion of the German Population From Czechoslovakia* (Bonn: Federal Ministry for Expellees, Refugees and War Victims, 1960).

Treaty Series No. 9 (1939), *Financial Assistance to Czecho-Slovakia*, Cmd. 5933 (London: HMSO, 27 January 1939).

U. S. S. R. Ministry of Foreign Affairs, *Documents and Materials Relating to the Eve of the Second World War*, vol. 1, November 1937–8 From the Archives of the German Ministry of Foreign Affairs (Moscow: Foreign Languages Publishing House, 1948).

Select bibliography

Are Refugees an Asset? Political & Economic Planning Pamphlets (London: Europa Publications, 1944).

Becher, Peter, and Canz, Sigrid, eds, *Drehscheibe Prag: Deutsche Emigranten/Staging Point Prague: German Exiles 1933–1939* (Munich: Adalbert Stifter Verein, 1989) [joint German/English].

Beneš, Edvard, *The Fall and Rise of a Nation: Czechoslovakia 1938–1941*, ed. and trans. Milan Hauner (New York: East European Monographs, Boulder/Columbia University Press, 2004).

Brinson, Charmian, '"In the exile of Internment" or "Von Versuchen, aus einer Not eine Tugend zu machen": German-Speaking Women Interned by the British During the Second World War', in Niven, William, and Jordan, James, eds, *Politics and Culture in Twentieth-Century Germany* (New York: Camden House, 2003).

Brinson, Charmian, and Malet, Marian, eds, *Exile in and From Czechoslovakia During the 1930s and 1940s: Yearbook of the Research Centre for German and Austrian Exile Studies*, vol. 11 (2009).

Brown, Alan, *Flying for Freedom. The Allied Air Forces in the RAF 1939–45* (Stroud, Gloucestershire: History Press), 2012.

Brown, Martin David, *Dealing With Democrats. The British Foreign Office and the Czechoslovak Emigrés in Great Britain, 1939 to 1945* (Frankfürt am Main: Peter Lang), 2006.

Burešová, Jana, *Proměny společenského postavení českých žen v první polovině 20. století* [*The Changing Position of Czech Women in Society In the First Half of the 20th Century*, with English Summary] (Olomouc: Katedra historie, Univerzita Palackého, 2001).

Buresova, Jana Barbora, 'Hana Benešová: The Forgotten First Lady', in Charmian Brinson, Jana Barbora Buresova, and Andrea Hammel, eds, *Exile and Gender II. Politics, Education and the Arts: Yearbook of the Research Centre for German and Austrian Exile Studies*, vol. 18 (2017).

Cresswell, Yvonne, M., ed., *Living With the Wire: Civilian Internment in the Isle of Man During the Two World Wars* (Douglas: Manx National Heritage, 1994).

Csikszentmihalyi, Mihaly, and Rochberg-Halton, Eugene, *The Meaning of Things; Domestic Symbols and the Self* (Cambridge: Cambridge University Press, 1981).

DeSantis, Alan D., 'Caught Between Two Worlds: Bakhtin's Dialogism in the Exile Experience', in *Journal of Refugee Studies*, vol. 14, no. 1 (2001).

Dove, Richard, ed., *'Totally Un-English'? Britain's Internment of 'Enemy Aliens' in Two World Wars: Yearbook of the Research Centre for German and Austrian Exile Studies*, vol. 7 (2005).

Duff, Susan Grant, *Europe and the Czechs* (Middlesex: Penguin Books, 1938).

Feinberg, Melissa, 'Democracy and Its Limits: Gender and Rights in the Czech Lands, 1918–1938', in *Nationalities Papers: Journal of Nationalism and Ethnicity*, vol. 30, no. 4 (30 December 2002).

Frisch, Shelley, ed., 'Women in Exile', Special Issue, *Germanic Review*, vol. LXII, no. 3 (Summer 1987).

Frommer, Benjamin, *National Cleansing. Retribution Against Nazi Collaborators in Postwar Czechoslovakia* (Cambridge/NewYork/Melbourne/Madrid/Cape Town: Cambridge University Press, 2005).

Griffin, Alan, *Leamington's Czech Patriots and the Heydrich Assassination* (Warwick, UK: Feldon Books, 2004).

Halliday, Fred, *Rethinking International Relations* (London: Macmillan, 1994).

Hermann, A. H., *A History of the Czechs* (London: Allen Lane, 1975).

Iggers, Wilma A., *Women of Prague: Ethnic Diversity and Social Change From the Eighteenth Century to the Present* (Oxford: Berghahn Books, 1995).

Isaac, Julius, 'Problems of Cultural Assimilation Arising From Population Transfers in Western Germany', in *Population Studies*, vol. 3: *Cultural Assimilation of Immigrants: Supplement* (March 1950).

Jewish Women's History Group, *You'd Prefer Me Not to Mention It … The Lives of Four Jewish Daughters of Refugees* (London: Calverts North Star Press, 1983).

Jurnečková, M., with Matheson, M. C., *Women of Czechoslovakia* (London: New Europe Publishing, 1944).

Kaplan, Karel, *The Short March. The Communist Takeover in Czechoslovakia 1945–1948* (London: Hurst, 1987).

Kapp, Yvonne, and Mynatt, Margaret, *British Policy and the Refugees, 1933–1941* (London: Cass, 1997) [largely written in 1940].

Kay, Diana, and Miles, Robert, 'Refugees or Migrant Workers? The Case of the European Volunteer Workers in Britain (1946–1951)', in *Journal of Refugee Studies*, vol. 1, nos 3 and 4 (1988).

Kocourek, Milan, and Slobodová, Zuzana, *Česko-slovenská Británie* [*Czecho-Slovak Britain*], UK Chapter of the Czechoslovak Society of Arts and Sciences (Trebon: Carpio, 2006).

Kushner, Tony, 'Domestic Service', in Mosse, Werner, E., ed., *Second Chance. Two Centuries of German-Speaking Jews in the United Kingdom* (Tubingen: Mohr Siebeck, 1991).

Laffan, R. G. D., *Survey of International Affairs 1938*, vol. II, *The Crisis Over Czechoslovakia January to September 1938*, Royal Institute of International Affairs (London: Oxford University Press, 1951).

Lafitte, François, *The Internment of Aliens* (Harmondsworth: Allen Lane, 1940).

London, Louise, *Whitehall and the Jews, 1933–1948. British Immigration Policy, Jewish Refugees and the Holocaust* (Cambridge: Cambridge University Press, 2000).

Luža, Radomír, *The Transfer of the Sudeten Germans, A Study of Czech German Relations, 1933–1962* (New York: New York University Press, 1964).

Malet, Marian, and Grenville, Anthony, eds, *Changing Countries. The Experience and Achievement of German-Speaking Exiles From Hitler in Britain From 1933 to Today* (London: Libris, 2002).

Mamatey, Victor, S. and Luža, Radomír, *A History of the Czechoslovak Republic 1918–1948* (Princeton, NY: Princeton University Press, 1973).

Morrison's Prisoners. The Story of the Czechoslovakian Anti-Fascist Fighters Interned in Britain, National Council for Democratic Aid (London: around May 1941).

Owen, Jean, and Segal, Naomi, eds, *On Replacement: Cultural, Social and Psychological Representations* (London: Palgrave, 2018).

Parkin, David, 'Mementoes as Transitional Objects in Human Displacement', in *Journal of Material Culture*, 4:3 (1999), 303–20.

Pavlik, Devana, 'Czechoslovak Publications Issued in Britain During World War II', in *Exile In and From Czechoslovakia During the 1930s and 1940s*, Brinson, Charmian, and Malet, Marian, eds, *Yearbook of the Research Centre for German and Austrian Exile Studies*, vol. 11 (2009).

Quack, Sibylle, ed., *Between Sorrow and Strength. Women Refugees of the Nazi Period* (Washington, DC: German Historical Institute and Cambridge University Press, 1995).

Rees, Neil, *The Czech Connection. The Czechoslovak Government in Exile in London and Buckinghamshire During the Second World War* (Buckinghamshire: Croxson's, 2005).

Robbins, Keith, *Munich 1938* (London: Cassell, 1968).

Rye, Gill, *Narratives of Mothering. Women's Writing in Contemporary France* (Newark: University of Delaware, 2009).

Schechtman, Joseph B., *Postwar Population Transfers in Europe 1945–1955* (USA: University of Pennsylvania Press, 1962).

Skilling, H. Gordon, *Mother and Daughter. Charlotte and Alice Masaryk* (Prague: Gender Studies, o.p.s., 2001).

Srba, Bořivoj, *Múzy v exilu* [*Muses in Exile*, re. cultural activities in London 1939–45, with English summary] (Brno: Masarykova univerzita v Brné, 2003).

Steinert, Johannes-Dieter, 'British Post-War Migration Policy and Displaced Persons in Europe', in Reinisch, Jessica, and White, Elizabeth, eds, *The Disentanglement of Populations* (Basingstoke: Palgrave Macmillan, 2011).

Taylor, Jennifer, 'Einheit', in Abbey, William, *et al.*, eds, *Between Two Languages. German-speaking Exiles in Great Britain 1933–45* (Stuttgart: Heinz, 1995), 169–88.

Turnwald, Wilhelm K., ed., *Documents on the Expulsion of the Sudeten Germans* (Munich: Association for the Protection of Sudeten German Interests/University Press, 1953).

Vinzent, Jutta, *Identity and Image. Refugee Artists from Nazi Germany in Britain (1933–1945)* (Kromsdorf: VDG Verlag and Datenbank fur Geisteswissenschaften, 2006).

Wasserstein, Bernard, *Vanishing Diaspora* (London: Hamish Hamilton, 1996).

Wardi, Dina, *Memorial Candles: Children of the Holocaust*, trans. Naomi Goldblum (London: Tavistock/Routledge, 1992).

Weber-Newth, Inge, and Steinert, Johannes-Dieter, *German Migrants in Post-war Britain. An Enemy Embrace* (London: Routledge, 2006).

Wiskemann, Elizabeth, *Czechs and Germans, A Study of the Struggle in the Historic Provinces of Bohemia and Moravia* (London: Oxford University Press, 1938).

Non-academic books

Albright, Madeleine, with Woodward, Bill, *Madame Secretary. A Memoir* (Basingstoke: Pan Books/Macmillan, 2004).

Bradbrook, Bohuslava, *The Liberating Beauty of Little Things. Decision, Adversity and Reckoning in a Refugee's Journey From Prague to Cambridge* (Brighton: Alpha Press, 2000).

Demetz, Hana, *The House on Prague Street* (London: Allen, 1980).

Emanuel, Muriel, and Gissing, Vera, *Nicholas Winton and the Rescued Generation. The Story of 'Britain's Schindler'*, 3rd edn (London: Vallentine Mitchell, 2001).

Frumin, Vera, '"You my Passengers" by a Clippie', in Kaye Webb, ed., *Lilliput Goes to War* (London: Hutchinson, 1985), 201–2.

Gissing, Vera, *Pearls of Childhood* (London: Robson Books, 1994).

Greenfield, Hana, *Fragments of Memory From Kolin to Jerusalem* (Jerusalem: Gefen, 1998).

Greag Bell, Susan, *Between Worlds. In Czechoslovakia, England and America* (New York, USA: Dutton, 1991).

Kain, Peggy, *Prague Winter. An Englishwoman Behind the Iron Curtain: A True Story* (London: REMprint, 1999).

Kavan, Rosemary, *Freedom At a Price. An Englishwoman's Life in Czechoslovakia* (London: Verso, 1985).

Kocourek, Milan, *Krajanská Farnost v Londýně. Pamětník: Otec Jan Lang S. J.* [*Compatriots in the London Parish. Survivor: Father Jan Lang S. J.*] (London: 1994).

Kundera, Milan, *Ignorance* (London: Faber and Faber, 2002).

Machacek, Karel A., *Escape to England* (Sussex: The Book Guild, 1988).

Margolius, Heda, *I Do Not Want to Remember. Auschwitz 1941–Prague 1968* (London: Weidenfeld and Nicolson, 1973).

Margolius, Ivan, *Reflections of Prague. Journeys Through The 20th Century* (London: Wiley and Sons, 2006).

Masaryk, Jan, *Speaking To My Country* (London: Lincolns-Prager, 1944).

Mayer, Gerda, *Prague Winter* (London: Hearing Eye, 2005).

Roth, Milena, *Lifesaving Letters. A Child's Flight From the Holocaust* (Seattle: University of Washington Press, 2004).

Šlingova, Marian, *Truth Will Prevail* (London: Merlin, 1968).

Vrbová, Gerta, *Betrayed Generation. Shattered Hopes and Disillusion in Post War Czechoslovakia* (Kings Lynn, UK: Zuza Books, 2010).

Select electronic material

Art. XIII, Orderly Transfer of German Populations, approved 2 August 1945 by Stalin, Truman and Attlee, <http://potsdamer-konferenz.de/dokumente/protokoll_en.php#XIII>, accessed 31 May 2018.

British Council, Allied Centres, <https://www.britishcouncil.org/organisation/history>, accessed 31 May 2018.

'Czech PEN club marks 85 years of promoting freedom of speech', Radio Prague, Czech Radio, <http://www.radio.cz/en/.../czech-pen-club-marks-85-years-of-promoting-freedom-of-speech>, accessed 31 May 2018.

'Czechoslovakia: "Island of Democracy" and Refuge Between the Wars', Radio Prague, Czech Radio (20 October 2005), <http://www.radio.cz/en/article/71864>, accessed 31 May 2018.

'Lady Luisa Abrahams – a Truly Remarkable Life', interview with Ian Willoughby, Radio Prague, Czech Radio (23 January 2006), <http://www.radio.cz/en/article/75025>, accessed 31 May 2018.

Steffen Prauser, and Arfon Rees, eds, *The Expulsion of the 'German' Communities From Eastern Europe at the End of the Second World War*, EUI Working Paper HEC No. 2004/1 (European University Institute, Florence), 18–20, <http://

cadmus.eui.eu/bitstream/handle/1814/2599/HEC04-01.pdf?sequence=1>, accessed 31 May 2018.

'US National Archives and Records Administration, Records of the Foreign Service Posts of the Department of State (RG 84) Czechoslovakia', <http://www.archives.gov/research/holocaust/finding-aid/civilian/rg-84-czech.html>, accessed 31 May 2018.

Index

EXILE STUDIES

Edited by Andrea Hammel

A series founded by Alexander Stephan

Exile Studies is a series of monographs and edited collections that takes a broad view of exile, including the life and work of refugees from National Socialism, and beyond. The series explores the different global and cultural spaces of exile and refuge as well as the specific historical, political and social concerns of exile writers and artists. The series engages with recent theoretical approaches to exile to shed new light on the unique conditions of mass flight from National Socialist persecution, with a particular interest in the work of Jewish refugees of the period. A plurality of theoretical approaches is encouraged, featuring research that reaches beyond national frameworks or disciplinary boundaries and takes multi-directional, transcultural or comparative approaches. The series aims to make connections to studies on more recent groups of refugees and to contribute to current debates. Themes include persecution, exclusion and delocalization, legacies of displacement, loss and acculturation as well as the creation of new homes and networks.

The series promotes dialogue among transnational, Jewish and memory studies, and among diaspora, Holocaust and postcolonial studies. It invites research that acknowledges questions of gender, race, class, religion and ethnicity as indispensable tools for understanding the cultural processes connected to the lives and works of refugees and exiles.

Vol.   1   Sonja Maria Hedgepeth, 'Überall blicke ich nach einem heimatlichen Boden aus': Exil im Werk Else Lasker-Schülers.
254 pp. 1994.
US-ISBN 0-8204-2219-3.

Vol.   2   Elfe Vallaster, 'Ein Zimmer in der Luft': Liebe, Exil, Rückkehr und Wort-Vertrauen.
278 pp. 1994.
US-ISBN 0-8204-2225-8.

Vol. 3   Waltraud Strickhausen, Die Erzählerin Hilde Spiel oder «Der
          weite Wurf in die Finsternis».
          500 pp. 1996.
          US-ISBN 0-8204-2623-7.

Vol. 4   Renata von Hanffstengel, Mexiko im Werk von Bodo Uhse:
          Das nie verlassene Exil.
          251 pp. 1996.
          US-ISBN 0-8204-2683-0.

Vol. 5   Harald Reil, Siegfried Kracauers Jacques Offenbach:
          Biographie, Geschichte, Zeitgeschichte.
          159 pp. 2003.
          US-ISBN 0-8204-3742-5.

Vol. 6   J. M. Ritchie, German Exiles: British Perspectives.
          344 pp. 1997.
          US-ISBN 0-8204-3743-3.

Vol. 7   Tibor Frank, Double Exile: Migrations of Jewish-Hungarian
          Professionals through Germany to the United States,
          1919–1945.
          501 pp. 2009.
          ISBN 978-3-03911-331-6.

Vol. 8   Nicole Brunnhuber, The Faces of Janus:
          English-language Fiction by German-speaking Exiles in Great
          Britain, 1933–45.
          240 pp. 2005.
          ISBN 3-03910-180-3 / US-ISBN 0-8204-6989-0.

Vol. 9   Lee Kyung-Boon, Musik und Literatur im Exil: Hanns Eislers
          dodekaphone Exilkantaten.
          306 pp. 2001.
          US-ISBN 0-8204-4938-5.

Vol. 10   Regina U. Hahn, The Democratic Dream: Stefan Heym in
          America.
          150 pp. 2002.
          ISBN 3-906768-53-8 / US-ISBN 0-8204-5865-1.